"No matter what you're interested in concerning Ireland, Monie Begley has something fascinating to tell you in her very diverting and offbeat book."
—**MYRA WALDO**, author of many travel guides

"As historians, scholars, and invaders of all stripes have discovered over the centuries, it is an impossible task to *grasp* Ireland. The moods and mysteries of this wonderful island remain intact to intrigue. Any visitor today would profit well from Monie Begley's RAMBLES IN IRELAND which instructs with charm, recommends with candor, and entertains with gusto."
—**WALTER J. P. CURLEY**
American Ambassador to Ireland 1975-77

"This is an absorbing and intelligent book about one of the least understood countries in the world—for all that has been said by so many for so long. The trite old bunk is dispensed with, the true magic of Ireland and her people remains."
—**DAVID McCULLOUGH**
author of *The Path Between the Seas*

N

| 0 | 40 | 80 |
KILOMETRES

| 0 | 20 | 40 | 60 |
MILES

Courtesy of Irish Tourist Board

Rambles in Ireland

A
County-by-County Guide
For
Discriminating Travelers

MONIE BEGLEY

With Photographs and Maps

METHUEN

New York   London   Toronto   Sydney

Library of Congress Cataloging in Publication Data

Begley, Monie.
    Rambles in Ireland.

    Includes index.
    1. Ireland—Description and travel—1951-
—Guide-books. 2. Ireland—Civilization. 3. Begley,
Monie. I. Title.
DA980.B43 1979   914.15′04824   79-27302
ISBN 0-416-00651-5

Manufactured in the United States of America by
The Book Press, Brattleboro, Vt.

Published in the United States of America by
Methuen, Inc.
733 Third Avenue
New York, New York 10017

Ireland, with thy faults,
    they follies too,
I love the still, still
    with a candid eye
    must view.
They wit too quick, still
    blundering into sense,
Thy reckless humor and
    improvidence,
And even what sober
    judges tallies call...
I, looking at the heart,
    forget them all.

—Maria Edgeworth
Edgeworthtown

CONTENTS

PART TWO
Along the Roads

A Guide to Hotels, Country Houses, Farms; Restaurants and Pubs; Antiques Trails; Buyers Market; Entertainment; Diversions

Race Map, p. 177
Dublin Pub Crawl, pp. 308-09
Photographs between pp. 184 and 185

AUTHOR'S NOTE

There's an expression in Irish, *Sé an scéal ó Shamhna go Bealtaine é*, which means "It's a very long story," or literally, "from November to May." It fairly expresses the limits of thanking so many who helped create this book. Whatever list I manage here in thanks can only possibly be a fragment.

My intention for the book has always been to extend an invitation to Ireland, and it seems appropriate to begin my thanks to Bord Fáilte (the Irish Tourist Board) in Ireland. My warmest gratitude: To Joe Malone, now Director-General, for his initial enthusiasm and support. To Sean Carberry and David Hanly for their tireless aid, keen perceptions, and constant humor. To Aideen Friel and Ellen Healey for smoothing the way. To John McCormack, patient good friend, who traveled every bog road, and often buoyed sinking spirits. To Patricia O'Donnell for her never ending hospitality and friendship. To Mark Stern, who has always been an original source of encouragement.

Also my gratitude to all those whose friendship, effort, optimism *and* criticism formed this book: Terry Keane, Edward Delaney, Nicholas and Eva Gormanston, Oonagh Delaney, Roderick O'Connor, Charles Haughey, Dominik Browne, Sean White, Ben Kiely, Stephanie Griffin, Michael O'Leary, Minister for Labour, Jeffrey Craig, the Hanley girls, Isabelle Penet, Denis Corboy, Desmond Fitzgerald, The Chieftains, Seamus and Maire Heaney, Winnie Hayes, Bart DeStefano, Patricia Tunison, Padraic O'Coileain, Deputy Consul General, Thomas Bevins, and all those others who appear throughout the book.

There's another expression the Irish have, *Ni bheidh ár*

leithéidí ann arís, meaning "His likes will not be here again."
It's a tribute rarely made, but is truly deserved by these
friends, without whom there wouldn't be this invitation to
Ireland. To them I am deeply indebted: Gerald Hanley,
Garech Browne, and Tony O'Riordan.

—1979

Introduction

It's been a little over a year since I stood in the March drizzle
on Fifth Avenue watching the Saint Patrick's Day parade. A
few weeks before I had been approached to write a book on
Ireland, so I was watching it all with a different view. The
celebration of Saint Patrick's Day registers on the emotional
seismograph somewhere just above the Declaration of In-
dependence, the Great Gold Rush, and Armistice Day
combined. Every ethnoeccentric becomes Irish for a day,
searches the wardrobe for *anything* green, and accepts for
twenty-four hours heaps of green food and drink and bou-
quets of green flowers. Crime takes a holiday, dispensing
what seems to be the entire force of "New York's finest" to
march and drink the city dry. Regardless of prevailing
national disaster, the Chief Resident of Pennsylvania Avenue arrives by helicopter at the Waldorf-Astoria to join the
leaders of every political party to address the black-tie
dinner of the Friendly Sons of Saint Patrick. The largest
concert hall in New York has been sold out for months for
the Clancy Brothers' appearance. And the Aer Lingus ter-
minal at Kennedy Airport enjoys an octave traffic jam
shuttling obscure societies, ceili bands, and Gaelic B'nai
Briths back and forth between Dublin and New York.

As I was standing there I couldn't help wondering how such a tiny island on the margin of the world — isolated, insulated, and desolated for so many years — could have accomplished this envious public relations scheme. Arousing the inhabitants of a city acknowledged to be the most blasé, indifferent, ethnically insular to go in passionately for "The Wearing of the Green." Something, though, didn't quite sit right. It couldn't be *all* for shamrocks, leprechauns, and "forty shades of green." There was an atavistic mystery somewhere.

Twelve months have gone by trying to find the secret of the celebration, and today I agree with the celebration. Only it's right for all the wrong reasons. Recently I asked an Irish friend why he thought the celebration had gone wrong. "It's a lot of Victorian b...s...." he said. "It suited the English that Paddy should be a comic dancing with a shillelagh and clay pipe, and the Wasps in America encouraged it. All those Americans today singing 'The Old Bog Road' have accepted it; perhaps because they know nothing about themselves other than overromantic notions. The real stuff is much more fascinating, poignant, and interesting."

The "real stuff" my friend was talking about is not easily revealed. The Irish have often opened themselves up too freely in the past and have been rewarded with ridicule and ended up in *Punch*. Seven hundred years of colonization have left the Irish well trained. "Give 'em what they want." And if the traveler isn't careful, he'll depart Shannon having watched the performance of his life.

One of my first days in Dublin a gentlemen at lunch advised me to "leave in forty-eight hours while you still understand it all." Not too long afterward a more cynical Celt warned I was "in a museum with a lot of fouled-up curators," and went on, "This isn't a country, it's a conspiracy." This type of fencing went on for a while, until we were all getting worn from the warnings.

The surest way to silence a group or incite a performance in Hibernia is to suggest that you are writing a book. The alternative reaction is yawns emerging from distant corners. "Another book on Yeats?...Lady Gregory?" Each year at least ten authors descend on the island for further dissection of the Irish. These pursuers, with all good intention, track overtrodden ground. I suggested to one I met that maybe his talent and purse would be better spent pursuing the possibility that Shakespeare was an O'Shaughnessy from Cork, descended from the ancient *filid*, and that some English navvy had muddled his name on a cross-channel passage. The writer moved away politely and permanently, convincing me he probably didn't even know about the ancient Irish or the *filid*.

I arrived *tabula rasa* on the Irish — Irish-American without the tears. No one in my family was particularly concerned with Ireland. We were at least fourth generation, with an unspoken skepticism of where a tracing of backways and byways would lead. Having arrived in this unbiased, innocent state, I was willing to believe anything — for a while.

These pages are not an attempt to unravel the "character" of the Irish, which has been done hundreds of times and is usually overly sentimental or vitriolic, depending on the author's frustrations. The Irish, like every other nation, have become a juke box of Freudian selections — only more likable than most. As Lord Macaulay said, "The Irish were distinguished by qualities which make men interesting rather than preposterous."

These pages are a glance at the tapestry of an ancient lady, a civilization dormant, submerged, and lingering until her eventual collision with a world she disappeared from centuries ago. When you travel Ireland today you are seeing only fifty-odd years of growth. There are some who sarcastically refer to it as the "New Ireland." And a porcupine reception greets any traveler's "tips to the natives" on what they can do with their little country. This advice is usually offered by returned Irish-Americans, the "returned empties," as they are called, though not limited to them. Brendan Behan's account of how he reduced one such missionary is worth the warning:

One of the hazards of traveling in the west of Ireland is the danger of meeting a certain type of Irish-American... They're always offering advice in a very patronising way... I was sitting in a hotel in Ballinasloe at breakfast one morning, not feeling well at all, and waiting on the waitress to bring me some whiskey, before I could encourage myself to look at a bacon and egg. Seated at a table not far from me was a person very like the unlamented Senator Joe McCarthy, wearing a suit of fine American cloth and a huge green tie, and though he looked across at me several times, I didn't encourage him to speak.

Finally, he looked across and said, "Say."

I said, "Yes?"

He said, "You could do a lot for this country. You could do a lot with this country."

"Well," I said, "you could blow it up" — that remark being more the humour of the moment than my permanent attitude.

"Oh," he said, "you're one of these people who don't believe in Ireland's future. Why don't you people try to do something practical? You could clean up that river at the end of town and you could get some good fishing there and a lot of Americans would come for that...."

"Friend," I said, "I only came in on the six o'clock train last night. Please give me a little time."

◇ ◇ ◇

What separates Ireland from the emerging uniworld culture, whose alleged accomplishments have created a fairly unbearable world, is what remains unchanged. Most of the Irish have a queer, inverted defiance of progress, probably rooted in their seven-hundred-year view from the bottom-side looking up. C. D. Darlington, in his ambitious genetic analysis of every civilization in the world, *The Evolution of Man and Society*, offered the comparative characteristics of the English and the Irish. The English he analyzed as "sober, industrious, mechanical, calculating and ruthless (characteristics invaluable in government)." The native Irish, on the other hand, were "imaginative, unpredictable and even irresponsible." The only exception I would take to that is the addition of "irresponsible." Thinking back over the months here, I can't recall ever asking any Irishman to do *anything* that was really *important* that didn't *eventually* get done. It's merely a variation of approach and emphasis, and they're the arbiters. For Americans everything is important and urgent. For the Irish life is merely a diversion rather than a plan. I remember last summer walking into a one-room tourist office in the West with a young girl handling at least ten tourists' requests. I asked her to make thirty hotel reservations for me and said I would be back in a few hours. When I returned, she was cordial and polite and very pleased to let me know she had made two reservations. Who was unreasonable?

The distillation of the myths of the Irish extends over two thousand years, embracing their ancient, aristocratic order and its mutilation by intruders; their diaspora, as wide-ranging as that of the Jews; and their final cycle of retrieval. An inevitable retrieval, evident far back in the art of the ancient Celts repeating endless circles in their designs, fascinated with the infinity of circles, hinting at the endless cycle of their race, crossed but never broken. There is a strange, haunting presence of its past in this island, which sits surrounded by water as an endless reflection of herself, forced into seclusion and restrained from the flow of seven centuries. Only fifty years ago, emerging exhausted from civil war, Ireland unfolded like a delicate moonflower, mysteriously responding to the cool calm of an evening, with her land settling peacefully for the first time in seven hundred years.

◇ ◇ ◇

Who were these ancients? Any sense of the Celts, until recently, has been blurred by the angular view of the progress of civilization under Graeco-Roman guidance, culminating with the British Empire piloting civilization through so many ancient cultures — East through China, South over Africa, East again over India, and North through the Celtic nations. History has suffered a myopia, relying on these cultures for an unsympathetic rendering of the "barbarian" fringes. Interestingly, the word "barbarous" was to the early Greeks all those "of foreign language." Only later it became a caste description of all those not settled within the Mediterranean world as primitive, savage, and vulgar. Only narrowly recognized are the Celts' advances in the arts, in a comprehensive and intricate law system, and later in their rescue of a Europe emerging from the Dark Ages.

At one time Celtic influence spread over one quarter of Europe, with their earliest home believed to be along the Upper Danube. Since ancient times great importance was placed on historical records, and the arrival in Ireland of the Milesians, the ancestors of the present Irish, is calculated at 1,000 B.C. These Milesians dispossessed the Tuatha de Danann, who had migrated from Northern Europe, and who, it is believed, displaced the Fir Bolgs before them. The ancient shanachies (storytellers) relate that the Milesians arrived from Spain, but this is generally argued by scholars, who insist that the mode of transportation at the time, wicker boats, could not have made the long journey; and they conclude that the Spain of which the ancients are referring was a land geographically inflated to the Spain recognized today. It is more reasonable to assume that the Milesians crossed from Gaul to Britain and then on to Ireland.

There's a temptation, to which I plan to yield, to move from 1,000 B.C. toward a general description of the Irish during the relatively settled centuries just before the arrival of Saint Patrick in the fifth century A.D. through to the twelfth, before Ireland became a port for invaders.

Untampered and largely ignored by Roman invasions, native Irish literature provides a limn today of the Celtic ancestors: the bardic volumes such as the *Dinnshenchas*, the lore of high places passed orally through generations until they were first recorded by the early missionaries. This description of the topography shows a land vastly different from the denuded countryside we pass through today. Gaelic scholar P. W. Joyce writes of the ancient land:

> ...All over the country there were vast forests, and great dangerous marshes, quagmires, and bogs covered with reeds, moss and grass.... Buried down at a depth of many feet in some of our present bogs, great tree trunks are often found, the relics of the primeval forest.

> The woods and wild places were alive with birds and wild animals of all kinds, and the people were very fond of hunting and fishing; for there was plenty of game both large and small, and the rivers and lakes teemed with fish. Sometimes they hunted hares and foxes for mere sport. But they had much grander game; wild boars with long tusks, deer in great herds, and wolves lurked in caves and thick woods...Kites and golden eagles skimmed over plains, peering down for prey; and the goshawks, or falcons, used in the old game of hawking, were found in great abundance.

The country was originally divided into five provinces: Leinster, East Munster, West Munster, Connacht, and Ulster. Gradually the two Munsters merged; then, in the second century A.D., a new province, Meath (or Mide) was established. Over the countryside were almost two hundred *tuaths* (tribes or families), each under the rule of a king or chief, all under the High King of Ireland. The High King and the lesser kings were all elected by the free citizens and were by no means all-powerful monarchs. Their power was restrained as prescribed by ancient customs and laws of the tribes, and further by the counsels of the chief men of the *tuath*.

This society, divided by degrees of nobility, learning, and wealth, aided the kings in their rule. Next in stature to the kings were the *filid* (learned poets), who in later times separated into the *brehons* (the interpreters of the law) and the *druids* (keepers of the supernatural). Class distinctions were in most cases determined by the ownership of land and were divided into five degrees: kings, nobles, non-noble freemen with land, non-noble freemen without land, and the nonfree, most often the *Daer Fuidirs*, "persons carried off from a conquered country."

One of the most notorious of this class, the Daer Fuidirs, was Saint Patrick, who had been brought to Ireland as a young boy after a raid on Britain. He remained as a slave and sheepherder until his escape to the Continent. He returned to Ireland as a Bishop in A.D. 432. In 438 he approached Laegaire, the High King of Ireland, to ask that a council be arranged to revise Irish laws in accordance with the new Christian teachings. The result of this council, which was attended by kings, two other bishops, and three filid, was the *Seanchas Mor*, the most revealing document of the blending of the newly arrived Christianity with the life of the ancients.

These filid, who shared the responsibility of the tribe, were insured position by talent rather than birth. It was the filid who would commit to memory the vast collections of history, lore, and law, as the Brahmins did in ancient India. They possessed

Purity of Hand: bright without wounding

Purity of Mouth: without poisonous satire
Purity of Learning: without reproach.

They actually possessed more power than the kings, for they could travel from territory to territory recognized by all.

Because interpretation of the native law was of such importance in ancient Ireland, a separate specialized group in the filid emerged, the brehons. These were the judges who interpreted the *seanchas* (law of the *fine*, or free landtillers) until the seventeenth century, when the native system was replaced. To the brehons were left all judgments of a system of laws of "vast technicality; no outsiders could hope to master their intricacies." One ancient account reveals the belief that a divine power watched over the rulings of the brehons: "When the brehons deviated from the Truth, there appeared blotches upon their cheeks." Joyce went on to describe: "Early times regarded them as mysterious, half-inspired persons...Great brehon Moraum wore a *sin*, or collar, around his neck, which tightened when he delivered a false judgement and expanded again when he delivered a true one. But later on the Penal Laws changed all that and turned natural love of justice into hatred and distrust of law, which in many ways continues to manifest itself to this day."

An Englishman, John Davies, the Irish Attorney General to James I, wrote in 1610 of the love of justice among the Irish, which the English were about to smash in the seventeenth century:

> For there is no nation of people under the sunne that doth love equal and indifferent justice better than the Irish; or will rest better satisfied with the execution thereof, although it be against themselves; so as they may have the protection and benefit of law, where upon just cause they do deserve it.

Of equal importance were the Druids, who maintained their influence long after the Christian missionaries arrived. In early times these Druids were "judges, prophets, historians, poets and even physicians," but later their most important function was that of divining curses and foretelling the future. The most dreaded of all their powers was that of producing madness. Though today it is difficult to believe in these powers, they were of great influence on the ancients and highly regarded: "In the pagan ages, and down far into Christian times, madness was believed to be often brought on by malignant magical agency, usually the work of some druid. For this purpose the druid prepared a 'madman's wisp,' that is, a little wisp of straw or grass, into which he pronounced some horrible incantations, and watching for his opportunity, flung it into the face of his victim, who at once became insane and idiotic." Throughout their literature the ancients reveal a tenderness and sensitivity, as this passage shows, toward victims of the Druid's power of inflicting madness:

> There is a valley in Kerry called "Glan na Galt" — the glen of the *galts,* or the lunatics — and it is believed that all lunatics, if left to themselves, would find their way to it, no matter from what part of Ireland. When they lived in its solitude for a time, drinking of the water of Tober no galt (the lunatics' well) and eating of the cresses that grow along the little stream, the poor wanderers get restored to sanity.

The ancients were devoted to extremes, whether feasting or warring. One account describes their fairs, which were popular for centuries:

> In most parts of the country open-air meetings or fairs were held periodically, where the people congregated in thousands and, forgetting all the cares of the world for a time, gave themselves over to unrestrained enjoyment — athletic games and exercises, racing, music, recitations by skilled poets and storytellers, jugglers, and showmen's representations, eating, drinking, marrying and giving in marriage. So determined

were they to ward off unpleasantness on these occasions that no one, at the risk of his life, durst pick a quarrel or strike a blow: for this was one of the rules laid down to govern all public assemblies.

On the other hand, he continues:

But outside such social gatherings, and in ordinary life, both chiefs and people were quarrelsome and easily provoked to fight. Indeed they love fighting for its own sake, and a stranger to the native character would be astonished to see the very people who only a few days before vied with each other in good-natured enjoyment, now fighting to the death on some flimsy cause of variance, which in all likelihood he would fail to understand if he made inquiry.

Long before the arrival of Saint Patrick there was a high cultural life in this island. In A.D. 254 Cormac MacArt, one of the High Kings, established three colleges at Tara: one for the study of military science, one for the study of history and literature, and one for the study of law. The arrival of the Christians merely augmented an established culture, hence later the description: "The Island of Saints and Scholars."

Though it may have pleased some to regard Ireland as the land of saints and scholars, the Irish themselves had only one devotion — pleasure in all forms, a devotion enduring to this day. Kuno Meyer's versions of ninth century *Triads* dispel the folktale of Ireland's immediate conversion to a holy land by Saint Patrick.

Three slender things that best support the world: the slender stream of milk from the cow's dug into the pail; the slender blade of corn upon the ground; the slender thread over the hand of a skilled women.

Three rude ones of the world: a youngster mocking an old

man; a robust person mocking an invalid; a wise man mocking a fool.

Three fair things that hide ugliness: good manners in the ill-favoured; skill in a serf; wisdom in the misshapen.

Three glories of a gathering: a beautiful wife, a good horse, a swift hound.

Three signs of a fop: the track of his comb in his hair; the track of his teeth in his food; the track of his stick behind him.

Three idiots of a bad guest-house: an old hag with a chronic cough; a brainless tartar of a girl; a hobgoblin of a gilly.

Three things that constitute a physician: a complete cure; leaving no blemish behind; a painless examination.

Three nurses of theft: a wood, a cloak, night.

Three false sisters: "Perhaps," "Maybe," "I dare say."

Three timid brothers: "Hush!" "Stop!" "Listen!"

Three sounds of increase: the lowing of a cow in milk; the din of a smithy; the swish of a plough.

Three steadinesses of good womanhood: keeping a steady tongue; a steady chastity; a steady housewifery.

Three candles that illumine every darkness: truth, nature, knowledge.

Three keys that unlock thoughts: drunkenness, trustfulness, love.

Three youthful sisters: desire, beauty, generosity.

Three aged sisters: groaning, chastity, ugliness.

Three services, the worst that a man can serve: serving a bad woman, a bad lord, and bad land.

Though there were classes of people ranging from kings to slaves, women in society equalled in rank to men in owning land and possessions. Consistent with other Aryan nations, it was the man who brought the dowry "to purchase his wife." This would consist of gold, silver, brass, cattle, horses, land, and the like. However, if the marriage was dissolved, husband and wife took the land and goods each had brought to the marriage. Fosterage was common with children during these centuries and practiced by all classes, but especially among the nobles. A child would be sent to be reared and educated by another family of the tribe "for affection" or "for payment." This was a close and sacred tie among the families and continued through to the eighteenth century.

"An oval face, broad above and narrow below, golden hair, fair skin, white, delicate and well-formed hands with slender tapering fingers..." These for the ancient Irish were the markings of beauty and aristocracy. They were enchanted by and devoted to beauty, both men and women, in their clothes, adornments, and appearance. Thousands of lines of their literature are devoted to portraits of their clothing. In one of the ancient tales, the *Táin*, is a description of the panoply of colored mantles of the Ulster Army "...some with red cloaks, others with light blue cloaks, others with deep blue cloaks, others with green, or blue or white, or yellow cloaks, bright and fluttering about them: and there is a young red-freckled lad, with a crimson cloak in their midst." Both men and women had long flowing hair down their backs, and its elaborate styling, curling, and plaiting is evident in the figures in the illuminated manuscripts, such as the *Book of Kells*. The combs they used may be seen in the National Museum. Unused to such sybaritic excesses in the care for appearance, one of the first things the English did was to set rules for the regulation of clothes for the Irish and the length of their hair (coolin). Today you often hear a traditional song called "The Coolin," which was composed in medieval times as a protest against the forcing of the Irish to cut their hair.

◇ ◇ ◇

The waves of invasions began with the Danes, then the Normans, and finally the English. The Danes were defeated at the Battle of Clontarf in A.D. 1014. The Normans settled and eventually became absorbed in the culture, but it was the English — "the country who came to dinner," with England playing Sheridan Whiteside — who stayed on and on and on for hundreds of years attempting to dissolve everything Irish.

Hibernia is a strange, ancient hydra, refusing to be extinguished, though often deserted. The desertion has conveniently and romantically been focused on the Famine, with starving wretches in rags pouring into ports, struggling to reach America. Hundreds of thousands did starve, die, and emigrate during the Famine, but the Irish diaspora began long before and had nothing to do with potatoes. Nor did everyone leave Ireland naked and destined for immigrant slums across the Atlantic. There were others who left for the Continent, for Russia, South America, and the Near East, and who became distinguished diplomats, soldiers, politicians, merchants, actors, writers or thieves, depending on their choice.

The first wave of departure was forced and vile and caused by Henry VIII's uncontrollable fear of the Irish. After Cromwellian defeat, confiscation of lands, and the fall of the Gaelic order, the English still worried over Irish resurgence and devised a scheme of outlawing and expulsion. Early records show that blacks were not the only ones exported West for slavery. One interesting account written in 1667, "Some Observations on the Island of Barbados," shows onto which rung of the social ladder the Irish landed in their new home:

> The negro slaves not being in the yeare 1643 above six thousand fower hundred were by computation in the yeare 1666 above 50,000, theire buildings in the yeare 1643 were generally meane, and within their houses only things for necessity....

> For first they are not above seven hundred and sixty consider-able proprietors; and not above 8,000 effective men of wch twoe thirds are of noe interest or reputation, and of little innate courage, being poore men, that are just permitted to live, and a very great part Irish, derided by the negroes and branded with the epithite of white slave...

> I have for my particular satisfaction inspected many of theire plantations and have seen 30, sometimes 40, Christians, En-glish, Scotch, and Irish at worke in the parching sun without shirt, shoe or stocking, wch theire negroes have bin at their respective trades, in good condition.

While brothers were being deported, others stayed, try-ing to take back their lands. The final blow came at Limerick in 1691, after which no hope was left. Treaties were broken, and the only alternative was desertion. Patrick Sarsfield left with the first of a stream of thousands to the Continent, illegally smuggled out of their country to join foreign ar-mies, listed on the ship's bill of lading as "Wild Geese." They fought and died for dozens of armies for a hundred years, hoping one day to defeat the English. One of these Wild Geese, Marshal Maurice Lacy, received two letters which reveal the tragedy of honor in foreign wars, while their own country still belonged to others:

Vienna, 19 February, 1790:

My Dear Marshal Lacy:

I behold the moment which is to separate us approaching with hasty strides. I should be very ungrateful, indeed, if I left this world without assuring you, my dear friend, of that lively gratitude on which you have so many claims and which I have had the pleasure of acknowledging in the face of the whole world.

Yes, you created my army; to you it is indebted for its credit and consideration. If I be anything, I owe it to you. The trust I could repose in your advice under every circumstance; your unbroken attachment to my person, which never varied, your success in the field, as well as in the Council, are so many grounds, my dear Marshal, which render it impossible for me sufficiently to express my thanks.

I have seen your tears flow for me. The tears of a great man and a sage are a high panegyric. Receive my farewells. I tenderly embrace you. I regret nothing in this world but the small number of friends, among whom you certainly are the first. Remember me, remember your sincere and affectionate friend Joseph.

— *Joseph II*, Emperor of Austria

June 25, 1807:

General: Your illustrious master permits me to address you. Your country and your faith have all my sympathies. The noble devotion of Ireland's sons which have produced so many sacrifices through so many ages inspires the hope that you will seek to benefit your country and your faith, and to restore to her proscribed sons. Your name will inspire confidence, thousands will flock to your banner, and the ancient enemy of our common faith might be humbled to the wishes of both your royal master and myself. Think of this, and if favourably let me know. Accept my high consideration of your renown and ancestry.

– *Napoleon*

It seems as though no matter how many thousands of soldiers died bemedaled in foreign wars, the Irish were incapable of retrieving their own small island. All that remains on the Continent today are a few uniforms in museums, Irish surnames in almost all European countries, and Hennessy's brandy in France and Garvey's San Patricio sherry in Spain, both founded by Irish Wild Geese.

One day I was talking to Liam O'Flaherty, one of modern Ireland's most acclaimed writers, and when he found I was American he began to sing a song he was surprised I had never heard and did not recognize. He explained it was a song of the Confederate Army, which he had learned on his native Inishmore, one of the Aran Islands. As a boy he remembered being brought into the pub and seeing the returned veterans of our Civil War sitting in their Confederate uniforms singing Southern songs they had brought back. He remembered a few Union soldiers, also in uniform. "They were the only ones that came back with pensions." So the Irish were still fighting other people's wars when O'Flaherty was a boy.

◇ ◇ ◇

Over the months, as I drove along the roads seeing the farmers working their lands in Mayo, or the islanders of Blasket rowing back to the Big Island to graze their sheep, or boys cycling down through Wicklow to escape Dublin for a weekend, it was hard for me to imagine the Irish deprived of their lands, to understand how an intruder could bear to disturb the rhythm. For months I heard endless stories of their lands, rivers, deserted raths, and fairy hills. A bond handed down from the ancient poets reciting the *Dinnshenchas,* leaving legends for today of granite cairns, distant hills, and holy wells.

One afternoon in Clare an old man told me a story of the Aranocks, the Aran islanders, who used to row over eight miles in their currachs to the mainland on the last Sunday in July, Garland Sunday, a pattern day in Lahinch. They would come to choose a wife to bring back with them to the islands. After they landed at Doolin, they would walk over the cliffs to St. Brigid's Well at Liscannor, make the round of the old pagan well, and spend the night singing. As the old man observed: "What in the name of Jaysus were they singing? Sure there isn't a song in Aran, they're tone deaf…like the Americans." The custom has all but died out, though he said that a few years ago four islanders arrived by taxi.

Sitting on the majestic, solitary cliffs of Mizen Head in Cork, I wondered what a strange people these disturbers must have been and how patient the Irish had to become. Not far from where I was sitting a gentleman called Langley, one of the Cromwellian planters of the island, had penned the most unusual will in 1674:

> My body shall be put upon the oak table in the brown room, and fifty Irishmen shall be invited to my wake and everyone shall have two quarts of the best aquavitae and each a skein, dirk or knife laid before him, and when their liquor is out, nail up my coffin and commit me to earth whence I came.

His friends, upon reading the will, were confused at the invitation extended to the Irish, for whom they knew he held no warm feelings. "Why, for that reason," he replied. "For they will get so drunk at my wake that they will kill one another, and so we shall get rid of the breed. And if everyone would follow my example in their wills, in time we should get rid of them all." An interesting legacy for a guest!

There were a few over the years who came to Ireland's side. In 1812 Percy Bysshe Shelley arrived in Ireland at the age of nineteen with his sister Harriet and his "Address to the Irish People." As M. J. MacManus says in his collection, *Irish Cavalcade,* Shelley had "come to Ireland on a mission — which was nothing less than the uprooting of the Constitution of the British Empire, restoring Ireland's Parliament and bringing about Catholic emancipation." Shelley wrote to a friend: "I stand on the balcony of our window and watch till when I see a man *who looks likely,* I throw a book to him."

Dean Swift's method was more vitriolic. He was born of English parents, but had been sent to Ireland and grew to abhor the treatment of the Irish. In 1720 he wrote his blistering satire, "A Modest Proposal," in which he recommended to the British people a scheme for the killing of year-old Irish children, whom he promised "a most nourishing and wholesome food."

Neither these nor other efforts curtailed the pamphleteers pounding up and down Irish roads denouncing the Irish. By the 1840's the island was becoming a floating pulpit, the last potato had rotted, and for many of the Irish nothing was left but the next boat to Boston.

Uprooted and forced to emigrate, the Irish began their "American wakes." Families and friends would gather for their style of bon voyage, since they knew they'd never be coming home. The legacy of the leaving was a hundred emigrants' songs, like "Spancill Hill," where a young man describes sailing into his childhood home:

 I went to see my neighbours,
 To hear what they might say
 The old ones were all dead and gone
 The young ones worn and grey.

He goes on about visiting familiar old fields and streams and seeing his first love he left behind, and then ends:

> The cock crowed in the morning,
> He crowed both loud and shrill
> And I woke in California,
> Many miles from Spancill Hill.

Emigration was the real bruise to the Irish, and it was only a backhanded pleasure that the "coffin boats" carried a generation to produce among them: John F. Kennedy, F. Scott Fitzgerald, Eugene O'Neill, John O'Hara, Eugene McCarthy, Spencer Tracy, Jack Dempsey, Gene Tunney, and many more. They were still Ireland's loss. The longing in the separation is touched in this fragment of an Irishman's letter to his brother: "When you get home, Michael, from America, we'll sit up and talk, and we'll wear out the stars."

◇ ◇ ◇

I can remember only twice being startled into realizing my connection with Ireland. One summer evening I was sitting on a wooden fence along the Dublin–Cork road just enjoying the calm sundown. For a moment, looking at the old road, I thought of someone a long time ago walking down that road, or one like it, to get to America so that I'd arrive back one day with a typewriter for a tour. I had no idea who they were, where they had gone in the States. I felt a sadness knowing nothing about them, and realized someone had been embarrassed by their poverty, forgotten about their courage, and wanted a memory only of yesterday's fortune.

I didn't think about it again until months later when a friend took me up to a cottage in the desolate hills of Connemara to try some poteen (Irish moonshine). An old

woman came to the door, about seventy-five, I guessed,
only five feet tall, in a long black dress and plaited grey hair
to her waist, and with the largest swollen hands I had ever
seen. We talked for hours, and she fixed us poteen the way
they used to drink it to survive the razor sharp winter
nights in the West — stirred with sugar in boiling water.
She told us pieces of her life. Twelve grown children —
eleven had emigrated — one son stayed with her. The
husband had died in Birmingham after the last child. There
was a bitter edge while she talked, not from complaint, just
a knowing. The lines on her face showed every season, and
her swollen hands every chore. While she was moving
around to get us another drink, I thought of another
woman I know about her own age. Her family name was
Martin, and she had married a man named Madden, both
Galway names. I saw her as she had appeared to me
throughout my childhood, a lovely lady with beautiful
dresses and furs and rings and such a soft face and soft
hands. My grandmother. That was the only other time I
wondered about those people I didn't know who had gotten us to America.

◇ ◇ ◇

Today people wonder in comfortable hindsight why no
one, especially the European countries — France, Spain,
Austria, and all the others — did not come to Ireland's
rescue in those years, after so many Irishmen had died for
their causes and freedom. In 1855 a Frenchman, Emile
Montégut, sensed why Ireland had been neglected:

> There is another and more profound reason. Our manner of
> judgement today is essentially prosaic and bourgeois; we
> weigh and we measure things, people, races, as we measure
> oil or we weigh stuffs. All that cannot be classed and num-
> bered is valueless in our eyes. A man has only a productive

and commercial value; and the more a people produces, the greater it is. The modern world, which only esteems what it can see and touch, is not grateful to Ireland for her seductive gifts, and, in fact, this unhappy race is entirely isolated in our Occident; in all that exists, nothing resembles it, nowhere does it find a reflection of itself.

Around the time of Montégut's article England's *Morning Post* said "The Celt is going, going with a vengeance. Very shortly an Irishman will be as scarce on the banks of the Shannon as an Indian on the banks of the Potomac." As Brendan Behan wrote, telling the story: "But I am very happy to report that the *Morning Post* is gone, and by Jaysus, we're here yet."

It was inevitable that the English couldn't win here. The Union had been a failure, and the reasons were best explained in a pamphlet, *An Irish Apologia*, written by an Englishman in 1917, Warre Wells.

He quoted Tom Kettle, who had died for both Irishmen and Englishmen on the fields of Ginchy in France:

> Ireland, unvisited by the legions and laws of Rome, had evolved a different vision of life of men in community, or in other words, a different idea of the state. Put very briefly, the difference lay in this: The Romans and their inheritors organised for purposes of war and order; the Irish for the purpose of culture. The one laid emphasis on police, the other on poets.

Another Anglo-Irishman, Horace Plunkett, summed up the years: "Anglo-Irish history is for the Englishman to remember, for the Irishman to forget."

◇ ◇ ◇

It would be unfair to assume that the English made no contribution to Ireland during their stay. Some of the most beautiful, whimsical architecture — their country houses and follies of that period — dots the Irish landscape. Desmond Guinness wrote in *Country Life* an amusing description of the free style of eighteenth century architecture:

> The most extraordinary fancy of Irish architecture appears in Castle Ward. Built by an unknown architect for Mr. Bernard and Lady Ann Ward in 1762. The story goes that they could not agree on the style of their new house — Mr. Ward wanted a classical house and his wife one in the Gothic mode after Strawberry Hill in England. The result was a compromise — a house that is classical in the front and Gothic in the back.

Though it may not be architecturally correct, it's an ingenious tribute to marriage!

Georgian Dublin in the eighteenth century became an enviable classical music center. During the year 1741-42 Handel directed more than eighteen concerts in Dublin, one of which included the first performance of his *Messiah* in the New Musick Hall in Fishamble Street. As one critic attending the evening wrote: "One would think that Apollo, the God of Music, had taken a long stride from the Continent over England to this land."

While the classical mode was entertaining in Dublin, the music of the Irish people developed in isolation as it had for hundreds of years. The harp, now the national emblem, which was known as the *criut* or *clairseach*, can be seen sculptured on the ancient high crosses. One of these high crosses at Monasterboice shows three pipers playing. Though often mistaken by the classicists in Dublin as peasants' music, Irish traditional music was in fact the court music of the ancients, and closely linked to Indo-European court music. An account by Giraldus Cambrensis in 1185 imparts the subtlety of the music of the harpers:

> For their manner of playing on these instruments, unlike that of the Britons to which I am accustomed, is not slow and harsh,

but lively and rapid, while the melody is both sweet and sprightly.

They enter into a movement and conclude it in so delicate a manner and tinkle the strings so sportively under the deeper tones of the brass strings, they delight so delicately and sooth with such gentleness, that the perfection of their art appears in the concealment of art.

There were many blendings between the traditional and classical musical cultures in those days. One young Irish tenor, Michael Kelley, who was influenced by both, became a friend of Mozart while he was abroad on the Continent, and played in his first performance of *Figaro*.

◇ ◇ ◇

As the twentieth century began, no one would have imagined that the first fifty years would be bracketed by two world wars, proving that empires could no longer exist and intruders were no longer welcome on native soil. No one but the Irish! A new generation of Irishmen crossed into the twentieth century. As one of them wrote anonymously:

I do not hesitate to assert that the existing generation in the country is half a century in advance of that which is dying off, and that the generation now at school will be a century in advance of us. We were reckless, ignorant, improvident, drunken, and idle. We were idle, for we had nothing to do; we were reckless, for we had no hope; ignorant, for learning was denied us; we were improvident, for we had no future; we were drunken, for we sought to forget our misery. That time has passed away forever.

So one day after the bloody "Troubles" in 1922, the intruders went home, and the Irish set about heaving the dust off their dreams.

◇ ◇ ◇

In his preface to *John Bull's Other Island* George Bernard Shaw wrote of his countrymen: "Oh, the dreaming! the dreaming! the torturing, heartscalding, never satisfying dreaming...an Irishman's imagination never lets him alone, never convinces him, never satisfies him...." Later Yeats said the Irish were men "who believed so much in the soul and so little in anything else that they were never entirely certain that the earth was solid under their foot-sole." Both descriptions deal with only half an Irishman. Like the double-faced Janus gods of the ancient Celts, they twine their dreams around a firmly rooted cynicism. After the Free State was formed, Eamon de Valera described the intentions of the country.

> The Ireland which we have dreamed of would be the home of people who valued material wealth only as a basis for right living.... who.... devoted their leisure to things of the spirit; a land whose countryside would be bright with cozy homesteads...with the romping of sturdy children, the contests of athletic youths, the laughter of comely maidens; whose firesides would be the forums for the wisdom of old age. It would be, in a word, the home of a people living the life God desires men should live.

Dev's statement was typically Irish. What seems utopian is merely obvious and practical to the Irish.

The Irish are far from obsessed by goals. You're free to be ambitious if you want, you merely don't have to be. If you stay with the Irish for a while, they have the facility for draining a frantic pace. John F. Kennedy visited Ireland in 1963, some months before he died, and said in an address before the Dail:

> Ireland is moving in the mainstream of current world

events.... Your future is as promising as your past is proud, and your destiny lies not as a peaceful island in a sea of trouble, but as a maker and shaper of world peace.

This ponderous proposal had a double-edged reception. Many Irishmen would *prefer* to remain a peaceful island, adding only some prosperity, and are fairly skeptical of world solutions. Nor do they want to be interfered with by the world's solutions for them. One evening during dinner an American journalist wrapped in a mist of nostalgia was challenging Ireland's entrance into the Common Market. A deputy of the Commission who was present quietly turned toward her and offered an apology: "Sorry, we can't be the Irish-American Azores."

◇ ◇ ◇

No other quality of the Irish is better known or more curiously regarded than their outrageous contempt for conviction or convention. The epigrams of Wilde, the paradoxes of Shaw, the lyrics of Yeats, the quotes of O'Casey, Synge, Beckett, Behan, a fisherman from Aran or a publican from Bohola have been printed, quoted, and repeated in almost every language on every continent. And the wit is pointed outward and inward. When George Moore left Dublin in 1911, he regretted being separated from his young friend, Oliver St. John Gogarty, "the arch mocker, the author of all the jokes that enable us to live in Dublin." Gogarty once wrote to Lloyd's of London asking them to insure him against knighthood. Upon hearing that another of his books had been banned by the Censorship Board in Dublin, he instructed his publishers to insert on the flyleaf of his next publication: FORBIDDEN TO BE SOLD IN IRELAND. Libraries and Dublin brim with these stories, but charm and outrageous irreverence are not the exclusive possession of the literati. A Dublin insurance broker made a pilgrimage to

Lenin's tomb a few years ago. While standing in the long queue, he broke away and approached the somber, armed guard, reached out his hand to the soldier, and said: "Sorry for your troubles." He spent the remainder of his Russian vacation in a Moscow jail.

In the evening, looking out from the Georgian farmhouse at the foot of the Dublin Mountains a generous friend lent me, the lights of Dublin bubble up the hill from the city's bay. It's a very different country from even twenty years ago when foreign countries were invited in tax free. Yet much remains the same. Industries have mushroomed, slicing emigration, curing a great deal of poverty. They seem important to the Irish only to free them for elusive pastimes. If there's an effort ever going on in Ireland, it's only to ease the spirit.

◇ ◇ ◇

A few years ago in Ireland an unusual individual made an unexpected effort on behalf of the arts. It would be rare to find a person, including publishers and gallery owners, who worries about how artists survive. Most people just assume they eat old typewriter ribbons and drink leftover paint. Charles Haughey, then Minister for Finance, proposed that artists and writers should live in Ireland tax free, the only country in the world to dream up such legislation. When challenged, Haughey remarked: "What's wrong with building a little Athens by the Liffey." A friend of mine, a writer, told me he arrived back at his house on the day the announcement was made to find an "AUCTION" sign tacked to his front door by the tax bureau for back taxes. Some Irishmen haven't come to terms with it all, especially regarding artists. One well-known artist told me: "There's always a few who come up to you in the pub, and the conversation turns to the tax. Aw, you're a chancer, they say to me. You see, they don't know anything about art." So I asked him why he stayed on, when New York, Paris, and London, with their culture buffs, awaited him. He told me a story. "A few years ago I had a show in Wexford, and I had found a piece of bog oak in the shape of a horse and mounted it and put it into the show. A farmer came up to me during the show and was annoyed, saying it was just bog oak. I talked to him for a while about form and all that, and the next day I came back to Dublin. A few weeks later I got a letter from the farmer, saying that he had been out in the bog and found more 'art' for me. I wrote back and told him to keep it for himself and have his own show. Can you imagine the conversation that went on with the old man and his friends out in the bog while he explained to them about forms and the oak."

Over the months, I've heard hundreds of these stories, and "Views and Overviews" are just conversations with some Irish people about their country — its history, its legends, its customs, its music, art, theatre. But remember the Janus gods. An Irishman's view today he will probably argue against tomorrow. The Irish aren't what they seem. And then they are.

PART ONE

Views and Overviews

1. Genealogy:

Seed and Breed

**with
Garret Roche**

The tourist in Ireland looking out from his car or bus from town to town may not know he is traveling across the oldest and best-documented tribal territories in Europe, and that the names of each tribal group – surnamed in the ninth or tenth century – are still thick on the ground of their traditional lands. Many an Irish-American Sullivan, Byrne, Sweeney, Brennan, or what-have-you, crosses the tribe-family lands on which those of his name once lived for a couple of thousand years and more without knowing it. Often he passes his own relatives, also without knowing it, relatives lost four, five, and six generations back when his ancestor left for America.

◇ ◇ ◇

There are very few Irishmen who do not realize, however vaguely, the antiquity and continuity of the Irish people. With the recent collapse of various empires, for which the Romans and the Greeks were such model political ancestors, the Celts, who once stretched from the Danube to Galway, have been rediscovered. Losers to the Romans, and later to the British, their monuments have proven irremovable, and the Irish are still the living artifacts of what was once an enormous tribal world.

C.D. Darlington, the English geneticist, in his remarkable book, *The Evolution of Man and Society* (1968), writes: "The most wide-ranging of all Aryan migrations and conquests, however, on the evidence of living languages, were carried out by the Celts. They completed their movement on the western fringe of Europe, but they went east as well as west." He describes "the first glimpse of the Celtic warrior in the thousand graves of Hallstatt dating from the beginning of the first millennium B.C.," and goes on to say that "they owe their lasting fame to what they did in their settled life in the west. They owe it to their military and agricultural, religious and artistic activities. And, in addition, to their languages and literature, which still survive."

One of these Celtic literary survivals is the huge corpus of genealogical compilations in the Irish language that miraculously survived the centuries of war and destruction in Ireland. The written compilations were already in existence in the eighth century. In Europe, Ireland is unique, mainly because the real assaults upon its unbroken tradition came late in the day.

When the Celtic warrior people known as the Gael invaded Ireland c.300-250 B.C., the gigantic tombs of Newgrange, glittering with their coatings of white quartz, were already about two thousand years old, and all kinds of arts and skills were practiced in the island. For bronze work alone Ireland was a famed workshop. From that invasion of the Gael (the Sons of Mil, called the Milesians) to the comparatively brief intrusion of the Norsemen a thousand uninterrupted years would pass, and it would be four hundred more years before the Normans came. Within two centuries of their arrival these Normans would be absorbed. Their genealogies are recorded from their arrival in the twelfth century, alongside those of the native Irish dating from the sixth century. Though the Normans brought turmoil, solutions were found, and the incredibly long tradition continued, until the English hammer blows of the sixteenth and seventeenth centuries, and it even survived the neurotically fretful and anti-Irish obsession that followed.

Because of the reverence of long-dead chroniclers for family history, many people of Gaelic and Norman descent are able to link up with the genealogies, which only ceased to be meticulously kept with the death of the Gaelic order in the seventeenth century. Until then various families of hereditary scholars had recorded the births and deaths of the ancient tribe families in every part of the island. For the English invaders of the sixteenth century Ireland was another world, totally alien in language and custom, in attitude and aspiration, a living museum of a culture that had existed at the very end of the known world for thousands of years. It was only a little over a thousand years since the Teutonic Anglo-Saxons had invaded Celto-Roman Britain, and Ireland, this strange Celtic museum, had completely missed the Roman yoke.

Darlington writes of the Anglo-Irish struggle as follows: "This quarrel can be understood only in terms of the profound racial difference between the Gaelic-speaking natives and the English-speaking invaders, a difference which even today, after twenty generations of limited hybridization, is still not seriously blurred." And Darlington, the geneticist with his detached view of man and history, looked even farther when he wrote of the Celts in Britain: "The Celts in their frontier city had failed to be assimilated by the Saxons: they were too equal for slavery, too different for marriage." There was another difference, about land and its ownership, the difference between the English primogeniture and the Irish joint-family ownership of land. The tribe-family or joint-family heightened the importance of detailed genealogical records, the basis of which was the Derbfine, which consisted of four generations of a property-owning joint family.

The Irish scholar, Professor James Hogan, describes the Derbfine as follows:

> Under the ordinary law of inheritance a family group of four generations formed what was termed a Derbfine, or legal family. This family group, consisting of the sons, grandsons, and great-grandsons of a common ancestor, constituted the legal family for purposes of inheritance. On the death of any one of its male adult members, his property was divided between the remaining members of the Derbfine in proportions fixed by law. This arrangement held good only so long as the Derbfine represented a joint family removed not more than three generations from a common ancestor. When the next generation came forward, that is to say, when the sons of the great-grandsons of a common ancestor came of age, the Derbfine thereupon resolved itself for legal purposes into a new set of derbfines or group families, the head of each new Derbfine being one of the sons of the man who was head of the older group.

A man had a simple way of explaining or remembering the layout of his own particular Derbfine, and Sir John Perrot, one of the many who arrived to conquer Ireland in the late sixteenth century, wrote of it as the law or custom "of the finger's end." The palm of the hand represented the common ancestor of the Derbfine and the three joints of the fingers the three generations coming down from the common ancestor. Commenting on this, Professor James Hogan states that ancient literary evidence shows this custom to have been in use in the distant past, long before Perrot.

The last of the traditional Gaelic genealogists was Dualtagh MacFirbis, who died in 1670, killed by a drunken Cromwellian. MacFirbis, in the introduction to his great

Book of Genealogies, speaks of the qualities required by the ancient historians: "As to the historians of Ireland," he wrote, "indeed scarcely any difference is found in ancient times between them and experts in law and the class called men of art (i.e., poets) today, for at that time the learned men of Ireland were often of one school, and they were arranged in seven grades, that is, *ollam, anradh, cli, cana, dos, macfuirmidh,* and *fochlag,* which were the names of those seven grades...." And along with every other law, the grades of poets were required to be free from the taint of theft and killing, from defamation and adultery, and from everything that was harmful to their learning.

He then proceeds to unfold the detailed tribal systems of the pre-Gaelic peoples of Ireland, and when he comes to the Gael he mentions the differences of "the two races that are in Ireland, that is, between the remnants of the Fir Bolg, Fir Domnann, and Gaileoin, and Tuatha de Danann and the Sons of Mil." Quoting from ancient documents, Mac-Firbis writes:

> Everyone who is white of skin, who is brown of hair, who is bold, who is honourable, who is daring, who is happy, who is bountiful of chattels, wealth, and gold ornaments, and who is not afraid of battle or combat, those are the descendants of the Sons of Mil in Ireland.

> Everyone who is fair-haired, who is honourable, who is tall, every spoiltaker, every musical person, professors of stringed-sweetness of music, of both hand and wind instruments, and adepts of every art of magic and all medical art besides, they are the remnant of the Tuatha de Danann in Ireland.

The Tuatha de Danann, or the People of the Goddess Danu, were in Ireland before the Gael, and when the Gael came they "agreed" to vanish into the Underworld of Ireland, and the new invaders would live on the earth above them, each leader of the Tuatha de Danann being assigned a tomb or *Sidh* mound, most of which exist to this day. Many manuscripts detail the names and traditions of these burial mounds of the magical Tuatha de Danann.

When he comes to the original inhabitants MacFirbis quotes again:

> Everyone who is black-haired, ill-doing, tale-telling, stringy, graceless, every thriftless, disorderly, vulgar, changeful, unsteady, crafty, and undignified person; every slave, every slavish thief, every inhospitable or unruly person, everyone that does not keep silent in the presence of music and playing of wind instruments, those who disturb every debate and every assembly, and set everyone at variance, those are the descendants of the Fir Bolg, and the Gaileoin, and Lioghmaine, and Fir Domnann. But, however, the descendants of the Fir Bolg are the most numerous of these.

A description, obviously, of the losers, the original inhabitants, the small, dark, Iberian people whose island had fallen at last to the new, tall, pale-skinned warriors.

MacFirbis gives details of the Bolg Tuath, the tribal territories assigned to the conquered Fir Bolg by the conquerors, and one of them is the Bolg Tuatha Bagna, a settlement allotted to them on what is now Slieve Baune, the mountain of Bagna. About two thousand years after the Gaelic invasion the Irish scholar, John O'Donovan, wandering the province of Connacht in 1837 for the Survey Department in Dublin, found himself on Slieve Baune mountain in Roscommon. "It was the market day of Strokestown, and I was struck with the prevalence of black hair in the district — 'hair black as the raven's wing.' Are these the Fir Bolgs of Bagna who have assumed Gaelic names? It is very probable that they are." (We can forget the modern idea that black hair in Ireland came from the descendants of the wrecked Armada seamen. From Spain, yes, but a few thousand years before the Armada.)

Summing up, MacFirbis quotes how the ancient Irish saw the various races of the world about them:

The architecture of the tall Jews
And their truly fierce envy,
The large size of the Armenians without deceit,
And the strength of the Saracens.

Astuteness in the Greeks with valour,
Great pride among the Romans,
The obduracy of the floating Saxons,
And the unruliness of the Spaniards.

Tell ye avarice in the Franks,
And anger in the true Welshman,
Here is the just knowledge of the stocks,
The gluttony of the Norse and their commerce.

I will not conceal the high spirits of the Picts,
The beauty and lust of the Gaels,
Giolla na Naomh tells it in verse,
Oh, Christ, let it be worthily preserved.

A hundred years earlier an English traveler in Ireland, Arthur Young, noted how the Irish passion about pedigree still lived, though the Gaels were long conquered and impoverished.

At Clonells, near Castlerea, lives O'Conor, the direct descendant of Roderick O'Conor, who was King of Connacht six or seven hundred years ago; there is a monument to him in Roscommon Church, with his sceptre, etc.... I was told as a certainty that the family were here long before the coming of the Milesians. Their possessions, formerly so great, are reduced to three or four hundred pounds a year, the family having fared in the revolutions of so many ages much worse than the O'Neills and O'Briens. The common people pay him the greatest respect, and send him presents of cattle, etc., upon various occasions. They consider him as the prince of a people involved in one common ruin. Another great family in Connacht is MacDermot, who calls himself Prince of Coolavin. He lives at Coolavin in Sligo, and though he has not above one hundred pounds a year, will not permit his children to sit down in his presence. This was certainly the case with his father, and some assured me even with the present chief. Lord Kingsborough, Mr. Ponsonby, Mr. O'Hara, Mr. Sandford, etc., came to see him, and his address was curious. "O'Hara, you are welcome. Sandford, I'm glad to see your mother's son" (his mother was an O'Brien). "As to the rest of ye, come in as ye can."

Not too long after that a poor blind harper, Arthur O'Neill, who was born in County Tyrone in 1734, recounted an experience showing this importance of a family name.

Lord Kenmare, the principal proprietor of Killarney, the lakes and the surrounding country, took it into his head to give a Milesian entertainment, that is, to entertain at Christmas time every Milesian that could be found that bore the name of an Irish chieftain, which names are the O'Neills, the O'Briens, the MacCarthys, the O'Donoghues, the O'Driscolls, the O'Connors, the O'Donovans, the O'Sullivans, the O'Connor Kerry (sic), the MacNamaras, the O'Keefes, the O'Meaghers, the O'Learys, the O'Callaghans, the O'Connells, the O'Mahonys, the MacGillicuddys, and some others of the Milesian race that my memory at present will not enable me to mention. At the feast there were one or more of every name (already mentioned) present but an O'Neill, which Lord Kenmare observed and mentioned.

"Och," says my patron, Muirrecertagh MacOwen O'Sullivan, "upon my honour I can soon fill up that gap for you, as I have now at my house a young man from the north who is blind and plays on the harp very well for his years, and from what I can understand from his own lips he has a good claim to represent on this occasion the O'Neills."

"Well, send for him," says my lord.

I was sent for and was without any ceremony seated amongst them in the Great Hall before dinner. Hundreds of questions were asked me concerning my descent, and on my giving them satisfactory answers I was dubbed and deemed an O'Neill, for they all said I had a very genteel mug (a good face).

When dinner was announced, very nearly two hundred of the O's and Macs took their seats, and poor self, being blind, I done what blind men always do — I groped for a vacancy near the foot of the table: and such a noise of cutting, carving, roaring, laughing, shaking hands, and such language as generally occurs between friends who only see each other once a year, I never before or since witnessed. But when Lord Kenmare hobnobbed me, he was pleased to say, "O'Neill, you should be at the head of the table, as your ancestors were the original Milesians of this Kingdom."

"Oh, my lord," says I, "it's no matter where an O'Neill sits, and let it be at what part of the table I am, it should be considered the head of it."

A universal burst of applause ensued, and my arm was almost shaken from my body by all present, and I believe it was in consequence of my reply to his lordship, which they remarked came by instinct to an O'Neill; and damn the O'Neill that ever was born or that will ever yet be born as well as myself but was drank by all the Milesians then present.

This feeling attached to a family name persisted, as John O'Donovan recorded in his account of his 1837 journey to Roscommon:

The present O'Conor Don is looked up to here with the most affectionate regard, and I believe most deservedly. Whenever the poor people see him in the Courthouse, their eyes glisten with joy at the very sight of his person, and from the idea that through him justice will be done. He would frank a letter for a beggarwoman as soon as he would for Mr. Wills. They call him in Irish "An t O Conchuir Donn" and in English always "the Don," never O'Conor. In old time their followers must have had great veneration for the chiefs of their own race.

The O'Conor don represented their dead kings and their ancient patrimony —

> *The fort over against the oak wood,*
> *Once it was Bruidge's, it was Cathal's,*
> *It was Aed's, it was Ailill's,*
> *It was Conaing's, it was Cuiline's,*
> *And it was Maelduin's:*
> *The fort remains after each in his turn –*
> *And the kings asleep in the ground.*

Anyone of Irish descent will want to know who his ancestors were.

◇ ◇ ◇

Comment

Dublin is the best for your genealogical tracing. Before you begin have as much specific information as possible — name, occupation, townland and the date of departure from Ireland — of your family. The Heraldic Museum in Dublin Castle (Hours: 9:45 A.M.-1:00 P.M.; 2:15-4:45 P.M.) has a vast collection of officially recorded pedigrees, register of armorial bearings, printed family histories, and other heraldic material. For a fee of £2.00 per hour (this usually takes 4-5 hours) a search may be done. For those who want to pursue more details the National Library in Dublin has a manuscript collection including directories, family histories, deeds, letters, and other papers on many Irish families.

2. Paganism and Antiquities:

Pagan Traces

with
Morgan MacSweeney

I who have sought afar from earth
  The Faeryland to meet,
Now find content within its girth
  And wonder nigh my feet.

– Æ

The "little people," leprechauns, the fairy folk became a joke outside of Ireland a long time ago, and a joke in Ireland not all that long ago – for they were once gods and goddesses worshiped long before Christianity came. Yet people still see the "fairy folk," privileged people, that is.

I met one of the privileged recently, one of the most truthful and reliable old men I ever knew. I had to believe what he told me, for he obviously believed it himself, and, anyway, there are places in Ireland that really do emanate a strong feeling of another world, the world of what has been, called the Middle Kingdom.

I have never seen any form of ghost or spirit, and don't expect to, yet I do believe what this old man described to me. There is nothing unusual in what he saw, because so many others have reported similar "sightings." What was unusual was that it came from him, a man I knew to be scrupulously truthful.

"I was coming across the field beyond the bridge," he told me, "and it was near dusk, when suddenly I could not move, and could not believe what I was seeing before me." He saw a crowd of small people, tiny men and women, running to and fro in the field — "playing they were" — and when they stopped and looked at him, he found he could not move. Significantly, as so often in these stories, there was a "fairy fort" not far ahead of where the "little people" were gathered. He said he could not move because of the curious power of the gaze of these "little people," and he was frightened, not because they were in any way malevolent, but because he had never really believed in such things, and never expected to.

The fact is that the people of the countryside still protect these "fairy forts" and other such relics, even if they only half believe in the "occupants" so long believed in by vanished populations. This has been a great help to archaeology, though another generation, with its bulldozers, may sweep them away altogether in the new Ireland now taking shape at great speed.

Journalists quite often have much fun with the "little people" and the Irish, and often forget that this harmless reverence for the monuments of long-forgotten gods and heroes has preserved them from destruction. Nearly every myth and legend has a basis of all-but-forgotten fact. In Irish literature there are many indications of the tenacity of pagan custom and belief and of the continuing influence of the Druids following the introduction of Christianity.

About a hundred years after Saint Patrick began to convert the Irish to Christianity, a Druid of the King of Connacht clashed with Saint Berach about land. The land was called Rathonn and was beside the Shannon near modern Kilbarry (the church of Berach) in County Roscommon. It happened that Saint Patrick had long ago "bequeathed" the land as a future religious territory, and now Berach claimed it for his monastery. The King, Aedh, son of

Eochaid Tirmcarna, had given the land to his Druid, Diarmuid in payment for a panegyric. The Druids were, like the
Brahmins of ancient India, the keepers of learning, and this
included poetry, medicine, law, history, and the gift of
divination. As poets they could curse and satirize, and
when Diarmuid and Berach took their case to the king, the
Druid threatened a satire if the king awarded the land to
Berach, a satire that would raise blisters on the king's face.
There was a terror of satire in Ireland (and it is not dead,
even yet).

The life of Berach is more than a "life." It is one more
"cover story" for tribal and religious history. Did Patrick
promise the land to Berach's ancestor as a religious foundation, or was Berach's tribe using the new religion to dispos-
sess the Druids? It is significant that Berach's tribe, Cinel
Dofa MacAengus, were to own the land for centuries (and
the descendants of the tribe still live there today). The ruins
of Berach's churches still stand there beside the Shannon.

Berach, during the argument, placed the palm of his
hand over Diarmuid's mouth and said: "Neither satire nor
panegyric shall cross these lips forever, and I declare that
this day, a year from now, shall be the day of thy death."
On the same day a year later Diarmuid, who played safe by
hiding out in a church, heard a great noise outside. When
he went to the window, he saw a crowd of people both on
horseback and on foot pursuing a stag. "And one of the
people who was pursuing the beast made a cast at it with
his hunting spear; and the spear went through the window
and hit Diarmuid in the throat, and he fell on the floor of the
church and died." One more victory in the struggle with
paganism, which went on for longer than was once popu-
larly supposed.

The ancient tales about Saint Patrick's mission in the fifth
century give many hints of the strength of pagan belief, as
when he reached the lands of the tribal group in what is
now County Roscommon. He was seeking the tribal king,

who was evading him. When the king saw Patrick coming, he snatched up a weaver's beam nearby and tried to look like a weaver, but he must have looked too kingly, for Patrick addressed him by name.

"Are you Ethin?" asked Patrick.

"I am not," said the king.

"Then you will not be, and no son or grandson of yours will ever be king either," declared Patrick — which is a genealogical explanation of why the tribe never rose to kingship of Connacht. Those who clung to paganism did not rule, but one of Ethin's brothers accepted Patrick and became king, and from him descended the O'Conors, kings of Connacht until the twelfth century.

The tourist who cares to can follow the course of the story of Berach, the Druid, and the King, and he can drink from Saint Berach's Well near Kilglass lake in Roscommon, almost certainly one more pagan site Christianized in the fifth century. The church in which the Druid, Diarmuid, met his death was at Baslic not far from the well.

The nostalgia for the old pagan world is typified in the tragicomic tale of Oisin, one of the heroes of the Fenian warrior band. This tale is one of hundreds told of Saint Patrick in Irish for centuries.

"Oisin," Patrick said. "It's time you were baptized."

"What's the point?" asked Oisin.

At the time, the story goes, he was dragging stones to build the church of Elphin in Roscommon. Elphin itself was a very ancient Druidical area, and the land for the Elphin church had been granted to Patrick by Ono, a Druid, ancestor of the MacBrennans of the Tri Tuatha. After some argument Oisin asked Patrick what the damning into hell of all the ancient pagan heroes of the Irish was all about, and Patrick patiently explained about the apple in Eden.

"If I had known your God was so narrow-sighted," Oisin said, "as to damn all those people for one apple, we would have sent horses and mules carrying apples to God in heaven."

Patrick himself had once been prey to such as Oisin, when Irish war bands used to land on the coasts of Britain as Roman rule crumbled. For he was taken captive and spent years in Ireland, where he learned the language. He was herd for a Druid called Liliuc, and the story is told that years after his escape from Ireland, when he returned as a Christian missionary, he sought out his old master. The Druid, when he saw his ex-slave approaching, no doubt to convert him, withdrew into his hut and set it alight, dying in the flames. Whether or nor you believe the story, it was a characteristic Indo-Aryan thing to do.

There's a popular legend that tells of Saint Patrick driving all the snakes from Ireland. In the twelfth century Giraldus Cambrensis gave his opinion on this banishment of the snakes:

> Of all kinds of reptiles, only those that are not harmful are found in Ireland. It has no poisonous reptiles.... Some indulge in the pleasant conjecture that St. Patrick and other saints of the land purged the island of all harmful animals. But it is more probable that from the earliest times, and long before the laying of the foundations of the Faith, the island was naturally without these as well as other things.... One reads in the ancient writings of the saints of that land that sometimes, by way of a test, snakes have been imported in bronze containers. But as soon as they reached the middle of the Irish Sea they were found to be lifeless and dead.... And if poison be brought in (to Ireland), no matter what it be, from elsewhere, immediately it loses all the force of its evil.

Even six hundred years after Patrick's labors among the Irish pagans the old spirits of the island were still alive, and men who were Christians still revered them, as if they could not give up such things so old. In the *Annals of Loch Ce*, under the year 1014, which records the battle of Clontarf (the battle in which the Irish shattered the Danish and Norwegian forces), the scribe casually notes a visit from the Other World. "Oebhinn (Eevin), daughter of Don-Oilen, came a short time before nocturns on that night from the Sidh of Craigliath (an ancient burial mound, home of the Spirits) to converse with Brian, and told him that he would fall on the morrow," and then advised him as to which of his sons should reign after him.

King Brian Boru was killed the next day at Clontarf, and the spirit who visited him was the guardian of North Munster, and in particular of the O'Brien tribe, or Dalcassians. Her home is still in Craigliath (now Craglea) near Killaloe in County Clare, but her clients today are few.

The island is covered with "fairy forts" where these guardian spirits of pre-Christian times resided. As the centuries passed, the dead gods and goddesses became the "little people," leprechauns, and fairies. In this guise they lived until quite recent times, and on occasion they live even today.

◇ ◇ ◇

The ancient Celtic year is divided into four parts. Spring begins on the first of February and is called *Oimelc;* it signifies the time of the "ewe's milk." Summer begins on the first day in May, *Bealtinne.* Autumn starts on the first of August, *Lugnasad,* a day of games instituted by the Tuatha de Danann god Lugh (whose name is commemorated in the names of many European cities and towns today). Winter, or *Samain,* falls on the first day of November, and it was on the eve of the first of November that the fairy hills and forts of Ireland opened, and the gods and goddesses who lived within came out and roamed the countryside.

Nearly every district in Ireland has its sacred site, such as Knockainy in County Limerick, which commemorates Aine, daughter of the Tuatha de Danann. The tourist interested in such things should ask old men or women in the districts they are visiting, for some still know the lore. But it is fast vanishing, though securely preserved in a thousand Irish books.

One of the most revered of pagan sites is briefly referred to in *Prehistoric and Early Christian Ireland* by Estyn Evans. Describing the antiquities of County Cavan, he says of Killycluggin: "There are many scattered standing stones. In this area, tradition says, the stone idol known as 'Crom Cruaich' (a pillar stone inside a stone circle) was over-thrown by Saint Patrick. The area was clearly a cult center in early Celtic times, and as elsewhere in Ireland (Tara, Meath), the site has associations going back to the Bronze Age."

In the older literature this pillar in the stone circle is called "King Idol of Erin," and an ancient poem in the *Book of Leinster* celebrating it was translated by the Irish scholar, Douglas Hyde, later the first President of the Irish Republic. The idol stood on Moy Slaught (the Plain of Adoration) in County Cavan. The poem states:

He was their God,
The whitered Cromm with many mists,
The people whom he shook over every harbour,
The everlasting kingdom they shall not have.

And it ends:

There was worshipping of stones
Until the coming of good Patrick of Macha (Armagh).

Always the tales of pagan places end with the coming of Patrick, when he overthrew them, or blessed them and Christianized them.

Three years before Patrick arrived King Laoghaire's Druids had prophesied it, saying that "Adze-head would come over a furious sea."

Their mantles hole-headed,
Their staves crook-headed,
Their tables in the east of their houses.

In Irish Patrick was always called *Tailceann,* Adze-head, a reference to his episcopal headgear.

A few years ago, in a pub near the river Shannon one night, an old man leaned over to me and in a whisper, pointing covertly to another old man, said: "He's still going out to the island in the middle of the river and throwing sticks. And at Mass every Sunday too, mind you." He was laughing now. "Sure the paganism's still in us all, so it is."

What fascinated me about this aside was that the island where this old man went to to "throw the sticks" was known to have been used by the Druids. More interesting still was that the old man who "threw the sticks" carried the surname of a tribe-family who had been the *coarbs* (successors), for a thousand years until the seventeenth century, of the Celtic Christian churchlands nearby, and of which the island was part. Curiously, I discovered, the old man had no knowledge of that, but almost certainly his grandfather would have known, for Irish was still spoken there a hundred years ago, and every tradition was remembered in Irish and faded when the English came.

The privileged traveler may sight the "fairy people." Good luck to him, but he must move fast, for only last week there was a meeting of archaeologists who appealed to the people of Ireland to stay staunch in their protection of the thousands of sacred pagan places inhabited by god and fairies for thousands of years. The bulldozers are more merciless than Christianity, which, through Saint Patrick, preserved these heathen sites.

In one district in which the fairies and banshees have not been seen for generations an old man was asked recently, "When exactly did they disappear?"

"I'd say when they brought in the Angelus," was his reply.

3. Language:

Renewing Gaelic Expression

**with
Sean MacReamoinn**

> *I am always sorry when any language is lost
> because languages are the pedigree of nations.*
> — Samuel Johnson/Boswell
> *Tour of the Hebrides*

*Language tends to be the ward of poets and scholars and its
fortunes the pursuit of philologists. Not so in Ireland. For the
Irish language became the stepchild of the vernacular in less than a
few generations, and in recent years the thrust toward its restoration has drawn the extremes of emotion and activity. Leagues are
formed to counter leagues. Newspapers and magazines offer vis-
ceral editorials. Columns of statistics reporting percentages of
Irish speakers are discredited as shockingly inadequate or irres-
ponsibly exaggerated, depending on the linguistic barometer of the
challenger.*

*Why the attempt at renewing Gaelic expression? And why the
fury on either side?*

To begin to have a sense of the confusion one must necessarily understand Ireland today, a relatively young state
only fifty-odd years old, as set beside its ancient corpus
thousands of years in the forming.

The chronicling of this disintegration of the national language contains the obvious — assaults, assimilation, and
the inevitability of surrender. Yet resting in the shadows is
a curious lingering thread of survival.

The tracing of the Gaelic language provides a passage to
the antiquities of civilization no less ancient than the cultures of Rome and of Greece. Through archaeological find-
ings, and documents, of civilizations dating back to 3,000
B.C., and in references to the Celts in the writings of Caesar,
the first historical recordings of the Celtic tradition and its
language appear after the arrival of Saint Patrick.

Early descriptions of the raucous Celts warring and
wenching over mountain, glen, and continent swing to
extremes and fall somewhere to the mercy of self-
propelling fantasy and images of Christian missionary
myth. What the Celts did reveal to these early arrivals was a
highly developed, aristocratic, and cultured society. Over a
hundred tribes spread across this tiny island, each politically autonomous under the paternity of a separate king
and bound by common language and custom. The filid, or
poet seers, were descendants of the Druids and the vaults
of Celtic tradition. Each was trained to memorize
thousands of verses of lyric poetry, mythology and heroic
tales, with the additional task of composing biting satire.
Their influence over the centuries survived to such an extent as to command singular assault during the siege of
Elizabeth I, describing them as "lewd rhymers."

Preservation of Celtic culture up to this time depended
on the skills of memory. With the gradual establishment of
monastic organization, oral tradition passed to written record.

Daniel Corkery in *Fortunes of the Irish Language* describes a unique situation emerging in the monastic tradition in Ireland. Based on a Roman structure, Latin was the sole language of these monasteries; yet for the first time the vernacular was recognized and recorded. This encouragement of tradition, along with the Celts' fascination and acknowledgment of the supernatural, are generally credited with enabling a smooth blending of the two. This enchantment and assimilation with the native culture was to continue for hundreds of years and through waves of invasions.

Secular schools flourished alongside the newly established monasteries of Clonmacnoise, Bangor, and Armagh. Early on, two significant contributions were offered by these monks. The one was a systematized alphabet giving form to a national language that had previously existed in four dialects. The other was the dispersing of native graduates to the classical learning centers of the Continent, carrying the first awareness of the Celtic culture. Centuries later these same European monasteries would hold the source of retrieval of the tradition lost. Transformation of this detached tribal community to a significant learning center had been achieved, and the seventh and eighth centuries unfold as the Golden Age of Ireland. For a time the custodianship of the language passed from the community to the literati.

As early as 795 the first thrust of aggressive foreign intrusion arrived with the Vikings. For the next few hundred years these Norsemen ravaged the country; yet their interest was in plundering the wealth, not the character, of the people. The most severe casualty to the culture was the establishment of *Dubhlinn*, forming a centralized area that was never to be retrieved as native or Irish-speaking. By the 1500's this area had passed to the English and was now referred to as the Pale. Its influence and boundaries waxed and waned for centuries, always remaining the source and fortification of all that was non-Irish.

With the arrival of the Norman settlers in the twelfth

century a new sphere of influence seeped into the existing culture. Norman institutions and monasteries paved over the relics of Saint Patrick's order; yet there was kindred response separated by seven hundred years. These families — the Burkes, Fitzgeralds, Delaceys, and others — became absorbed by the native tradition. They became Irish speakers, became enchanted intruders — *Hiberniores Hibernicis ipsis* (more Irish than the Irish themselves). This romanticizing of the Norman settlement of the next few hundred years refers only to a description as it relates to the language and culture. The inherent oppression and tyranny bound to any invasion seem self-evident. By the fourteenth century this facile assimilation alarmed the Anglo-Norman leaders, and in 1366 the first penal assault on the Irish culture, the Statutes of Kilkenny, manifested an attempt not solely to suffocate Irishness, but to maintain Anglo-Norman culture. Demoralizing strictures were sent down from Dublin forbidding marriage with the Irish, use of the language, and observance of Brehon Law. The consequences of these statutes were neither as serious nor effective as the intention, but the course of integration of the Anglo and Irish was set.

A shifting of custodianship of the Irish language takes place again in the seventeenth century. With the Flight of the Earls in 1607, the loss of bardic schools under the kings' patronage meant a fragmentation of the Irish culture. One of the last poet seers, Egan O'Rahilly, envisioned the death of the Celtic tradition and expressed his bitterness at the desertion of their kings, the O'Neill and the O'Donnell whom he addresses in this lament:

> *My heart is withered and my health is gone,*
> *For they who were not easy put upon,*
> *Masters of mirth and of fair clemency,*
> *Masters of wealth and gentle charity,*
> *They are all gone, Mac Caura Mor is dead,*
> *Mac Caura of Lee is finished,*

Mac Caura of Kantuck joined clay to clay
And gat him gone, and bides as deep as they.

Ease thee, cease thy long keening, cry no more:
End is, and here is end, and end is sore,
And to all lamentation be there end:
If I might come on thee, O howling friend:
Knowing that sails were drumming on the sea
Westward to Eire, and that help would be
Tramping for her upon a Spanish deck,
I ram thy lamentation down thy neck.
                                  —Clann Cartie
                                  (James Stephens, trans.)

The inheritors are the peasants, and the classic tradition of folktales and bardic poetry retreats to the firesides as generative entertainment. Irish culture without patronage returns to oral tradition. Though native scholarship had vanished during this century, Michael O'Cleary, a Franciscan at Louvain, was sent home to walk the countryside for over a decade tracing the submerged vine of Celtic tradition. His collaboration with fellow monks produced the *Annals of the Four Masters,* the singular attempt at capturing a race dissolving.

The scourge of brutality and confusion marked the records of the sixteenth and seventeenth centuries in Ireland. Henry the VIII had ascended the throne and, driven by the Reformation and rabid nationalism, set upon his scheme to de-Irelandize Ireland. The Elizabethan and Cromwellian plantations meant wholesale destruction and confiscation of lands. Only a fragmented rural society with sporadic but ineffectual European assistance faced the tyranny of these invasions.

As the English were establishing towns and crafts around the country in the seventeenth century, the Irish themselves were set on sand — no institutions or structures of unity, no schools, no laws, no courts. One cohesive element remained through to the nineteenth century — the language. Gaelic scholar Sean MacReamoinn insists that the disintegration of a language depends on two intertwined elements: the language being deinstitutionalized and its loss as the vernacular. The first had been accomplished. Institutions were dissolved and, as he describes it, "the seeds of its death as a vernacular had begun." English had become the language of authority and economy.

After two hundred years of debasement it was not the Anglo-set economic sanctions or the penal laws that silenced the vernacular of Ireland. The ending was accomplished within one generation by the subtle belief of a people convinced of self-evident inferiority. The vitality of what had once been an enviable expression had shriveled to an embarrassed whisper of wearied voices.

Sean MacReamoinn describes the course.

"Why did the Irish stop speaking Irish? It was not a matter of persecution...economics.... They had lived for so long just balancing on the edge of living. When they got the chance to break through to real life, they seized at the key — the English language. And they did this terrible thing. They stopped speaking Irish to their children. Out of an act of love and hate and fear and most of all an act of economic and social purpose. A necessity."

The famines of 1845-46-47 sapped the life force of the colony. The stun of survival at the hands of the indifferent released inward bitterness. Masses died, their corpses to haunt their survivors. Thousands fled, infuriated by their obvious impotency. A few dropped back in the flush to remain scavengers and receivers of immigrants' generosity. All that was Irish seemed cursed. Often in defeat people seem unable to set the blame outwardly and grasp at self-loathing. In Irish clubs abroad fists would rage at the sound of Irish spoken. For many the sound of Irish was now the keener's echo.

The process of recovery pressed over the next fifty years. The momentum for political autonomy coincided with a revival of interest in the Gaelic tradition. In 1893 an attempt was made to reverse the tide of cultural anomie by a young member of the Ascendancy — Douglas Hyde. Hyde was Anglo-Irish, in a sense traditionless, regarded as Irish by the English and English by the Irish. Like Yeats, Lady Gregory, and others of the Revival, Hyde as a child had become familiar with, and fascinated by, the folktales and traditions of the peasantry, and at university he had pursued Irish. Aware of the growing national spirit, he was appalled by the irony of a people clutching at identity and at the same time discarding "language, traditions, music, genius and ideas" of their past. For Hyde two possibilities were available to the Irish. The first he dismissed as unlikely in an address to the Irish National Literary Society of Dublin in 1892:

> It has always been very curious to me how Irish sentiment sticks in this half-way house — how it continues to apparently hate the English, and at the same time continues to imitate them.... If Irishmen only went a little farther they would become good Englishmen in sentiment also. But — illogical as it appears — there seems not the slightest sign or probability of their taking that step.

The alternative for Hyde was to de-Anglicize, and the means was through language:

> In order to de-Anglicise ourselves we must at once arrest the decay of the language. We must bring pressure upon our politicians not to snuff it out by their tacit discouragement merely because they do not happen themselves to understand it. We must arouse some spark of patriotic inspiration among the peasantry who still use the language, and put an end to this shameful state of feeling — a thousand-tongued reproach to our leaders and statesmen — which makes young men and women blush and hang their heads when overheard speaking their own language.

To set in motion this alternative Hyde and his friends formed the Gaelic League. For twenty-odd years, fired with enthusiasm and idealism, they organized schools, published texts, wrote in Irish, and translated poetry and tales of this tradition back and forth. They naively intellectualized the revival as halcyon days of renewal. Their motives were more securely placed than their sensitivities. Their plans and ideas were met more often with ambivalence than mutual enthusiasm. This had not been their source of shame, and their revival presented a sting to memories still keen.

Seven hundred years of chaotic colonization ended with the establishment of the Irish Free State in 1923. Ireland was faced with giving a form to a new nation. Institutions that at best were joint efforts with the English — parliament, the courts, the law systems — still carried an Anglo ring. Some leaders envisioned the restoration of traditional names for Ireland — Eire, Banba, Fohlar — as a guarantee of identity. Ideals were set to rules, and the new constitution declared Irish the national language and first official language. English was recognized as the second language, although less than a quarter of the people had any knowledge of Irish at all. For the next few years confused demands were made: Irish was compulsory in the schools, a requisite for civil service employment and even acceptance at the Abbey Theatre. Government subsidies were offered for living in Irish-speaking areas. This well-intentioned nationalism carried the thistles of exclusion in a reversed direction. The whirling aspirations of revolution have mellowed over the years, and today pursuit is fired by individual preference rather than compulsion or questionable economic enticements.

Today both scholars and politicians would agree that the latter-day goal, though they shun "goals," would be a bilinguality of sorts, an awareness of the Irish language if not an exclusive application of it. The enigma of the survival of their language is this mysterious tenacity of the Irish to cradle a tradition chartered for oblivion.

◇ ◇ ◇

COMMENT

The "Gaeltacht" are areas of the country where Irish is still spoken as the first language. Generally they are clustered along the Western coastline from Donegal to Kerry, where the Irish were driven during Cromwellian times. (One exception to this is the coastal town of Ring in County Waterford.) During the summer months Irish courses are taught in special sessions at local schools and universities. More specific information on these summer programs and accommodations with Irish-speaking families is available through the Irish Tourist Board.

4.   The Wild Geese:

"Irish Wanted: Must Be Brave—Able-Bodied..."

with
Gerald Hanley

The word "mercenary" has a nasty meaning today, but once it was quite an honorable thing to be a mercenary soldier in the more or less permanent state of war in which Europe lived. Gentlemen mercenaries carried swords in battle, but would trail a pike in the ranks while they waited for a commission. The Irish "Wild Geese," as they were called, were the most famous mercenary soldiers from the sixteenth to the early nineteenth century.

In Dublin I talked with novelist Gerald Hanley about these mercenary soldiers. He told me of the wealth of documentation in Europe, still being researched, on the hundreds of thousands of Irishmen who formed their own units in the armies of France and Spain. For several years he did research for an old historian whose sight was failing, and himself became involved in the history of the "Wild Geese." "It's a wonderful subject for a writer," he told me, "but it needs time, money, and research. The material is so vast."

Hanley was an officer in the British Army during World War II, "young and wide-eyed about the new world of freedom to come," he told me. "But the two end results of that war seem to have been to get Hitler married to Eva Braun, and make communism a colossus." His attitude toward the "Wild Geese" seems about the same: wry, dry, yet compassionate. His view of the Wild Geese and their world follows here.

Somebody, someday, preferably one of the new breed of young Englishman who is a liberated person first and an Englishman second, must write a book about the English obsession with Ireland and the Irish. It is a phenomenon, this continual complaint from the English down the centuries about the thing still known as "the Irish Problem." The English would have had no Irish problem if they had never invented it by invading Ireland and staying there, hating, loving, despising, ordering, persecuting, recommending, wrecking, rebuilding, preaching, and always, always, explaining to the world about the impossible problem they were faced with — the Irish Problem.

And while this has been going on for centuries all around them in their occupied country, the Irish have had to try hard to get on with their lives, which included their private lives, to live as Irishmen, whether watching their people killed, their lands taken from them, or, later, seeing how they looked in *Punch*, which meant in rags with a clay pipe stuck in the hatband, a bottle of whiskey held on high, and in the other hand a string to which was tethered a pig.

The English just could not leave the Irish alone. They alternated emotionally throughout the centuries from fear to contempt to guilt to rage. But they would never leave the island. They had invented the Irish Problem, and they loved it and needed it and were able to hold onto it by telling the world over and over that they had it, this Irish Problem, and had found yet another solution to it, it didn't matter what. One can only assume, in explanation of this phenomenon, that, in fact, they do *love* the Irish. Always have, and always will, but must, in order to maintain it, be in a position of authority as a setting for the public sermon to the world about this insoluble love affair they have called the Irish Problem.

So, having been loved for so long in this way, in these many and varied ways, by the lecturing intruder in his house who would not go home, the Irishman had either to flee the country or stay and play the most difficult role in the world — England's favorite Irishman, a lion of courage and loyalty when serving in the British Army, or a comical unmannered ingrate who imagined he could run his own life while wilfully refusing to admit what had been done for him by the intruder upon whom he had inflicted "The Irish Problem." A rebel in fact.

The guest-intruder was at his most sententious and boring at the beginning of the eighteenth century. The loved one was in a pretty bad way at the time. Having recently raped the beloved again, the lover now set up the most incredible of all the sets of rules for living — known always, for some reason only to the lover, as English Law. Ireland never really hated the English, only the bad manners and the insufferable pretentions that went with the lectures about the Irish Problem. The new rules for Irish behavior were called the Penal Laws, for England had tried everything else, and it had become obvious that if Ireland was to receive the threatened benefits she had so perversely fought against throughout the guest's unbearably long stay, the firmest line possible must be taken with the Irish, who was shortly to become "Paddy."

It had been fifty-odd years since Cromwell, and the country was, more or less, a desert, sprinkled with odd mansions, for it had been burned down again and again in the varied dementias unrequited, passionate love can bring on. Cromwell's savage affair with Ireland — he came over in the mid-seventeenth century with yet another final embrace, The Solution — was deeply religious, fiercely serious, with many-sermoned promises of more to come if misbehavior continued. He ripped Ireland apart and smashed the remains of the framework in which the Gaelic Irish still owned their ancestral lands. He ruthlessly solved the Irish Problem, one more time, and gave it a real future as well. As a bonus he extended the Irish experience into a new area. He shipped about thirty thousand of them to the plantations of the West Indies. In fairness to Cromwell it should be remembered that he may have had his own secret inner racial hang-up. A terrible, determined public Englishman, he was of Welsh descent, and his real name was Oliver Williams. "The curse of Williams on you" would somehow lack conviction.

If the Irish had only been black, it would have helped England so much in her long struggle with the Irish Problem. The thing would have been seen more clearly for what it was. Even now, in the North of Ireland, the problem of the oppressed minority being white prevents the business being seen for what it was and is — Wasps have problems with the Niggers. Yet those thirty thousand Irish shipped to the West Indian plantations, treated as blacks, caused problems there by the anomaly of their whiteness, even while sending the Negroes up a social step by giving them, at last, something to look down upon. In the English report from Barbados in 1667 quoted earlier there is a comical note of self-satisfaction when it describes the Irish shipped there as "derided by the Negroes and branded with the epithet of White Slaves," and "at worke in the parching sun without shirt, shoe or stocking...(the) negroes at work at their respective trades, in good condition." The blacks were looked after, of course, because they were valuable and had cost money to capture, ship, purchase, and maintain. The Irish cost nothing, for they were part of the solution to their own Problem, being alive and fit and wilful on their own island, which England so loved to everybody's distraction.

There was no doubt that the native Irish in Ireland had now got the message; either they must win back their country some day or perish, vanish as an ancient people with ancient native rights. Great numbers, who missed the West Indian solution, went to France and became part of the French army, a thin framework for what was to come after their final effort to get rid of the unbearable guest, ending in their surrender to the Williamite armies in 1691.

On the heels of the Treaty of Limerick the best of the defeated Irish army, over ten thousand of them, many heads of ancient Irish families, sailed for France rather than live at the whim of the new land-and-power-hungry anti-Irish crowd that would now own and misrule their island. The guest had taken over the whole house and put the owners out into the garden with spades.

King James II, who had been tossed off the English throne to make way for Dutch William, had set up a court in France, and for well into the eighteenth century the Stuarts would hope, with the help of the Irish troops, to regain their lost throne. As time and wars passed, while the Irish in Ireland struggled to exist in the maze of new repressive laws designed to break and harness them as a humbled peasantry, the Irish on the Continent built a world of their own. The regiment was the family, the tribal group as it were, in which could be found every ancient Gaelic surname, along with those of Norman and Anglo-Irish stock, and to these military families a steady stream of fresh recruits would find its way from Ireland for more than a hundred years.

Romantic hindsight has often painted the Wild Geese as men who made a new Ireland of their own on the Continent, and who lived only to retake the real one by force of arms. Yet there was an irony in their situation. Like their fathers, they were actually fighting for one English king against another one, for Charles against Cromwell, and now for the deposed Catholic James against Protestant William, for an Ireland ruled by an English king anyway. Nationalism, as we know it, lay a long way off in the future, and as the Stuart hopes faded, the Irish brigades of France and Spain fought for honor and glory — until the machine gun men really believed in honor and glory.

Their reward was their reputation for staunchness and bravery, and if they were mercenaries they were mercenaries of a very special kind, who fought for more than pay and rations. They stayed Irish, yet became French, Spanish, Austrian: two loyalties, one immediate that claimed their military allegiance, their blood, their lives in battle, and the older one to their ancestral land, the tradition and antiquity of the Irish race. They descended from the oldest military caste in Europe, the Indo-European people known as *Keltoi* to the Greeks, and they were conscious of it. For thousands of years to fight and die well in battle had been considered an honorable and noble thing. War was permanent, a fact of life, like kings, and the Irish regiments became experts, trusted and acclaimed, as they could not hope to be under the new English rule transforming Ireland.

In Ireland they could not even be English soldiers and remain Catholic, nor could they own land, own a horse worth more than five pounds, be educated, practice their religion in peace, carry arms. The final stipulations were almost endless. But they worked. For a young Irishman to escape from this prison that had been his home, landing on the Continent after a journey made in secrecy with other recruits for the Irish Brigade, the excitement and hope must have been as high as that thousands of others would feel when they landed in America after the Famine ("the starvation" to the Irish) of the 1840's.

The Stuarts were, in Irish terms, a useless pack, and in no way worthy of the military fame the Irish troops achieved in their name on the Continent. But a Stuart was the only king they had. Some of the Irish leaders in France vaguely envisaged a free Ireland they might achieve under the French. It seems never to have been a serious and lasting hope, however, especially for the French, whose plans ranged far beyond Ireland now that it was lost.

The Irish troops engaged and defeated the Williamites in Holland. One of the heroes of the war in Ireland, Patrick Sarsfield, died of wounds in that action. Before dying he said to his friend, Gerald O'Connor, "I am dying the most

glorious of deaths; we have seen the backs of the tyrants of
our race. May you, Gerald, live to behold other such days;
but let Ireland be uppermost in your thoughts." His son
would join another Irish Brigade soon to be formed in
Spain.

By 1698 the Irish in France could field two regiments of
cavalry and thirteen regiments of infantry and dragoons.
They had fought in Germany and in Italy, and at the battle
of Marsaglia, in the fierce charges for which they had become famous, they again overcame the allied troops of
William, killing over a thousand in close combat. Most of
these officers and men had fought in the battles of Ireland,
and these victories over the Williamites must have tasted
sweet to them, if undertoned with bitterness that they
should come on fields so far from their lost Ireland. Their
lands were now owned by Englishmen; they were out-
lawed and could not return to Ireland, where the native
Irish were drawing in upon themselves, as if for a long
siege. Dean Swift watched this new oppressed Ireland
forming about him with anger and disgust, and writing to
an Irish officer, Sir Charles Wogan, serving with the
Spanish army, he said:

> Although I have no great regard for your trade, from the
> judgement I make of those who profess it in these Kingdoms,
> yet cannot but highly esteem those gentlemen of Ireland, who
> with all the disadvantages of being exiles and strangers, have
> been able to distinguish themselves by their valour and con-
> duct in so many parts of Europe, I think above all other na-
> tions, which ought to make the English ashamed of the re-
> proaches they cast on the ignorance, the dullness, and the
> want of courage in the Irish natives; those defects, wherever
> they happen, arising only from the poverty and slavery they
> suffer from their inhuman neighbours, and the base, corrupt
> spirits of too many of the chief gentry.... I do assert that from
> several experiments I have made in travelling over both King-
> doms I have found the poor cottagers here, who speak our

language, to have a much better natural taste for good sense, humour and raillery than ever I observed among people of the like sort in England. But the millions of oppressions they lie under, the tyranny of their landlords, the ridiculous zeal of their priests, and the general misery of the whole nation, have been enough to damp the best spirits under the sun.

Swift's correspondent, Charles Wogan, had risen to the rank of colonel in the Spanish army, and for his many distinguished services was appointed Governor of the Province of La Mancha. One of the Wogans of Rathcoffey in Kildare, in his youth he had been a friend of Alexander Pope and had later become a captain in the Jacobite forces.

In 1719, with three officers of the Regiment of Dillon, Captain Lucius O'Toole, Captain John Misset, and Major John Gaydon, he took Princess Clementina Sobieski from her imprisonment at Innsbruck and got her over the Brenner Pass into Italy so that she could marry King James, the Pretender. Pressure from England had caused her incarceration, King George being so anxious to prevent the marriage that he offered £100,000 toward her dowry if she would marry the Prince of Baden instead. For this extraordinary feat all four officers were advanced in rank, Wogan and Misset being made colonels in the Spanish army. O'Toole was killed in action later on the Moselle. Wogan was to see much military action in North Africa, whence he wrote to Swift: "I would not shed one ounce of blood in anger or enmity to make all the world Catholics, yet I am as staunch a one as any Pope in the universe. I am all for the primitive church in which people made proof of their religion only at their own expense. But I laugh with great contempt at those who will force others to Heaven their way, in spite of charity."

In these letters to Swift, Wogan revealed a great deal about what it felt like to be one of the Wild Geese, who watched from afar as his country's image was reshaped for a comedy role. "In the days of King Charles II," he wrote, "the Irish bravery and fidelity had the applause of whole theatres; but now nothing but Irish stupidity and wretched small craft will go down even upon the Dublin stage...and when that Demogorgon, Ireland, is to be run down it is wonderful how almost every English heart bounds for joy." He goes on to say that

> Nothing can be more distinguishing in regard of an unhappy people than your character of those abroad; nor more just than your remarks on the genius and suffering of those at home. But the set of people you mean can no longer be looked on as a nation, either in or out of their country. Those who have chosen a voluntary exile, to get rid of oppression, have given themselves up with a great gaiety of spirit to the slaughter, in foreign lands and ungrateful service, to the number of 120,000 men, within these forty years. The rest, who have been content to stay at home, are reduced to the wretched condition of Spartan helots. They are under a double slavery. They serve their inhuman lordliness, who are more severe upon them because they dare not yet look upon the country as their own, while altogether are under the supercilious dominion and jealousy of another overruling power.

Of the "honor and glory" sought by those like himself, he writes:

> The only fruit the Irish have reaped by their valour is their extinction, and that general fame which they have lost themselves, to acquire for their country, already lost to them.... They had always the post of honour allowed them, where it was mixed with danger, and lived in perpetual fire, which was all they could bequeath as an inheritance to their issue, who are extremely few, on account of the little encouragement given for begetting them.

He was writing in the 1730's, and he shared to the full Swift's contempt for what was being done in Ireland.

It is impossible for an upright and good-natured spirit not to look with concern upon the inhuman slavery of the poor in Ireland. Since they have neither liberty nor schools allowed them; since their clergy, generally speaking, can have no learning but what they scramble for, through the extremities of cold and hunger, in the dirt and egotism of foreign universities; since all together are under the perpetual dread of persecution, and have no society for the enjoyment of their lives or their religion, against the annual thunders of the English Vatican.

The recruits for the Irish regiments continued to flee from Ireland. In 1756 an act passed in Dublin stated that the punishment was death for all "natural-born subjects in the service of France" who should land in Ireland, and on their abettors and concealers. Commenting on this, a French historian wrote: "Les Irlandais répondiront à cette sentence capitale, en s'enrolant avec plus d'empressement sous les drapeaux de la France" (The Irish will respond to this death penalty by enlisting more readily under the flags of France).

Another comment on the act came in a letter from Daniel O'Connor, one of the Roscommon O'Connors whose kingship of Ireland had ended in the twelfth century after six hundred years. He was a captain in the Regiment of Dillon in the Irish Brigade in France. "Banishment," he wrote, "is frightful to every man but a robber or a murderer, and what man of common sense would submit to the condition of an exile on account of a post in the French service? But are we to get anything from what we are obliged to renounce? Or will there be an Act passed to prevent our breathing?"

Irish officers went secretly to and from the Continent, and on one occasion a batch of one hundred fifty recruits, about to leave for France, was informed upon and twenty-four men were captured. Three of them were hanged at Stephen's Green in Dublin. Those heading for service in Spain left from obscure coves and harbors and sailed to La

Coruña, and were then passed on to the depots of the Irish regiments. No matter how much thoughtful exiles like Wogan and O'Connor might regret the slaughter of thousands of young Irishmen in Europe's monarchal pastime, continuous war, it seemed that anything was better than slavery in their prostrated Ireland.

By the middle of the eighteenth century a few of the Irishmen on the Continent, who had been young men when they fought at the Boyne and Limerick, had risen to great positions. Four of them who died in mid-century were typical: Peter Lacy, who rose to Field Marshal in Russia; Major General John Nugent, fifth Earl of Westmeath, also Field Marshal; Major General Richard Talbot, third Earl of Tyrconnel and Ambassador for France to Prussia; and Daniel O'Conor, Sligo, over ninety when he died, a Lieutenant General in the Austrian army.

A few years ago, after long dusty travels in the back waters of Spain, I got off the train at Gerona and asked the taxi driver to take me to the best hotel in town. In the darkness he pointed to the tall new hotel as we neared the entrance. Its name, announced in neon lights, was the Hotel Ultonia.

"Very odd," I said to the taxi driver, "to find the antique version of the name Ulster over a hotel in Spain."

"It is the name of the famous Irish regiment, Ultonia, which commanded the long defense of our city against Napoleon's army in 1809," he said. "It was called 'Ultonia el Inmortal' — Ultonia the Immortal. There is still a regiment with that name today. Its base is in Gerona."

Colonel José Garabatos Gonzalez welcomed me to the barracks. I had telephoned and explained that I was on my way back to Ireland and had "discovered" Ultonia el Inmortal and wished to know if there were any records of the Irishmen who had established the regiment.

The first thing you see when you enter the barracks is the regimental crest, splendidly painted on the yellow wall, the gold harp of Ireland and a blue background, surrounded by laurel leaves and surmounted by the crown of Spain. Beneath is the regimental motto, *In Omnes Terram Exhibit Sonus Eorum* (Our name will resound throughout the world).

It was over two hundred fifty years since the Chevalier, Colonel O'Mahoney, had organized the embodiment of this and many other Irish regiments, the most famous of which were Ultonia, Hibernia, and Irlanda, the three that formed the long-lived Irish Brigade of Spain.

The Colonel showed me the list of regimental commanders, starting with the founder in 1709, and ending with the last of the Irish commanders in 1811.

Demetrio MacAulif, 1709
Tadeo MacAulif, 1716
Guillermo de Lacy, 1737
Juan Sherlock, 1765
Diego Aylmer, 1771
Francisco Comerford, 1773
Juan O'Slattery, 1775
Juan MacKenna, 1777
Pedro Tirrell, 1781
Miguel Knaresborough, 1784
Juan de Kinelan, 1791
Antonio O'Reilly, 1806
Enrique O'Connor, 1808
Rodolfo Marshall, 1808
Pedro Sarsfield, 1811

The regiment marches ceremonially through the city every Saint Patrick's Day, and when the flag of Ultonia is brought on parade, the actual flag carried throughout the eighteen months' defense of Gerona, it is attended with the honors of a Captain-General of Spain.

When one reads of what the few hundred men of Ultonia

achieved during the terrible siege, while training hundreds of Spaniards to fight alongside them, one can understand why Gerona honors them, and why the Spanish army called the regiment "El Inmortal."

The quality of their comradeship during the siege was described by a German officer who was there. He relates how he saw an old soldier of Ultonia searching among the dead, during a lull, until he found the body of his officer, Lieutenant Colonel MacCarthy. MacCarthy's tunic had been blasted from his body. The old soldier knelt down, kissed the face of his soldier and embraced him. Then, weeping, the soldier said to the corpse: "Ah, *mi señor*, thirty years I have served you, and thirty years you fed and clothed me. Now, *mi señor*, it is I who clothe you," and, taking off his cape, he wrapped MacCarthy in it.

The Spaniards regarded the Irish as a branch of the Iberian race, a relationship they date from the Bronze Age, and often showed it by honoring them with the greatest trust, as generals, ambassadors, admirals. The Irish more than repaid that trust. Spain for the Irish was a home away from home.

In Ireland I found in the archives a list of two hundred and sixty-five Irish officers who had served in the regiment of Ultonia, and sent it to Colonel Garabatos Gonzalez for his files.

Probably the best monument there is to the half a million Irishmen who served and died in the armies of France, Austria, and Spain is the barracks of Ultonia el Inmortal at Gerona. In glass cases in the officers' mess stand the flags the regiment carried in all its battles. There are very few other reminders of those dispossessed thousands.

Once, in a Schloss in Austria, I looked at a collection of old pottery in a tatty, tired glass case, memoirs of a vanished officer caste, and there, painted on the pottery, were the names of the O'Rourkes and the O'Reillys.

In 1959, on the anniversary of the Battle of Fontenoy, the

French General, Frederic Souard, arrived in Dublin carrying replicas of the colors of the Irish Brigade that had served France throughout the eighteenth century. At a ceremonial parade of troops of the modern Irish Republic he presented these colors in the name of France to the President of Ireland, and then spoke movingly of all the Irish soldiers who had shed their blood with Frenchmen on so many battlefields.

The man behind this solemn occasion was General de Gaulle, and few people knew at the time that, as well as celebrating the ancient links between the two countries, there was a personal involvement as well, for a Lieutenant McCartan, an ancestor of de Gaulle, was one of the Irish soldiers commemorated. Was it all worth it, the place of honor on a hundred battlefields throughout the eighteenth century in a "perpetual fire"? The figure of half a million Irishmen who served and died on the Continent seems incredible.

5. Country Houses:

Life in the Big House

with
Desmond Fitzgerald
Knight of Glin

"Ah! Sir," said an Irish Gentleman, who found me in admiration upon the staircase. "This is all very good, very fine, but it is too good and too fine to last; come here again in two years and I'm afraid you'll see this is all going to rack and ruin. This is too often the case in Ireland; we can project, but we can't calculate; we must have everything upon too large a scale. We mistake a grand beginning for a good beginning. We begin like princes, and we end like beggars."

— Maria Edgeworth
Ennui (1809)

This Irish Gentleman's reply to Lord Glenthorn's reaction to the magnificence of the Shelbourne Hotel on St. Stephen's Green best describes the inevitable decay of Ireland's anachronistic elite. It would take another hundred years before only a handful of the aristocracy remained in the country attempting to maintain their great houses and demesnes.

Generally today the Big House is regarded as a posses-sion of the "Anglo-Irish," a reference that has evolved more as a description of a class than a race and draws in an ethnic hodgepodge almost impossible to define. George Bernard Shaw attempted a definition describing himself. "I am," he said, "a genuine typical Irishman of Danish, Norman, Cromwellian, and of Scot invasion. I am violently and arrogantly Protestant by family tradition." Brendan Behan reduced these qualifications considerably, describing the Anglo-Irishman as "a Protestant on a horse."

Residence in the Big House varied over the centuries on the power of the day's reign, yet always depended on ownership of the land. One of the few remaining descendants of medieval Ireland, Desmond Fitzgerald, the Knight of Glin, explains the feudal life of the time. "The leading Gaelic and Anglo-Irish chieftains and barons owned vast tracts of forest, bog, and grazing land, among which stood the great walled castles such as Trim, Liscarroll, Askeaton and Roscommon. These are real castles in the English sense of the word, but below them in the feudal hierarchy ranked the smaller tower houses of the cadet branches of the great Norman families and the lesser chieftains. There are literally thousands of these towers all over the country. This feudal life continued well into the middle of the eighteenth century."

An interesting description of this period is given by Edward Willis, Lord Chief Baron of the Irish Exchequer around 1758. He tells of an invitation from a local chieftain, possibly one of the Joyces, to his house.

...a magnificent palace, where there were two long cabins thatched opposite to one another. The one was the kitchen and apartments for the family; the other was the entertaining room, neatly strewed, according to the Irish fashion, with rushes, and the upper end of the rooms was a kind of platform raised above the ground with boards and two or three blankets on each, which was the lodging for strangers and visitors. A bottle of brandy was the whet before dinner, and the entertainment was a half sheep, boiled top, half sheep, roasted at bottom; broiled fish on one side, a great wooden bowl of potatoes on the other and a heaped plate of salt in the middle. After dinner pretty good claret and an enormous bowl of brandy punch which, according to the old as well as the modern Irish hospitality, the guests were pressed to take their full share of.... The visiting servants were given a bottle of brandy each and later in the evening when the Chieftain began to mellow, he called his favourite girl to sing, which she did very well, and was a neat, handsome, jolly girl. Before he called her in, he stipulated with the guests that they were welcome to any liberty with her from the girdle upwards but he would not permit any underhanded doings. Later the bag-piper and a bard sang about the glorious deeds of the Chief's illustrious and warlike ancestors. At last the visitors were allowed to go to bed, but the next morning, after a breakfast consisting of another bowl of punch, they had the greatest difficulty leaving. In fact, when they tried to get into their boats, which they had anchored on the lake, they were chased on horseback and just managed to get into their boats when the Chief called them in Irish "a load of milksops." A case of too much and too little hospitality.

If you hear an Irishman refer to "the gentry crowd," it will more than likely have nothing to do with the Irish chieftains described above. Their escape to the Continent after the Battle of Kinsale — the Flight of the Earls — virtually marked the elimination of the Gaelic and Catholic aristocracy. After the Cromwellian purge the old Gaelic landlords were forced to surrender their lands and were given a choice to move West past the Shannon (hence the familiar "to hell or Connacht") or to leave the country altogether. Of these chieftains only a few remained: The O'Donovan of Lissarda, The O'Hara of Annaghmore, The O'Grady of Kilballyowen, The MacGillycuddy of the Reeks, the O'Briens of Thomond, the Quins of Adare, and man-aged to sustain themselves through advantageous mar-riages to the new tenants of the Big House. This particular section of the aristocracy developed a curious attitude to-ward themselves and Ireland. To quote one writer: "They belonged to Protestant quality and claimed Brian Boru as an ancestor." These Anglo-Gaelic lords prided themselves on a special relationship with the tenantry; and yet years later they fought for the union with England.

The English were, obviously, anti-Irish and often made curious assessments of the "natives." One gentleman named Richard Lawrence, a Cromwellian adventurer and political economist, settled in Ireland and calculated how much vice was costing the country.

To Drinking, Gaming and Swearing (1682)

Gaming including peasantry and mechanick gamesters at Cards, Dice, Shovelboard, Bowling Allies and Ninepins, say, 10,000 persons obstructing wealth of the country to the extent of per annum: £52,000

Profane swearing cost the country, p.ann.   20,000

Drunkenness: 3 wine-bibbers to each parish
    at 10 per wine bibber per
    ann., 25,000 parishes   75,000

Ale topers — 5 to a parish at 4 each per ann.   50,000

Second Sale of Ale topers or fuddicups generally
    artists or husbandmen at 2 each per annum   25,000

Tapsters and Drawers who might be employed in
    profitable arts cost the country per annum   4,000

Loss through bad work of the sots per annum   20,000
                                ————

                                £246,000
                                ————

If the Irish "gentry" were enigmatic ethnically, they

seem to have gone to great lengths to keep secret their style of life. Only rare documents, diaries, and letters remain to suggest their portrait. Extracts from Sir Jonah Barrington's (1760-1834) *Personal Sketches* give the most amusing and probably the most accurate limns of country living as the eighteenth century closed.

On his family residence "Cullenaghmore" –

The Old Mansion (the Great House as it is called) exhibited altogether an uncouth mass, warring with every rule of symmetry in architecture. The walls of the large hall were decked (as is customary) with fishing rods, firearms, stags' horns, foxes brushes, powder flasks, shot pouches, nets, dog collars; here and there relieved by the extended skin of a kite or a kingfisher, nailed up in the vanity of their destroyers: that of a monstrous eagle which impresses itself indelibly on my mind, surmounted the chimney piece, accompanied by the name of its slaughterer — "Alexander Barrington" — who not being a rich relation was entertained in the Great House two years, as a compliment for his present. The library was a gloomy closet, and rather scantily furnished with everything but dust and cobwebs. There were neither chairs nor tables. *Gulliver's Travels, Robinson Crusoe, Fairy Tales,* and the *History of the Bible,* all with numerous plates, were my favourite authors and constant amusement. I believed every word of them except the fairies and was not entirely skeptical as to those good people neither.

On a Match of Hard Going –

My older brother, justly apprehending that the frost and snow of Christmas might probably prevent their usual occupation of the chase, determined to provide against any listlessness during the shut-up period, by an uninterrupted match of what was called "hard-going," 'till the weather would break up.

A hog's head of superior claret was sent to the cottage of old Quin, the huntsman, and a fat cow was hung up by the heels.

All the windows were closed to keep out the light. One room was filled with straw and numerous blankets and was destined for a bedchamber in common, and another was prepared as a kitchen for the servants. Claret cold, mulled or buttered was to be the beverage for the whole company; and in addition to the cow above mentioned, chickens, bacon and bread were the only admitted viands. Wallace and Hosey, my father's and my brother's pipers, and Doyle, a blind but a famous fiddler, were employed to enliven the banquet, which it was determined should continue till the cow became a skeleton and the claret should be on its stoop.

From Barrington we gather the outdoor sporting life of the country gentleman. However, closer to the city a more refined lifestyle had been introduced. A young lady writes to a friend of her visit in 1779 to Carton House, the home of the Duke of Leinster:

The house is crowded, a thousand come and go. We breakfast between 10 and 11, though it is called half past nine. We have an immense table — chocolate, honey, hotbread, cold bread, brown bread, white bread, green bread and all coloured cakes and breads. After breakfast, the Duke's Chaplain reads a few short prayers, then we go as we like. A back room, a print room, a drawing room, and a whole suite of rooms, not forgetting the music room. We dine at half past four or five, courses upon courses, which I believe takes up two full hours. It is pretty late when we leave the parlour. We then go to tea; to cards 'till about nine, play 'till suppertime.... It is pretty late by the time we go to bed. I forgot to tell you the part you would like best...French horns playing at breakfast and dinner. There are all sorts of amusements.... The gentlemen are out riding and shooting early in the mornings.

Meals seem to have become only slightly more refined since the days of Gaelic chieftains' banquets. In a letter to a friend in 1764 a Mrs. Delaney sent along an "Irish Menu for 12 persons":

Turbot and soles, remove ham; force meat, etc.; two partridges
and two grouse; rabbits and onions; pies; sweetbreads and
crumbs; salmigundi; soup; boiled chicken; collop veal and
olives; pease; cream pudding; plumb crocant; chine of mutton;
turkey in jelly; hare; lobster fricasse. Dessert: Nine things: six
of them fruit out of the garden and a plate of fine Alpine
strawberries.

Life in the Big House ranged from elegant to raucous, but
by the beginning of the nineteenth century it contrasted
dangerously with the life of the tenants. In 1778 Arthur
Young, a prolific chronicler of Irish life during his travels
here, wrote of the "Droit de Seigneur," and prophesied the
destiny of the aristocracy, so indifferent to the tenantry of
their land.

A landlord in Ireland can scarcely invent an order which a
servant, labourer, or cottar dares refuse to execute. Nothing
satisfied him but unlimited submission...landlords of consequence have themselves honoured by having their wives and
daughters sent for the bed of their masters; a mark of slavery
that proves the oppression under which such people must
live.

If a poor man lodges a complaint against a gentleman, or any
animal that chooses to call itself a gentleman, and the Justice
issues out a summons for his appearance, it is a fixed affront
and he will infallibly be called out. Where manners are in
conspiracy against law, to whom shall the oppressed people
have recourse?

The residents of rural Ireland at the time were divided
into three main strata: farmers, with a reasonably firm hold
on their land provided they paid the rent; the agricultural
laborer, who paid rent in labor and received no wages; and
the final and most impoverished group — laborers with no
fixed land who merely cast their lot with the crops. Of this
situation one analyst wrote: "Land was the sole intervening

bulwark between the Irish rural family and starvation."

As the eighteenth century closed, the shades were being drawn on "The Big House" of the anachronistic elite, but it would take another one hundred years before the decline would be complete. They were a strange set, lingering in another century protected by their isolation. They were able to maintain a curious insularity. Though their demesnes were scattered over thirty-two counties, their social migrations moved along narrow venues: hunt meets, dinners, dances, agricultural fairs, the local church, shooting parties, and, in Dublin, the Shelbourne, the Horse Show, and the Kildare Street Club.

With such inbred socializing, marriage prospects were confined to those who shared common caste and interest. Burke's *Landed Gentry of Ireland* lists two and three generations marrying cousins, no doubt to protect the "purity of the race" and set them apart from the "mere Irish" in all speech, manner, and dress. Edith Somerville, a member of the gentry community of Castletownshend, where intermarriage circled among the Townsends, Beckers, and Somervilles, described in her *Irish Memories* their prospect for marriage:

> Each estate was a kingdom and in the impossibility of locomotion, each neighbouring potentate acquired a relative importance quite out of proportion to his merits, for to love your neighbour — or at all event to marry her — was almost inevitable when matches were a matter of mileage and marriages might be said to be made by the map.

The common alternative used to the gentry's conventional method of marital arrangements was abduction. In 1797 the Earl of Clare wrote to Lord Auckland concerning a recent court case involving this practice:

> Sir Henry Hayes and Murphy were indicted and tried on the same statute, each carrying off a woman by force with intent to

marry her. Murphy succeeded in ravishing his lady. Sir Henry
Hayes attempted to ravish his lady but did not succeed because the cock would not fight, and after standing out all legal
process for five years and bidding defiance to two proclama-
tions offering a reward of £500 for apprehending him, he was
at last brought to trial, found guilty and respited by Mr. Day
upon a silly doubt in his mind on a point of law. Poor Murphy
has been hanged and Sir Henry Hayes has been pardoned.
Another poor wretch of the name of Lupton was hanged
almost at the same time upon the same statute. His crime was
assisting a friend in carrying off a woman whom he wished to
marry. And certainly if any crime deserved punishment in a
civilised country, Mr. Murphy's, Sir Henry's and Lupton's did
merit it. But it will be difficult to persuade the lower orders of
the people that equal justice has been administered to rich and
poor.

Diversion and deviation were not qualities aspired to by
the Anglo-Irish, and many families even went so far as to
confine themselves to limited interests. There were hunting, shooting and fishing families; writing families; and
Army-Navy families. They were consistent in their interests and sadly consistent in their disinterests. They
seemed unaware or unable to sense the diminishing allegiance of their tenants and remained not so blithely detached. Elizabeth Bowen was remarkable in that she was
one of the first in the Ascendancy to come to terms with
their unreal existence. She wrote in *Bowen's Court:* "The
Irish landowner, partly from laziness but also from an
indifferent delicacy, does not interfere in the lives of the
people around. Sport and death are two great socialising
factors in Ireland, but these cannot operate the whole time.
On the whole, the landowner leaves his tenants and work
people to make their own mistakes while he makes his."
    There are as many versions as there are viewers to the last
days of the Big House. Some insist that decay from within

was the root, while others insist that external political factors prevailed. Certainly, most would agree that the decline began with the Act of Union. Prior to the Union with England 269 peers and 300 Members of Parliament resided in Dublin, whereas by 1821 only 34 peers, 13 baronets, and 5 members remained, but these were urban dwellers. The power of the country gentleman was declining for other reasons. Elizabeth Bowen writes of that period after the Union: "From the big lord to the country gentleman they were edged back upon a track of clouds and obsessions... The sense of dislocation was everywhere. Property was still there but power was going."

By the close of the nineteenth century even the property was gone. A new generation, inspired by the American and French revolutions, had produced rent boycotts led by Michael Davitt; advocacy of Home Rule was championed by Parnell and Gladstone (the latter regarded as madmen by their fellow Anglo-Irish). The fair distribution of land among the tenantry had begun.

To many of the Protestant Ascendancy this separate identity thrust upon them by the Gaelic nationalist was incomprehensible. They felt Irish by virtue of residence and duration and found no ambiguity in their allegiance to a separate island. Stephen Gwynne, in his *Experience of a Literary Man*, tells his reaction to this strange new duality.

I was brought up to think myself Irish, without question or qualification; but the new nationalism prefers to describe me as Anglo-Irish. Æ has even set me down in print as the Anglo-Irishman *par excellence* – or, to put it more modestly, the typical Anglo-Irishman. So all my life I have been spiritually hyphenated without knowing it.

Another Anglo-Irishman, Brian Inglis, later echoed the same sentiment in his evaluation of the Anglo-Irish predicament in *West Briton*.

We were unaware that anybody could believe we were not Irish, and if we had been told that there were actually people...who thought of us as alien parasites, and who made no distinction between us and the British from whom we were descended, it would seem a rather bad joke.

During the "Troubles" in 1921 torches were put to many of the Big Houses; others were spared, by accident or intent. Memories are long in Ireland, and many of the Anglo-Irish were regarded kindly by the locals. The Knight of Glin recalls the story of Glin Castle during the "Troubles." His grandfather, the Knight, was an invalid, and when he arrived down to the foyer they had already spread the kerosene over the entrance way. He locked his arms in the rim of the wheelchair and informed them if they intended to burn Glin Castle they would have to burn him also. Shaken by the prospect the rebels retreated to the local pub, where the publican poured enough whiskey into them until they passed out and slept the night on the pub floor. The next morning they got up and went on to their next assignment.

By the end of the "Troubles" the Ascendancy was finished and a new Ireland had been founded. The fate of the Big Houses varied. A few of the Anglo-Irish stayed on, and as one wrote: "It was those who tried to atone for that wrong and to break down this barrier who did most of the paying."

Today the Big House will more than likely be a hospital, convent, guesthouse, or castle hotel. Others have been salvaged and refurbished by the Irish Georgian Society. There will always be a fascination, if not a secret envy, of the elite, those pursuers of power and pleasure. They were exciting but too costly for those on the perimeter, and, like all other aristocracies, their end was inevitable.

6. Theatre: Two Views

Dublin's "Dying" Darling

with
Alan Simpson

When you begin to ask about the Irish theatre, the first thing you are told is "it's dying." Then, if you pursue the patient back over the years, each contemporary prognosis assures you it's been dying for almost as long as it has existed. With calm, wry assurance, Alan Simpson, Artistic Director of the Abbey Theatre, fends the black prophecy: "The theatre has been collapsing ever since I first went into it. My earliest recollections of the theatre were people like Anew McMaster cursing the cinema for ruining the theatre. Then the war ruined it. And finally it was laid to television. And now it's being finished off by inflation. So there will always be something about to finish off the theatre if it hasn't already been finished, and you should have seen it fifteen years ago, twenty, fifty!"

◇ ◇ ◇

It's a strange paradox in a country where imagination has been attributed with near genetic certainty and spontaneous flights of oratory for centuries have peppered otherwise dull parliamentary proceedings that the theatre in Ireland is a twentieth-century invention. The inventors were a visionary trio captured by their discovery of a rich submerged tradition they unearthed and from which they developed the Celtic Renaissance.

Then only thirty years old, William Butler Yeats had already established himself as the poet of the revival with his volume of lyric folklore, *Celtic Twilight*. He had come to Ducas House, Kinvara, in 1898 to discuss with Lady Augusta Gregory his plans for producing drama in Ireland and finding a patron to do so. Also attending the luncheon was Edward Martyn, a wealthy Galway landlord and aspiring playwright. The three agreed on the need for an experimental theatre in Dublin comparable to those in London and Paris. In a letter to friends they explained their intentions for their adventure, the Irish Literary Theatre, later to become known as the Abbey.

> We propose to have performed in the Spring of every year certain Celtic and Irish plays, which whatever be their degree of excellence will be written with a high ambition and so to build up a Celtic and Irish school of dramatic literature. We hope to find in Ireland an uncorrupted and imaginative audience trained to listen by its passion for oratory, and believe that our desire to bring upon the stage the deeper thoughts and emotions of Ireland will ensure for us a tolerant welcome, and that freedom of experiment which is not found in the theatres of England, and without which no new movement in art or literature can succeed. We will show that Ireland is not the home of buffoonery and easy sentiment, as it has been represented, but the home of ancient idealism.

Michael MacLiammoir once said of the venture: "Nothing that is worthwhile has a practical ideal as a basis." For this endeavor aims could not have been more lofty. There was no dramatic tradition in Ireland. Neither Yeats, Lady Gregory, nor Martyn had any formal theatrical experience. There were no trained actors. And for a hundred years the literary expatriates — other Wild Geese — had fled to

London and the Continent, beginning with Congreve and Farquhar, later followed by Sheridan and Goldsmith. Even their contemporaries, Boucicault, Wilde, and Shaw, were taking their subjects and bows from England and its audiences. Fortunately, the most amateur beginnings can result in the most astonishing professional results.

The following May the Irish Literary Theatre launched its first production in the Ancient Concert Rooms in Dublin. Lady Gregory chose a tandem production of Martyn's *The Heather Field* and Yeats's *The Countess Cathleen*. Martyn's play was well received by the audience, who seemed unruffled by the upheavals of a mismarriage and the eventual mental breakdown of the groom. However, the following evening, before the curtain rose on Countess Cathleen (she sells her soul to the devil to ransom her starving tenants), controversies seethed. The clergy, never accused of imaginative abandon save for the odd miracle, threatened to close the performance on theological grounds. The imbroglio was mild compared to future opening nights, as Yeats's dream of a "tolerant audience" suffered the pains of prematurity.

The next few productions of the Irish Literary Theatre were in the main almost totally forgettable. Those high ideals were floundering in practical pursuit as the founders were at cross purposes. Edward Martyn, influenced on the Continent by Ibsen's sociointellectual plays, resigned in a fury over Yeats's finespun intention of creating a theatre for poetic drama, "spiritual, ideal and remote," that began to fail early on. The end arrived on the opening night of his coproduction with George Moore of *Diarmuid and Grainne* at the Gaiety in 1901. The play was a camp fiasco of imported Shakespearean actors struggling to make sense of this ancient Celtic legend set to music. The production distinguished itself only in that it marked George Moore's singular entanglement with the *aes dana* of Irish theatre. He later described the collaboration:

Moore was to write in French; Lady Gregory would then translate his French into English; Taidg O'Donahue would then translate the English into Irish; and then Lady Gregory would translate the Irish into English! After all that Yeats would put style upon it!

Yet in typical Celtic convolution, the simple second billed play — Douglas Hyde's *Casadh an tSugain* (The Twisting of the Rope) — cast with amateurs and written in Irish, was the precursor of Ireland's unique dramatic contribution, the pure folk, or peasant, play. This was the beginning of a literary strain of poetic dialogue and sparse rural settings that would shortly explode onto international stages in the genius of John Millington Synge.

Among a kaleidoscope of links missing in Yeats's theatre was either producer or director to train Irish actors. Backstage at the Gaiety one evening he met a team of brothers, William and Frank Fay, who had been training amateur drama groups around Dublin for a few years. Yeats eventually persuaded them to collaborate with him and to become founding members of a new national theatre. Over the next few decades the naturalism of the Fay Brothers would influence such Abbey players as Sara Allgood, Marie O'Neill, F. J. McCormick, Barry Fitzgerald, and others. "They were unique," says Simpson, "in that they made the actors behave like human beings. Not to say that they didn't exaggerate somewhat. Dublin audiences are very seductive to an actor, and they can egg him on to overdo things a bit. But the Fay Brothers' technique was to make the actors more like ordinary people behaving in a room, while most of the actors up to then were what we would call wildly stylized."

The wandering years ended for the troupe when an English heiress and former secretary to Yeats, Miss Anne E. Horniman, volunteered to donate a permanent home for the national theatre. On December 27, 1904, a renovated morgue and savings bank became the residence of a drama

company that would soon become one of the most glittering in the world — the Abbey Theatre. Miss Horniman
stayed on with the theatre for a while, but Lady Gregory
remained the grande dame of the Abbey, and soon Miss
Horniman resigned when the board refused to close the
theatre on the day of King Edward VII's funeral.

The plays of the Abbey from its inception were highly
personalized limns of the language, moods, and mysteries
of the Irish people. Reactions to this staged reflecting mir-
ror were at times overvain and overviolent. Often claimed
as an inspiration for the 1916 insurrection, Yeats's play,
Cathleen ni Houlihan, caused him to wonder at the force of
such drama. He wrote of it later:

Did this play of mine send out
Certain men the English shot?

"The big impact of the Abbey, in those days," suggests
Simpson, "and what their reputation rests on, is that they
were the first people to portray what you would call ordinary people on the stage in any sense at all. Chekhov and
Gorky displayed peasants, but the plays were about the
landed gentry. The Abbey plays in those years were actually not only about peasants but the silent majority."

The revelations of this shadowed society began with the
plays of John Millington Synge. Yeats had met Synge in
Paris and had encouraged him to return to Ireland and
begin his writing career there. "Go to the Aran Islands.
Live as if you were one of the people themselves; express a
life that has never found expression." The result of his
return to Ireland — *Riders to the Sea, In the Shadow of the
Glen,* and *The Playboy of the Western World* — were micro-
cosms of the Irish life he had found, as spontaneous as they
were complex. Their ancient language he translated into
poetic prose, and his characterizations, at once overpower-
ing and gently primitive, dominated international stages
for years. A few found his plays an intrusion, a raw expo-
sure they translated into blasphemy. And in 1907, as the

curtain fell on *The Playboy of the Western World,* the audience hurled shoes and vegetables onto the stage.

Unfortunately, Synge was dying of Parkinson's disease by then, but in his relatively brief writing career he had proven Yeats's idea: "Words alone are certain good." He inspired other Abbey playwrights, such as T. C. Murray, Padraic Colum, and Lady Gregory, to continue to bring to the stage this unique source of drama.

> In Ireland we have a popular imagination that is fiery, magnificent and tender; so that those who wish to write start with a chance that is not given to writers in places where the springtime of local life has been forgotten and the harvest is a memory only and the straw has been turned into bricks.

If Synge was the romantic retriever of an ancient culture whose life was found in Ireland's outposts, Sean O'Casey, some twenty years later, was the chronicler of a new Ireland, urban and revolutionary, set in the rubble of Dublin tenements. The romantic glow of the Celtic twilight was about to be extinguished by O'Casey's trilogy of realism. His plays were invective responses to the blind national delirium of post-revolutionary Ireland and drew bitter, vicious attacks. After the opening of *The Plough and the Stars* in 1926 one critic accused O'Casey of portraying Dubliners as "prostitutes and cowards." While the mob violence in the Abbey that evening brought Yeats to the stage shouting at the audience, "You have disgraced yourselves again! Is this to be the ever recurring celebration of the arrival of Irish genius? The fame of O'Casey is born here tonight. This is his apotheosis."

Throughout the years Yeats was at once ever disappointed and ever drawn to Ireland and the Abbey. He once wrote in a letter to Lady Gregory entitled "The People's Theatre": "We did not set out to create this sort of theatre, and its success has been discouragement and defeat."

Of Ireland he could never manage to abandon her, yet

her provincialism and limitations rankled him. He described Dublin as "this rude, unmannerly town" with "great hatred, little room." O'Casey, Joyce, and, to an extent, Beckett shared this frustration with Yeats and like ambivalent lovers sought freedom in separation and settled elsewhere, somehow compelled to spend their lives writing exclusively about what they had fled.

Toward the end of the twenties the Irish Theatre was a triumph — prolific, raging, innovative...and myopic. Except for the efforts of Anew McMaster traveling around hundreds of villages with his Shakespearean company, every stage in Ireland was becoming imperiously Irish. In 1928 two young actors who had met touring with McMaster, Michael MacLiammoir and Hilton Edwards, founded the Dublin Gate Theatre. Their collaboration over the next forty years almost singly rescued Irish Theatre from chauvinistic exhaustion.

Their plan for the Gate was one only two youths would approach. Irish theatre depended on talk, and a great deal of it. However, both actors had been London trained, MacLiammoir at His Majesty's and Edwards at the Old Vic, and they intended to bring to Dublin the theatrical disciplines of technique and visual sense whose importance both eluded and disinterested the Irish. "The country," wrote MacLiammoir, "long since habituated to the image of herself as an entertaining slattern, has acquired a certain indolence of approach, which together with her inherent indifference to visual style could easily lead her theatre into a placid and mediocre acceptance of the second best, into a facile reliance, where voices rich, tongues eloquent, and ears receptive on sound alone; and these things were the many pitfalls we determined not merely to avoid, but to cure if we could."

Their method for the cure was to bring to provincial Dublin an international view. They began in the Peacock Theatre with an ambitious production of Ibsen's *Peer Gynt*.

Two years later the Gate was in permanent quarters, in which over the next few decades MacLiammoir and Edwards would produce a staggering repertory, including Shakespeare, Ibsen, Tolstoy, Sheridan, Wilde, Cocteau, Strindberg, O'Neill, Stein, Chekhov, and others. It would be impossible to define in what way either man influenced one particular area of the Gate or another; their combined talents blended into a peerless form. MacLiammoir emerges as the Renaissance man. Not alone is he an ingenious actor, fluent in many languages, including his native Irish, but he turns with facility to painting and writing, while Edwards is the firm hand of direction, training at the Gate such actors as Orson Welles, James Mason, Geraldine Fitzgerald, as well as many Irish-born actors and actresses.

They were joined at the Gate in 1936 by Lord Longford, a member of one of the most prolific literary families in Ireland, the Packenhams. His Longford Productions alternated residence with the Gate company, since both traveled extensively abroad in those years. Each founder of a theatre has a personal intention to create in a void. For Lord Longford his passion was the classics of Greece. His translations of Aeschylus and Sophocles, along with the plays written with Lady Longford, supplied the source of the Longford repertory. MacLiammoir, Edwards, and Lord Longford hoped by creating their theatre to provoke a new style of Irish playwrighting, and in this they concede failure. Other than MacLiammoir's plays, Denis Johnston's *The Old Lady Says No!* was the only new Irish play to be produced at the Gate. Their qualities were specific and demanding for a new play.

Often youthful, experimental ventures like the Abbey and the Gate grow rigid with age and less flexible with young talent. So in the fifties Brendan Behan's *Quare Fellow* and Samuel Beckett's *Waiting for Godot* were first produced in one of Dublin's fringe theatres, The Pike, run by Alan Simpson and his wife, Caroline Swift. Eventually The Pike was closed by the censorship board over a production of Tennessee Williams's *The Rose Tatoo*. Simpson minimizes the effects of those years of censorship — that scheme of clerics and nationalists to save the Irish from themselves — which dragged over three decades.

"There were lots of plays written and they caused furores, but it didn't stop them from being written. Censorship — what it did do, it gave the theatre a kind of excitement that perhaps it may have lost. As in Central Europe about ten years ago, they wrote nasty things about the government dressed up as ancient Rome or something. There is a certain fun in writers such as O'Casey and others twenty years ago of seeing how near to the bone they could get without actually causing a riot. That's gone slightly."

But the writers themselves were not quite as cavalier about the lunacy of censorship. Brendan Behan once wrote a few verses on the attacks of the censorship board banning almost all his works:

My name is Brendan Behan
I'm the best banned in the land.

It's not poverty nor oppression
That's hardest to endure,
But the derision unending,
A wound none can endure.

By the end of the fifties many of the theatres that had mushroomed over Dublin were vanishing. The Abbey Theatre had burned to the ground in 1951 and had moved to the Queens Theatre for a stay of fifteen years until the new theatre was opened in 1966. MacLiammoir's and Edwards's Gate Theatre had closed because of rising financial pressures. Also gone were Alan Simpson's Pike Theatre, Austin Clarke's Lyric Company (a company closest to achieving Yeats's dream of a theatre for poetry), along with Liam Redmond's Players' Theatre.

Then in 1957 Lord Killanin and Brendan Smith decided to produce the Dublin Theatre Festival as an annual fortnight of presentations combining new plays by both Irish and international writers. As the crowds increase each year attending the festival, the ritual laments of Dubliners for the end of Irish theatre begin again. A few years ago Mac-Liammoir warned against the Irish penchant for derision: "Never in a brief thirty years or so has a public, once so diffident and uncertain of its own significance, gained such an overwhelming and, in the main, unfounded self-confidence as the Irish."

If there is a dearth of good writing being done for the theatre, the same reason has also caused most of Ireland's great acting talent, such as Siobhan McKenna, Cyril Cusack, Liam Redmond, and the late Jack McGowran, to tour abroad most of the year — they have to make a living. "There are so many more outlets today for writers," explains Simpson, "notably television. In the thirties and forties Hollywood was a rather distant place. It wasn't possible for the writers, except the exceptional ones, to get there. But nowadays, at our own doorstep and certainly across the channel, they can write well enough, if not brilliantly, for television. They expend their creative ability. TV takes as much creative effort for a writer, and so this applies an effect on theatre. The writer will put out his genius on a one-hour play. Because of the nature of it, he would never have a chance to develop his talents as O'Casey or Chekhov or O'Neill developed theirs. The theatre was the only available medium then. All those people wrote an awful lot of boring, second-rate plays, but they got the chance to write the occasional masterpiece."

There are still playwrights writing today: Brian Friel's *Philadelphia Here I Come!* had the longest run on Broadway of any Irish export. Hugh Leonard produces at least one play a year that is remarkable by any standard. And Tom Murphy, author of *Whistle in the Dark* and *The Morning After*

Optimism, is better known in England. Kenneth Tynan once offered his evaluation of Irish theatre: "It's Ireland's sacred duty to send over every few years a playwright who will save the English theatre from inarticulate dumbness."

Since the festival was established new playwrights have at least a showcase for their works with critics and producers from London and New York. A far better situation than any nostalgic summons of the "good ole days." For over seventy years the clouds have been gathering over the Irish stage, though they now seem to have become more like familiar old props on opening night than nefarious portents of doom.

◇   ◇   ◇

DUBLIN THEATRES

ABBEY THEATRE
Lower Abbey Street
Telephone: 744505
Performances at 8 P.M.

This modern home of the National Theatre was opened in 1966, replacing the original Abbey destroyed by fire in 1951. A continuous repertory of works by Yeats, Lady Gregory, Synge, O'Casey, Behan, are presented along with new plays by Irish writers.

PEACOCK THEATRE
Lower Abbey Street
Telephone: 744505
Performances at 8 P.M.

This experimental annex was added to the Abbey to enable the theatre to expand its productions to include concerts, one-man shows, poetry readings, plays in Irish, and childrens' drama on Saturday afternoons.

PROJECT ARTS CENTER
Essex Street
Telephone: 781572

Dublin's vital center for new talent. This artist's workshop presents a lunchtime theatre for young playwrights. (As performances and times vary, check daily newspaper.)

GATE THEATRE
Cavendish Row
Telephone: 744045
Performances at 8 P.M.

For over forty years the home of the brilliant collaboration of Michael MacLiammoir and Hilton Edwards. Their "outward look" has brought to Dublin audiences over 350 productions of staggering international range. In 1978 MacLiammoir died, but Edwards plans to carry on their formula of presenting imported works along with modern Irish drama.

GAIETY THEATRE
South King Street
Telephone: 771717
Performances at 8 P.M.

Entertainment in this elegant old theatre, built in 1871, is the most diverse in Dublin. During the summer months a mad Celtic revue, *Gaels of Laughter*, stars Maureen Potter, Ireland's homebound Bea Lillie. During the remainder of the year are performances by the Radio Telefís Eiréann Symphony Orchestra, the Dublin Grand Opera Society, and at Christmastime a special pantomime show.

EBLANA THEATRE
Store Street
Telephone: 746707

Don't wander around aimlessly for too long, the theatre is tucked away in the basement of the new central bus station. The repertory is usually proven international hits of high quality, along with occasional "adults only" productions — which have a long way to catch up to Broadway's hard porn.

OLYMPIA THEATRE
72 Dame Street
Telephone: 778962

Ireland's old-time variety palace. The repertory is usually plays, variety shows, and pantomimes.

FOCUS THEATRE
off Pembroke Street
Telephone: 682993

Deirdre O'Connell came to Dublin after Actors' Studio in New York and started her own Stanislavsky studio. Completely self-supporting, the theatre presentations are fewer than a half dozen a year.

LANTERN THEATRE
38 Merrion Square
Telephone: 761741
Performances at 8 P.M.

Located a few steps down in the basement of a Georgian house on Merrion Square, this small theatre stages a new production each month of a wide repertory. Seating is limited

Advance booking is advised and may be done directly with the theatre or Brown Thomas (776861), or Switzers (776821) on Grafton Street. Most Dublin hotels will arrange tickets if you inquire with the hall porter.

DUBLIN THEATRE FESTIVAL

An unusual gathering of Irish and international playwrights, actors, producers, and critics for a fortnight of presentations. The Festival is usually held during the first two weeks of October.   A Theatre Club is open each evening after the performances with generous licensing hours for the celebration. Each year dates vary slightly, but the Irish Tourist Board will supply specifics and make reservations.

The Sprawling Adolescent

with
John B. Keane

The tide of expression carried Joyce, O'Casey, and others to foreign homes to spend their lives setting down the reflections of their native anamnesis. Unlike these Irish writers, John B. Keane broke the familiar tradition of exile. The teenage emigrant returned from the grey suffocating sacks of Birmingham and Northampton to open a pub in his native Listowel to observe and detail the vitality of his rural tradition. Some ten plays, numerous sketches, and fifteen years ago John B. sent off his first play Sive *to the Abbey Theatre. Five weeks later it was returned without comment. Soon after that the Listowel Drama Group produced a rather rough* Sive, *and John B.'s ingenuous descriptions of rural Irish life began traveling the thespian circles not only of Ireland but England and America.*

The early years of the rural theatre he recounts in his book, Self Portrait:

> In many aspects it's still a sprawling adolescent, but not for long, because the theatre is experiencing the pangs of rebirth in rural Ireland. It is taking a strange shape, but the stranger the better, and the more independent of outside help the better.

A decade later John B. described for me the survival of this unique tradition in its present form – more defined, more sophisticated, yet still rooted in the ethos of the people. To understand the rural theatre he shares a glimpse of the character of its participants. John B. is a Kerryman possessing, or possessed by, unbridled flights of conversation. What follows is simply his answer to one query: "What became of the Sprawling Adolescent?"

◇ ◇ ◇

(Author's note: Italic passages in this chapter are from Keane's *Self-Portrait.*)

You see, the rural theatre in Ireland really complements the professional theatre in Ireland. The vast majority of actors who graduate to the professional ranks come from the amateur dramatic societies of Cork, Kerry, Galway, Clare, and so forth. Also, the audiences that you get in Dublin for the plays, say, for the Abbey Theatre, the Olympia, and for the Gate Theatre, which does the sort of sophisticated European plays as distinct from the folk Irish plays or the purely Irish plays, have been nurtured in appreciation of drama at festivals all over the countryside. At the present time, while we sit here, you have at least six different drama festivals running concurrently. For instance, there is a festival in County Cork tomorrow, a festival in Galway, in Wexford, in Clare. There are several others that don't come to mind at once. Next week we have five or six new festivals. Now, the culmination of all these festivals is the All Ireland Drama Festival at Athlone. This is a fairly unique thing in any country in the world. In a small festival in County Cork plays by twelve different playwrights will be seen during the festival, and all these quite well done. This means that, for example, this year, just for curiosity, I went through all the festivals and discovered that every major playwright in the world is represented at these festivals in

Ireland. Plays ranging from Ibsen to Shaw to Chekhov to O'Neill. In fact, anybody you care to name. Any playwright in the world of any importance or significance is being done.

These are available to country audiences, and consequently there is no earthly hope that the theatre will die in the cities. Because of this stream of appreciative youngsters nurtured in drama, often actors, almost everyone is a potential theatregoer. This is unique. Another unique thing about this is that these people, because of the fact that they have a sort of innate appreciation of the theatre, form their own opinions and are not led by the critics. For instance, in Dublin, as distinct from London or New York, the critic carries no weight whatever. May we say that you have there the major newspapers in Ireland, the *Irish Times*, the *Irish Independent*, the *Irish Press*, and the *Cork Examiner*. Now, if the four of these were unanimous in their condemnation of a play, it would not have the slightest effect on audiences. This is a unique thing, a marvelous thing. The reason for this, as I say, is that the theatregoers can make up their own minds. Another thing that I have discovered from talking after plays to young boys and girls from, say, eighteen to twenty-five is that they are very well up on almost every aspect of theatre. They can discuss lighting, they can discuss cues, prompting, grouping, the whole lot. And this is unique. I go to London every year to see the current crop of plays, and I find that when I listen in the bar between acts, there is nothing like the same level of conversation.

The point is, people will say to me, "Yes, fine, but tell me what this thing has done. It's there for fifty years, sixty, seventy." What it has done is this: We have three Nobel prize winners, each of whom is a playwright — Shaw, Yeats, and Beckett. No country in the world has this sort of distinction. Now, instead of deteriorating, it is getting a firmer grip. Since I first wrote about this thing ten years ago standards have improved immensely. At that time very few groups would dare to do a play like *The Rainmaker*. I see at this year's festival there are five different groups, rural groups from tiny little villages, producing *The Rainmaker*, which is a subtle, very delicate, and very lovely play. And this is just one of the many. Now this can do nothing but good.

In places like Plymouth, where you have some good drama groups, you find nothing like the range of appreciation that the Irish theatregoer has. For the simple reason that people there tend as a rule to go by the London critic or the box office success, which is never good theatre. If you wanted to put on *The Rainmaker* in any West End theatre in London, it would not survive. If you were to put on Noel Coward's *Blithe Spirit*, it would run for possibly a year. Well, the point is that here in Ireland, if you had a choice of seeing a play by Tennessee Williams — a bad play by Tennessee Williams — or an all-out London smash hit, everyone would opt for Tennessee Williams.

When I first started writing I had seen very little theatre, except plays when I was working in England. There was very little then to see at home. On the other hand, almost every Lent you could for forty days see a play every night somewhere in the vicinity. Some of these weren't done so well. There would be no such thing as lighting in many cases, and there were times when some of the actors, when they got on stage, would speak some of their own lines as well. I remember one fellow in particular. They took to tying a big piece of fishing string around his leg to pull when he kept talking on and on.

There is no awareness of this incredible movement that is doing so much for the arts in this country. The culmination of all these festivals is about March in Athlone, where you have a continuous fortnight of amateur drama and the fourteen best groups in Ireland competing, most of them better than you would see off Broadway or in greater London, because these men are devoted. Fellows like Tommy MacArdell. Most of them have been offered jobs in the Abbey. Your American critic was here, and listen to his review of the Ballintra Players: "Ballintra Players presented *Indians* by Arthur Koppit at the Meath Drama Festival at Navan last night." The adjudicator said: "How can you present tribes of Red Indians, herds of buffalo and cavalry horses onto a stage and mix them up with the Grand Duke Alexis of Russia, and throw in Annie Oakley, Billy the Kid, and the President of the United States and hope to present this fantasia on the normal-size stage? Well — the Ballintra group has succeeded in combining all these elements in a memorable production." Apparently this is a marvelous production. There is a man in the bar tonight named Jimmy Boylan, and he was telling me about this thing and he said to me, "Where in the name of Jaysus is Ballintra?"

◇ ◇ ◇

New plays by country boys are springing up like mushrooms all around us. Maybe some of them are crude and clumsy, but it must be remembered that you cannot build a new native drama in a generation.

In a festival of one-act plays this year I saw five by new writers. None of them was any good, but that's not the point. This year so far there is one new play written by a playwright in Ballyduff, which is seven miles from here. He said that the reason he was writing a play was that he was fed up with smutty plays by other Irish playwrights...I wonder whom he meant? The point is that he had this play excellently mounted and beautifully produced. It's an average play, but it was well received. Now, that is a play done locally that would never see the light if its author were in the Abbey Theatre. I would say that this year there have been four new full-length plays by amateurs, one of them pretty good.

But there is an enemy at the moment, a thing called Bingo. All the local parishes in Ireland are running Bingo games for the purpose of improving churches, parish halls, and so on. It would seem that the ultimate goal of the Catholic Church in Ireland just now is the propagation of Bingo. It's a threat, but it's not winning. We're too firmly entrenched.

◇ ◇ ◇

Some others resented Sive, *said it was blasphemous and ungodly and noisily gave vent to their opinions while the play was in progress. Some – the more sanctimonious – even waited 'till the show was over and tackled us as we left the hall. One night we were pelted with clods and small stones and one of the girls got a nasty cut on her neck.*

The business about the violence in the Abbey at Synge s *The Playboy of the Western World*. Now the elements that kicked up their feet that night were a sort of pseudoliterati, jumped-up countrymen, who suddenly found themselves in suburban homes and wanted to divorce themselves as much as possible from their natural background. So when they saw the shift on the stage, they became disgusted. I found this to a certain extent with my early plays. I learned that the League of Decency were after me once in Dublin. They said that they were going to parade outside the theatre that evening, and I said: "Fine, but at your peril. I'll be there with my pals." They didn't show up.

This has never happened in rural Ireland. I've found that the rural audiences are much nearer to nature. They can understand, and accept homosexuality and buggery, for instance, because they live in the countryside where these things are wide open and above board. Here you have life, with sex in its very beginnings. Nothing shocks these people. We have always found that no matter what you put on in rural Ireland, the audience never revolted against the playwright.

Every townland and parish is vibrant with the ballads of our departed poets. They're there waiting to be adopted and woven into the fabric of living theatre... And look at the characters all around you, the genuine, earthy, soft-spoken wits who surround you.

The language that I speak and write in, I wouldn't call it English. I would say that it is a mixture of folk Irish and Elizabethan English. The language we speak now evolved from the marriage of bardic Irish and Elizabethan English. It's a very colorful language. You see, there was a wholesale movement away from the Irish at the time of Elizabeth I, because it was the first time ever the Gaelic poets showed any respect for English writers such as Spenser and Shakespeare. The languages married there, giving us what I would prefer to think of as a language with its own peculiarities, its own uniqueness. The language I use, and that of many Anglo-Irish writers, is greatly indebted to Irish. Without it we wouldn't be half as colorful. From this marriage of the two — bardic Irish and Elizabethan tradition — a unique, quirky character emerges whose mind is like quicksilver, conceiving so much that you will never know what goes on beneath. This is what makes man priceless and what gives him dignity and strength. That he knows so much about himself. He knows enough, in short, to live his life to the fullest. This is life. This is what it means. People in the city are missing this. But they have no field to walk in. They have no river. They haven't made their own community.

When you live in a community which has had its ups and downs for a thousand years you begin to realize that you can't have the moon and the stars. And when you have realized this, you have come to terms with yourself and your surroundings. And it means that you can embrace a great lump of life sufficient to satisfy all your needs. And this is living at the very highest level.

◇ ◇ ◇

COMMENT

This vital amateur drama movement varies in staging and standards around the country. As John B. has described for the more adventuresome, almost every Irish town offers at least a school hall production and a check in the local pub will give you more specific information. For those who prefer the security of more organized efforts, Cork offers the Theatre of the South and its own resident ballet company. (Cork claims the birthplace of Alicia Markova's mother, and the ballerina spent many of her holidays there.) During the autumn months Wexford draws an international audience for its Opera Festival, and neighbouring Waterford has recently staged a light opera festival gaining in popularity. In Galway there's the only all-Irish Theatre *Taibhdhearc*, where Siobhan McKenna began her career playing Joan of Arc in Irish. Over the summer Risteard O Broin presents *Seoda* (the word for jewels in Irish), an evening of the most authentic traditional music, song, dance, and drama in the country. The Limerick Theatre launched its premiere season last summer, alternating repertory and new plays by Irish writers. During the summer months all of Ireland is an exuberant theatre festival. Detailed information concerning programs and times of performances may be obtained from local tourist offices.

7. Literature:

A Way with Words

with

Benedict Kiely
Sean White
John Ryan
Thomas Flanagan

Irish literature evolves from the thousand roots in its past. One afternoon in Dublin four friends gathered, as they often do, to sift through its many and mercurial strands and to puzzle over Ireland's staggering contribution to literature. They were Irish novelist Benedict Kiely, Gaelic scholar Sean White, John Ryan, Editor of Dublin Magazine, *and Thomas Flanagan, Chairman of the English Department at the University of California at Berkeley.*

◇ ◇ ◇

SEAN: We are taking Irish literature, whether in the Irish language, Latin, or English, as a kind of whole body, and I think this is the proper way to take it. Not to divide it into

Anglo-Irish, and so on. It is literature written by Irishmen from the fifth century onward.

I think that the question that does present itself is why the Irish express themselves in literature rather than in any of the other arts. I think it is a very interesting question, because there are certain periods of the Golden Age of the tenth, eleventh, and twelfth centuries when the Irish express themselves in metal work, stone work, and manuscript, but apart from that Ireland's contribution to the plastic arts is fairly minimal and remains so. But why in literature?

Just to suggest a few quick reasons. From the beginning I feel that the Irish were a verbal race. Their literature was composed in words. At first orally in speech, poetry, saga, mythology — "story and poem." And even their legal documents — for genealogies were necessary for law — had a certain literary and poetic element in them. When they came to write a lyrical kind of literature and made the little annotations we find on the sides of manuscripts, I think they were responding to something very real within themselves. Now, as time went on, there was this particular Golden Age of gold work, but a great deal of this was done under Continental influence. There is no doubt about that. But this opens another large subject that is rather interesting. The Romans never invaded Ireland. It is one of the few countries, perhaps the only European country, that totally escaped Roman influence.

TOM: That was the first oppression — Rome never came!

SEAN: But it's what makes a certain individualistic thing about Ireland. Rome didn't come. But it did come in a second coming in the form of Christianity. We had, as it were, the Second Version of Rome.

TOM: Second comings are never as good.

SEAN: Again, why do the Irish express themselves in literature? After the Golden Age the age of invasions started — the Danes, the Normans. Ireland never again had the possibility of becoming a wealthy stable country. Now, maybe it never had it from the beginning. It was always a tribalistic kind of a country anyway, and a great deal of time seems to have been spent, right up to the present day, fighting each other for tribalistic reasons. When you have this kind of society you don't have either the calm or the establishment or the money to produce painting, sculpture, or architecture. The one thing you have, though, is a form of art, the minimal form of art — literature. All it requires is a good memory, an ability to compose orally, and some paper or parchment to write it all down. So the minimum was there for that. And it doesn't need a rich Florentine or any other kind of patronage system. Literature became the art of Ireland, and has remained the Irish art.

TOM: You can see it existing to the present day perfectly. If you go to a pub in the country, you hear people talking or singing, and you realize that it's an auditory culture, not a visual.

SEAN: There is something in the nature, lacking as far as we can observe, having to do with the visual. However historical and environmental reasons must affect us, I do believe that affluence and a period of stability would possibly lead to a flowering of the other arts too. To draw a parallel with England. England has a superb literature. Its contributions, frankly, to the visual arts are minimal, though not quite as minimal as Ireland's. It has been muted. Their architecture is vernacular and provincial. Their painting and music is not "of the center," as Matthew Arnold would say.

TOM: They too are an island.

SEAN: They too are a Western island, on the edge, peripheral to the center. And so again my vague generalization — literature is very much the art of the "deprived." I don't mean in a pejorative sense. Perhaps it is good to be cut down in a way.

Ireland's Reflecting Pond

TOM: What I feel is important and relevant to Irish literature is that the literary values are far more closely associated with how people live and feel in this country than, say, in America. In a way we have been talking about literature, but, in fact, all we have been talking about is the way people live. And we have never believed we weren't talking about literature, and we were quite right — literature and life are far more closely combined in Ireland.

When people are arguing here about literature and brush off into politics, it might well be thought an irrelevancy; or when they begin to argue about politics and they begin drifting off to literature. Neither of those things is irrelevant. What is important about literature in Ireland, and what is interesting, is that the two are so closely related that they are virtually functions of one another. What might seem an irrelevancy, or going up a tributary or down a tributary, whichever way you go, you are really arguing about the same thing. Because Ireland is a remarkably close, cohesive society, where what people say is what people write.

SEAN: Literature here is a critique of life, whereas literature in the States is part of "show biz." Philip Roth has as much influence on American life as he does on Irish life. Whereas Ben Kiely *has* an influence on Irish life. He is as important a figure as Conor Cruise O'Brien.

A friend of mine, a visiting American professor, was asked at the end of his stay what were his conclusions. He said in a distant and vaguely nonapproving way, "It seems a very personal society."

TOM: What other kind of literature could a personal society produce but a very personal literature, and, in fact, what other society but a personal one could produce a *genuine* literature. It is when a society ceases to be personal that you cease to get an actual literature and get an abstract literature. Do you remember Yeats wondering: "Did this play of mine send out certain men the English shot?" That is a personal literature.

SEAN: Critics arrived and were embarrassed by the nearness of the life to literature. They want to talk about it in the abstract — in a *New York Review of Books* sense. They are horrified that writers should be so accessible. Life should be observed, but they shouldn't be part of the scene. It's too rich for them.

TOM: It's as though Shakespeare drank at the Mermaid Tavern! Life and literature are cramped into an actual community; which was also true of Shakespeare's London, Samuel Johnson's London, and François Villon's Paris. Actual living was written about. From this Ireland has produced a number of outstanding *town* novelists, culminating in the greatest, James Joyce.

SEAN: The writing is not always morally healthy, and in small spaces you are going to find hatred and tremendous emotions. As Yeats said of Dublin, "Great hatred, little room."

Literature ... Libel ... and Litigation

JOHN: The Irish are very litigious. Every Irishman is a hob lawyer. But not about crime. All civil actions.

SEAN: This is the Irish libel thing. There is a sort of continuous series through the thirties. First, Oliver St. John

Gogarty wrote *As I Was Going Down Sackville Street*. He libeled the Sinclair family, and he was sued. Then Patrick Kavanagh libeled him. Then Gogarty sued Kavanagh.

JOHN: Kavanagh described in an article coming up from Inishkeen to Dublin for the first time. He walked, and it took three days. He called on Gogarty, as indeed he called on Æ and Seamus O'Sullivan. He wrote that "the door was opened and I didn't know whether it was a maid, his wife, or his mistress. I presumed all writers to have at least two wives or a mistress." So Gogarty sued him and won.

BEN: That made Gogarty's attitude all the nastier. You see, Gogarty had been defying convention all his life and was now prepared to accept a cover of convention in his status as a practicing surgeon. So it was a vile thing, Gogarty's attitude. And he ruined a book by a young poet and it was kept out of circulation for years. But the real reason was that Gogarty was offended by something on the previous page, which I didn't realize for years. Kavanagh described going into the National Library when he arrived in Dublin and asking for Æ's address. As they hadn't Æ's address, they gave him Gogarty's address. Then Kavanagh made a very typical Kavanagh remark: "Is that the best you can do?" This is what offended Gogarty.

SEAN: Paddy really never recovered from the humiliation of the trial.

JOHN: They were trying to prove there was no libel contained. Now, they have two ways of doing that. First, to prove that there isn't libel or intent; and second, to so disgrace you in front of the jury you're humiliated.

BEN: You see, Paddy brought the action. But you can't win in the courts. Wilde was the worst example of that. He thought he was quick, and Carson gave him just enough rope. In the Kavanagh trial John Costello said at one stage: "I put it to you, Mr. Kavanagh, that your entire testimony has been nothing but a tissue of lies." What can you say to that?

JOHN: You can't take an action against him!

BEN: Poor Sam Beckett came over to testify at the Gogarty trial. He was appearing as a character witness.

SEAN: Billy Fitzgerald was the most relentless cross-examiner. "Ah, Mr. Beckett, yes. Ah, Mr. Beckett you've come home. You're the Mr. Beckett who writes the obscene books."

BEN: Oh, he didn't use the name, Sean. He said: "So nice to see you home. How is that book doing, *Whoroscope?*" "Very well," said Beckett, delighted that anybody would have heard of it, you see. "And that other book, Mr. Beckett, *More Pricks than Kicks?* Thank you, Mr. Beckett." This with a jury of tobacconists and sweet-shop owners!

SEAN: Sam didn't come back to Ireland for twenty years.

BEN: Oh, there's more to it.

JOHN: In the trial Costello came across the word schizophrenia, which he pronounced "shitsophrenia." He said, "Ah, *nice* word, I must say." And with this his junior, Neil McCarthy, had to take him aside. He returned: "Ah yes, well, we'll get on to the next question." The ignorance, the incredible ignorance!

SEAN: Later Costello went on:" Will you explain an incident in the Irish Club in London." "No, I don't mind," said

Kavanagh. "I was going up the stairs and some fellow shouted at me 'How's Shakespeare?' And so I came down and taught him manners."

SEAN: Well, let's face it, the libel element in the suit wasn't really all that big. Paddy wrote worse about everybody else.

BEN: You know, the only person who ever really turned Paddy apart was Sean O'Faolain, when Paddy wrote the article "Coloured Balloons" — the attack on Frank O'Connor. It was a vile article.

JOHN: Paddy really got off to a good start by jumping on the grave of Fred Higgins. The same thing Cyril Connolly had done to Housman. To get a good start on a literary life, you must jump on somebody's grave.

BEN: Paddy had done Fred Higgins and Frank O'Connor, and he went up to Brinsley MacNamara in an art gallery one day and said, "Brinsley, I want to borrow your books." "I haven't many of them," said Brinsley, "and what do you want with them, Paddy?" "I want to write an article about you." "Well, I'll tell you," said Brinsley, "you see my large stick here, Patrick. Apart from not loaning you my books, most of which I don't have, if you write an article on me, I will *beat* you to death with this stick." Brinsley meant it.

SEAN: Who was it, Brinsley or Larry Morrow, who was writing his autobiography and putting everybody in it?

BEN: It was Brinsley. The title for his autobiography — alas, only a few pages of the manuscript are around — was *The Long Vexation*. Which is a great title for an autobiography. But he met Frank Hugh O'Donnell on the street, and years had passed since they had shared an apartment, and Frank said: "Brinsley, how's the autobiography getting on?"

Brinsley said: "Wonderful, Frank. I'm on chapter thirteen, and it's all about you."

SEAN: There were quite a few libel cases, and they all made a tremendous impact.

JOHN: Suddenly people found that they had to sell the family homestead to pay the lawyers, and then it came to an end.

A Curious Censorship....

SEAN: We changed from being a part of a great empire to being an isolated African-style state. We were the first to leave the British Empire, and the door closed behind us. As has been said, "The Empire ends where it begins." This is where the British Empire began.

TOM: When you talk about censorship — which I abominate as much as anybody here — when you consider the problems of a country beginning anew in the year 1921, as abominable as censorship was, still it was milder than the evils that beset other countries starting out on their own. There was never political censorship. Only stupid moral, religious nonsense that was relatively innocuous. "Dark Rosaleen" (Ireland) emerged and was disillusioned by reality.

JOHN: Ours was the only purely literary censorship. It had nothing to do with politics whatever. Here it had to do with morals.

BEN: The court was no way to settle something. The only way to settle it was to laugh it out of existence. You see, they established a real de Valera way out of a crux. They established an Appeals Board. And it got to the stage where at least 99 per cent of what was banned by the censors was immediately unbanned by the Appeals Board. A publisher wasn't going to bother his hoof about all this, but it did hurt the sales of a book. You'd run into the oddest things. Old Liam O'Brian, who died recently, was a professor of French in Galway University. A nineteenth-century curate, but a friend of mine. I had a book banned that was based on my memories of the Jesuits' novitiate. And as far as I am capable of writing a religious book, this was a religious book. I remember I was in Hamburg with Kevin Howlin, and he was on the phone to his wife, who said the book had just been banned. I remember blinding all over Hamburg that night about this. When I returned to Dublin, it was appealed. A few days after the Appeals Board met I met Liam O'Brian on O'Connell Street. He had always been very forthright and frank, and he said he had voted against unbanning of the book. He was afraid I might have heard, so he decided to tell me. "What for?" I asked him. "That incident," he said, "of the woman getting more or less nude into the lake. You know, for a book about the novitiate, that was incongruous." I said: "Liam, with all due respect, you are not here to tell me how to write novels. You are here to administer an act of the *Oireachtas* (Senate), and the phrase is '...in general tendency indecent or obscene.'" We didn't speak to one another for many years after that. This comes from a rather good man who was vastly acquainted with French literature! So there are rather curious warps in the Irish mind that you come up against. I'm talking about the forties and fifties. Not now. It is all gone except in a few instances.

JOHN: The irony of the fact is that Donleavy is living here, not having to pay taxes as a writer on the royalties of books that are banned here.

BEN: *Man Alive,* the Irish version of *Playboy* (or "Ploughboy," as we call it), was banned here. But they are taking an action against the Censorship Board. This is most interesting, because they can't *find* the Appeals Board! And they can't appeal the censorship. They can't find the censors, and nobody has been in the office for the past six months. This may be the death of the Censorship Board. You see, it was always a very expensive thing to take it into court.

Unending Cycles

JOHN: I believe we are thinking in terms of a literary move- ment. Yeats was a one-man literary movement. But Æ gave a definition to a literary movement as "eight or nine writers living in a city who cordially hate one another."

BEN: What you had at the end of the last century and the beginning of this century was a very unusual period. Quite seriously, you can't see it as a simple Irish thing. It was part of the whole development of what is called the British Empire. It was all part of that. It also had to do with native Gaelic literature and the discoveries made by scholars such as Sir Samuel Ferguson. This had to do with the origins of Yeats and where they came from. That scholarship had gone on for a century before. There were a lot of things joining together, but then it may have been just accidental that people like John Synge, George Moore, William Yeats, Lady Gregory, Sean O'Casey, James Joyce, and James Stephens were all born in the same period. It was a good period, and when I talk of that period, that particular period, I would begin about 1890 to roughly 1930. Forty years. It's difficult to talk about periods at all in this way. You can't cut off periods like that. Yeats bestrode sixty years of English poetry!

JOHN: There is a ferment of ideas here today, I would say

more so, and probably more honest. You see, we are a very small country and we have produced Yeats, probably the best poet of the century, and Joyce, clearly the greatest novelist since Rabelais, and then Synge and O'Casey could be considered great playwrights...and, of course, this tends to inspire everybody here to think "well, maybe I...tomorrow."

The Myth of the Exiles

BEN: Yeats never left. The way Yeats was brought up, he lived a little in London, a little in Ireland. That was the nature of the society.

JOHN: Yeats sent Synge back.

BEN: Yes, but there was a specific literary reason for that. Yeats thought Synge was wasting his time in Paris. Also, I suspect that Paris was not any good for his health, which is not in any document, but I am quite sure considering the circumstances. You see, Yeats overexaggerated when he said that he sent Synge back. Synge knew the Aran Islands better than Yeats did. He also knew Irish better than Yeats did, and he knew the people of Ireland, in some ways, better than Yeats. But it is no question that it was Yeats's suggestion. I think all this love/hate is grossly exaggerated. I suppose in my time I have written more vitriolic things, not specifically about my compatriots, but about certain aspects of Irish life, and I still say them. Some of my friends agree with me; some very definitely do not.

When O'Casey left he overreacted. He was a very sensitive man. You see, O'Casey was reared in a curious background. He was a poor, Dublin Protestant. Poor comparatively, no Protestants were that poor. So that O'Casey was always in the minority setup. And then you had the ruckus about *The Silver Tassie*, in which, I think, he was rather badly treated. Some people were trying to lay the blame on Brinsley MacNamara. This is untrue. Lay the blame squarely where it was...on W. B. Yeats. It was a mess, and there was no doubt that Yeats was responsible for it. He was wrong about O'Casey. A man who has been so successful is entitled to his own failures. You must be fair.

SEAN: And Beckett...

BEN: Beckett left because he wanted to live in Paris. That's simple. That's as good a reason for going to Paris as any I can think of. Joyce did the same thing. And not only that, Joyce made a game out of it, or an act out of it.

If you look at the images of exile in Joyce, you will find that they refer to political exiles. And he is always wearing the mask of the exile, the artist in exile, the man removed from society. Parnell, his Fenians on the run. That was part of the act. Now when it comes down to base material, Padraic Colum told me that Joyce would have stayed in Ireland if he could have got a job at a pound a week in 1913. He couldn't get a job. He went for sheer ruddy economics. There was an offer of money in the States, and he went. This was not a rich island, and the opportunities were small. Remember this, that a man can live as well here in Ireland, as a writer or as anything else, as he can in the United States. Communications have improved. If I want to get to Paris, London, or New York, I can be there in a few hours. I specifically don't want to. I'm quite content in Dublin. But remember that fashions have changed. But do *not* think that Ireland drove out Joyce or anybody else. This is a fantasy. A man goes out because he wants to.

Another Cycle

JOHN: I think one important person that the Northern Situation has produced is the poet, Seamus Heaney. A lot of his verse has been inspired by the North. Seamus is a product of the British education system, as was Bernadette Devlin. You know his "Bog People" poems, where he compares the people found intact, preserved by the texture of the peat over two thousand years ago in Denmark, to the Irish imprisoned in their own culture for over five hundred years. As he says himself, "they arose from the dark." Though it's an appallingly dreadful thing — but still, there is the Resurrection. In his recent collection of poems, *North*, is a poem entitled "The Grauballe Man" about a warrior found preserved in the bog with a deep gash in his neck. He draws a parallel to the sectarian murders in our community and then toward the end contrasts the realities of the death of this warrior to the aesthetic beauty representing death in the famous Roman sculpture "The Dying Gaul." (See end of Chapter 11 for text of "The Grauballe Man.")

BEN: Also you have the poetry of John Montague, who is also from the North. In his collection, *The Rough Field*, you have a very good example of man taking three hundred years of history and his own personal life as well and making a great poem out of it. They're considerable poets. As far as the novel — the novel requires quite a period of gestation.

JOHN: Kavanagh said: "Art is life squeezed through a repression" — and you need a repression — something to fight against.

BEN: And it comes out of a wish to write.

8. Art: Two Views

Custodian of the Past

with
James White

"The Irish have no visual sense" is a popular generalization belied by an afternoon's visit with James White, Director of the National Gallery. As we walked through its halls and galleries, he described to me the ancient history of Celtic art through the ages.

◇ ◇ ◇

The history of Irish art as far back as we can go begins with the great burial places in Knowth, Dowth, and New-grange. These passage graves, dating somewhere around 3,000 B.C. contain remarkable abstract ornament. Little is known concerning the meanings of these ancient Celtic motifs, shown inside and out, other than that all three were similar in design and were connected with sun worship. Recently archaeologists have discovered at Newgrange that the sun pierces the entrance and beams onto the center of the cave only once a year at midday a few days either side of the summer solstice.

From that point onward there are only occasional remains to be found until the fifth and sixth centuries before Christ, when beautiful ornaments, such as the Boighter collar from the La Tene civilization, were discovered and can now be seen in the National Museum. This artistic tradition was eventually absorbed in Ireland with Christianity in A.D. 432 and turned into Christian art based on Celtic designs. One of the most famous examples of this tradition is the Ardagh Chalice, also displayed in the National Museum. Throughout this period there is a multitude of early Christian objects of metal, of stone, of wood and enamel, and of course there are the famous manuscripts of the seventh, eighth, and ninth centuries — the *Book of Durrow* and the *Book of Kells* — all of which have been discussed in the remarkable books of Françoise Henry.

The activity of art in Ireland during the thirteenth and fourteenth centuries was centered almost totally in the churches being established then by European missionaries. These Romanesque churches were rich in ornament and design. Unfortunately, they were destroyed during the Cromwellian era, and all that remains of them today is stone shells. The fifteenth and sixteenth centuries were almost barren, a time of continuous destruction as the Irish fought and lost wars, culminating in the Battle of Kinsale in 1609.

Then, in the early seventeenth century a new Ireland began to be built by the people who settled from England. That new Ireland is depicted in the great buildings rather late in the century like the Royal Hospital at Kilmainham, which is dated 1670 and was designed by Sir William Robinson. From that moment forward there is a third age of Irish civilization, based on the classical models taken from France and which England also copied.

An attempt by certain historians to gather the architecture, furniture, silver, and other objects of this period into a singular reference — Georgian — has resulted in a misnomer of works derivative of classical models. The word quite incorrectly associates with an English king art that was in fact universal in Europe at the time and was really a revival of the models of Greece and Rome. The word is a good one in that it helps us to understand a style, but it is relevant only to an English-speaking style, and it is wrong to assume that Irish art is purely English-speaking in origin.

Irish art reflects also a strong French and Italian influence. In fact, many of the plasterworkers, such as the Francini brothers, came to Ireland from Italy, and they had nothing to do with King George. The same is true of the Flemish painters who came to Ireland and England at that time. For instance, much of the painting of the eighteenth century in England is associated with Georgian styles, but in fact it is based largely on the existence in England of Lely, Kneller, and Van Dyke, who were the originators of such portrait painting. This is a very important point, because to some extent there is an overemphasis on English influences in Ireland. Some of our earliest Irish landscapes are signed works by Van der Hagen of the towns of Waterford, Drogheda, Derry, and the interiors of country houses. Van der Hagen lived and worked in Ireland and was the originator of the style of landscape painting that grew up in Ireland in the eighteenth century. So we must not allow ourselves to be swept off our feet by too close an association with the Georgian historians in England.

The development, of course, of civilized life in the eighteenth and nineteenth centuries closely parallels that in England, for the wealthy people who came and lived in Ireland were moving to and from the English court. On the other hand, let us not forget that the Catholic Church, which was the strongest influence in Ireland, sent its young men to be trained on the Continent in the famous monasteries of France, Switzerland, Italy, and Spain. They were so influential in making the people of Ireland anti-English and anti-Empire in their spirit that the British introduced in the early nineteenth century a seminary at Maynooth, which they actually paid for in order to change the attitude of the Church. The only rule they imposed was that all the Irishmen entering the seminary of Maynooth must take the oath of allegiance to the king.

During the nineteenth century, as a result of the oath of allegiance and the changed emphasis in the teaching at Maynooth, the Church became anti-Irish. So that when the revolution broke out in the early twentieth century, the Church was opposed to the Republicans and sided with the English. This was seen, of course, as a carefully arranged ploy by the British Government in the early nineteenth century. Here we have yet another example of the many attempts of historians to make facts fit their own ideas. So there are two great conflicts running through recent art history in Ireland. One of them is the natural instinct of the Irishman to return to his own ancestry, the other is the natural instinct of all English art historians to try to make it appear that they are only following a good English tradition.

What is often missed when considering the development of Irish art is the situation of the people in the sixteenth and seventeenth centuries. Education in Ireland was prohibited to Catholics unless they gave up their religion. As a result, the people of Ireland had to be taught under the hedges on the edges of fields in what was known as hedge schools, where the village schoolmaster passed on his lore orally. There they learned by word of mouth from their teachers about the history, law, and religion of their great ancestors. And so there came into being in the seventeenth and eighteenth centuries the most extraordinary oratorical tradition that exists in the world today. As a result certain Irishmen have a remarkable gift of words and can speak without preparation on almost any subject wherever they find themselves. This gift of words, this feeling for the sound of words, this use of them, appeared early in the extraordinary period of Yeats, Wilde, Shaw, Synge, Joyce, O'Casey, and Beckett. All of them were able to spin words with such skill that they created a new revival of English theatre and poetry.

The early twentieth century appeared to be much influenced by Irishmen and Irish thinkers, with their extraordinary songs and stories. At the same time this gave rise to the idea that the Irish were a race lacking in vigor in the visual field. Overlooked was the fact that if you deprive a people and prevent them from having the materials to make works of art, the only thing they can do in small, dark, lonely places is to pass on their stories and if possible write them down. A recent example of this is in Russia, where during these past fifty years of great troubles those who were banished to distant places wrote wonderful books on little bits of paper when it was impossible for them to paint, to sculpt, or to make anything. Something of this happened in Ireland. In the late seventeenth and early eighteenth centuries the people were once again given the opportunity to paint pictures and make furniture and create glass and silver; work of the highest quality was executed. In fact, the glass and silver of the eighteenth century in Ireland holds a high place alongside that of any culture by any standard. The Irish, then, were not visually unconscious people, they were merely a visually deprived people.

During the nineteenth century, when writers like Yeats came in contact with some of the great Fenians like John O'Leary, they discovered that O'Leary had gone to Paris, had lived and worked there with many of the great painters, and had come to be an intimate of Whistler. At their meetings the ideas of the modern artists were invoked. As a result a great many Irish artists of the day were trained in, and influenced by, the art centers of the Continent. Around about 1850 Nathaniel Hone, a landscape painter, went to the school of Barbizon painters at Fontainebleau and lived there for seventeen years. He was a friend of Corot, Millet, and Henri Joseph Harpignies, and became closely associated with them. His style of painting until his death in 1917 is clearly describable as of the school of Barbizon at its best. Other Irish painters, such as Walter Osborne and Sarah Purser, went to Paris and saw the work of the Impressionists. Walter Osborne, who, sadly, died at the age of forty-three, made a real contribution to Impressionist painting with his translations of light into color. Some of his great masterpieces — *Tea in the Garden* is one of the best known — in the National Gallery in Dublin are often mistaken by visitors for the works of Monet. Another artist of a slightly different genre was Roderic O'Connor. He belonged to the Pont-Aven colony and became an intimate of Gauguin, lending and sharing his studio with him. Nowadays it is quite easy to confuse the works of Gauguin and O'Connor. Roderic O'Connor was a rich man; that is to say, he did not have to earn his living by painting, and he painted for pleasure and didn't try to propagate the sale of his own works. This economic situation has had a strange effect on the history of art — when a painter doesn't need to sell, he is regarded as an amateur, and his work is not discovered until after his death. This is true of Roderic O'Connor, who is now esteemed as an important artist of the curious genre of Cubist primitive painting that Gauguin fathered.

Another artist active in Dublin toward the end of the last century was Æ. He was a theosophist, and his work was deeply influenced by such ideas. Recently the National Gallery was able to acquire an entire room painted by Æ about 1900 full of weird symbols and images of gods and ghosts of past times. These murals have been restored and placed on stretchers so that they can be exhibited in this gallery.

John Butler Yeats, the father of William B. and Jack B., was a splendid and neglected painter who went to New York rather lonely and sad in 1908, perhaps retreating from a city where his two sons were so famous and where he was

little known. From 1908 to 1922 he lived in a small hotel —
the Petit Pas — run by two French ladies, where he became
the center of a circle of great artists living and working in
New York at that time. Many of these artists painted John
B. Yeats into their works; the best known of these is a
portrait by John Sloan in the Phillips Gallery in Washington
called *Yeats at the Petit Pas*. At that time there was a generous Irish-American lawyer in New York named John
Quinn, who befriended Yeats. One of the most enchanting
stories about Quinn was that when he saw how poor old
John B. Yeats found it difficult to survive without patronage, he commissioned him in 1913 to paint a self-portrait
and told him he was not to hurry. He was to take his time
and Quinn would pay him as he went along. When J. B.
Yeats died in 1922, the picture was still in his studio — a
full-length portrait, several inches thick with paint that
was laid on lovingly and continuously in repayment to
John Quinn for the support received from him. This famous
painting has recently been exhibited in three cities in
America — in Columbus, Toledo, and St. Louis.

Quinn befriended not only Yeats but many other artists
of the day. When he died his art collection was sold; it was
found to contain some of the greatest paintings of the
Impressionists and of modern art, including Picasso,
Braque, and a large number of Irish artists, such as Æ,
Nathaniel Hone, Yeats, and his son Jack B. Yeats.

Jack B. Yeats is perhaps the most important painter of the
twentieth century in Ireland. He inherited, like so many
people of his age and generation, a tremendous love of
Ireland and a tremendous affection for the countryside. He
was brought up in Sligo, and he incorporated in his early
drawings the life of the tinkers, the fairgrounds and fair
days, and the circus. He took an attitude toward life in
Ireland in which the ordinary farming people, the fisherman, those concerned with outdoor life were the main
subject matter. Later, developing an Expressionist tech-

nique rather like Kadinsky, he built up a rich pallette and a method that in its freedom truly belongs to the finest tradition of Expressionist art.

Naturally, since the Irish people are an intellectual people seeking ideas — like Joyce, who went to Paris at the beginning of the century, and Sam Beckett, who went there later to write about the social-realist predicament of people — so also the painters went abroad and became involved with the theories of modern art. In 1922 two women, Mainie Jellet and Evie Hone, went to Paris and attached themselves to Albert Gleizes for ten years, and exhibited with the most illustrious of the Cubists — Leger, Picasso, among others. Their works are represented in the publications of the Cubists of those days. They returned to Ireland in 1930, and Mainie Jellet became the most important modern painter in the Cubist technique. Her friend, Evie Hone, diverted herself to stained glass and turned the Cubist style and color of the painter Rouault into a series of great stained glass windows. One of the most famous of these is the large window at Eton College, Windsor, placed there after an earlier one had been bombed out during the war. This remains as one of the largest windows made in the twentieth century.

Between 1939 and the end of the war Dublin became the center of an ingrown civilization cut off from the rest of Europe by virtue of the fact that Ireland was a neutral country and not involved in the war. And to Dublin came many poets, painters, and others trying to avoid the disaster that had overtaken Europe. An extraordinary hotbed of intellectualism developed during those years in Dublin, effecting exciting painting and many forms of art. Ever since then the works of Irish artists, such as Louis le Brocquy and Patrick Scott, in the Metropolitan Museum in New York and the Modern Art Museum in Paris, have carried Ireland beyond the parochial into international recognition.

GALLERIES, MUSEUMS, AND LIBRARIES

NATIONAL GALLERY
Merrion Square, West
Telephone: 767571
Weekdays: 10 A.M. —
    6 P.M.
Thursdays: Until 9 P.M.
Sundays: 2 P.M. — 5 P.M.

This collection of over 2,000 paintings and sculpture testifies that at least *some* Irish have a visual sense. Opened in 1864, the gallery was originally based on the collection of railway entrepreneur, William Dargan, whose statue, along with that of another patron, George Bernard Shaw, stands on the gallery lawn. Shaw generously placed one-third of his estate in trust to the gallery to be used for new acquisitions.

One of the most comprehensive collections of small Dutch masters in the world is on view, along with rooms filled with works of almost every European school, including Goya, El Greco, Valdez, Rembrandt, Titian, Tintoretto, Rubens, Millet, Corot, Monet, Degas, Turner, Gainsborough. Many paintings of famous Irish men and women hang in the National Portrait Gallery. W. B. Yeats penned this special invitation to visit him and his friends:

You that would judge me, do not judge alone,

This book or that, come to this hallowed place,
Where my friends portraits hang, and look thereon
Ireland's history in their lineaments trace;
Think where man's glory most begins and ends,
And say my glory was I had such friends.

Only recently given recognition, the eighteenth- and nineteenth-century portrait and landscape paintings by Irishmen are well represented, along with the more contemporary works of Hone, Osborne, Yeats, and others. An excellent overview of this period is *Aspects of Irish Art*, which was compiled as a catalogue to accompany Ireland's first major exhibition to the United States in 1974, which can be purchased in the museum shop. Here too can be found tasteful jewelry, based on ancient Celtic designs. Information about lectures, special exhibits, and films is available at the main desk in the gallery's entrance. Also available are touraphones for a one-hour taped tour by Director James White. The gallery's restaurant is one of the most popular in Dublin for lunch, and you may stop for a pot of tea or be tempted by a nine-course feast and a better-than-average wine list.

MUNICIPAL GALLERY OF MODERN ART

Parnell Square
Telephone: 741903
Weekdays: 10 A.M. —
   6 P.M.
Sundays: 11 A.M. —
   2 P.M.
Closed: Mondays and
   Bank Holidays

After the 1905 retrospective of Irish art in London's Guildhall, the director of the exhibit, Sir Hugh Lane, a Cork-born art dealer and patron, decided to found a gallery in Dublin where Irish artists could exhibit their work without having to cross the Channel. Charlemont House, designed and built by William Chambers in 1765, was chosen. Lane's devotion was to the artists themselves, and he donated his personal collection of works by Monet, Rodin, Bonnard, Renoir, Ingrès, Corot, Augustus John, Hone, Lavery, and others as a stimulation to them that they might otherwise never view. The new gallery lacked sufficient space for the entire collection, so Lane sent part to the National Gallery in London for display. In 1915 Lane drowned on the *Lusitania* at the age of forty, and a codicil to his will bequeathing all the works to the Municipal Gallery was declared invalid because it lacked the required signatures. Legal battles continued until 1959 when the two galleries agreed to halve the collection and alternate the exhibitions every six years between Dublin and London. As Lane intended, the gallery has acquired over the years such a large collection of Irish artists that the works have now outgrown Charlemont House. Unfortunately, besides those on display, the gallery has over five hundred paintings and sculptures stored away until the corporation can find a means of display.

NATIONAL MUSEUM

Kildare Street
Telephone: 765521
Weekdays: 10 A.M. —
   5 P.M.
Sundays: 2 P.M. — 5 P.M
Closed: Mondays

Ireland's vault of artifacts spans a thousand years of civilization, dating as far back as the Bronze Age. Attempting to make sense of such a vast collection, the museum has separated the displays in three areas: Antiquities, Folk Life, and Natural History. A hint of the Celts' richly ornamented society is salvaged in the Broighter Collar and the Petrie Crown. Later, early Christian artisans merely translated these pagan luxuries into appropriate Christian ornaments like the Ardagh Chalice, the Cross of

Cong, the Tara Brooch, and the Lismore Crozier. The Folk Life area shows the unusual inventiveness developed over the years for survival, from crude farming tools to variations of architecture based on climate. The wooden vessels on display were recovered only a few years ago in this primitive refrigeration. The Military section has the weapons and letters of soldiers and other memorabilia of the famous Irish rebellions. Around through the Merrion Street entrance is a gathering of Irish flora and fauna, bird life, skeletons of Irish elks... sorry, the dinosaurs bypassed Ireland.

TRINITY COLLEGE
LIBRARY
College Green
Telephone: 772941
Weekdays: 10 A.M. —
  5 P.M.
Saturdays: 10 A.M. —
  1 P.M.
Closed: Sundays and
  Bank Holidays

Just having been the library of such brilliant alumni as Goldsmith, Burke, Swift, Ussher, Berkeley, Congreve, Moore, Le Fanu, Leckey, and so on would make Trinity an interesting visit, but it's the unique Irish treasures of illuminated manuscripts, brilliant pages of jewels woven through paper, that draws every visitor to Dublin. The eighth-century *Book of Kells* is the most well known, but three other centuries of this early Christian artistry are on view: the *Book of Durrow* (seventh century), the *Book of Armagh* (ninth century), and the *Book of Leinster* (twelfth century). Trinity was founded in 1601 by Elizabeth I, and for those interested in such things a volume of her letters from 1565 to 1570 dealing with Irish affairs is there. The library has over one million volumes from an act of Parliament in 1801 entitling Trinity, like Cambridge and Oxford, to a copy of every book published in England and Ireland. Also on view are other manuscripts — Roman, Egyptian, Greek, and early Irish, along with a first edition of Dante's *La Commedia*. Near the *Book of Kells* is Brian Boru's harp, the oldest in existence. It was restored in 1961 and played long enough for a recording of its ancient sound for musicians interested in reviving Ireland's famous instrument. The name is misleading, though, since this harp is thought to be about seven hundred years old and the Celtic hero whose name it bears died some two hundred years earlier!

ROYAL IRISH ACADEMY

Dawson Street
Telephone: 762570
Weekdays: 9:30 A.M. —
   5.30 P.M.
Saturdays: 9:30 A.M. —
   12:45 P.M.
Summer: July, August,
   September
Closed: 12:30 — 1:30 P.M.
Closed: Last three weeks in
August

One of the oldest existing academic societies in Europe, the Academy's library contains manuscripts for the Irish scholar and may be heavy going for the novice.

MARSH'S LIBRARY

St. Patrick's Cathedral
Telephone: 753917
Monday: 2 P.M. — 4 P.M.
Tuesday: Closed
Wednesday — Friday:
   10:30 A.M. — 12:30 P.M.
   2 P.M. — 4 P.M.
Saturday: 10:30 A.M. —
   12:30 P.M.

This tiny library in the shadow of St. Patrick's Cathedral is the oldest in Dublin and has remained almost unchanged since 1707, when it was begun by Narcissus Marsh, the Archbishop of Dublin. Sympathetic to the weakness of man, the Archbishop attached chains to his books and required readers to sit in cages to avoid the temptation of theft. Along with volumes of Hebrew, Greek, Latin, and French are a number of Swift's books with the Dean's acerbic comments in the margins.

CHESTER BEATTY LIBRARY

20 Shrewsbury Road
Ballsbridge
Telephone: 692386
Weekdays: 10 A.M. —
   1 P.M.
   2.30 P.M. — to 5:30 P.M.
Saturday: 2:30 P.M. — 5:30 P.M.
Closed: Sundays and Mondays
   Bank Holidays

During his lifetime Sir Chester Beatty was devoted to art and Ireland. He was a patron of the National Gallery and one of Ireland's few honorary citizens. Upon his death in the late sixties he bequeathed to Ireland his private collection of Oriental manuscripts, regarded as one of the most complete and valuable in the world. This unique collection contains original manuscripts of the New Testament, Manichaean papyri, illuminated Korans of several Islamic countries, as well as hundreds of Oriental and Far Eastern miniatures.

Contemporary Impressions

with
Edward Delaney

*A friend once described Edward Delaney as "walking anarchy."
He has been one of Ireland's leading artists and sculptors for
almost two decades. His work is at once haunting, innovative and
ancient...more Celtic than any of his contemporaries. After eight
years studying in Europe, he returned to Ireland and has relent-
lessly brought an interest and an awareness of Irish art both at
home and abroad – usually in the eye of controversy. If you want to
sense an Irishman's view of modern art, stand by a Delaney
sculpture anywhere – in Galway, Dundalk, St. Stephen's Green –
and ask a passerby what he thinks...you may be captured for
hours. But that's Delaney's point, at least they're thinking. Here
he shares a few of his impressions of contemporary Irish art, a
struggling form, born in a vacuum, often regarded with suspicion,
only recently even regarded.*

◇ ◇ ◇

You always seem to have to go back a bit to explain *anything*
about the Irish, and that includes contemporary Irish art.
Irish painting and sculpture in recent years have followed
much the same patterns. There was the academic traditional school and the mid-twentieth-century moderns. In
the traditional group were those who still carried on the

portraiture of the eighteenth and nineteenth centuries. And then the abstract pop art, a conceptual group much influenced by what was and is going on in Europe and America.

To explain a little of the evolution of Irish art, I'll take the course of Irish sculpture. During the nineteenth century we had a number of very competent Irish sculptors who went to England and were commissioned to do great memorials there — British Empire sculpture. Even in Dublin we have examples of this kind of work, such as John Henry Foley's (1818-1874) O'Connell Memorial on O'Connell Street. Personally, I like this statue, but it was produced by ten to fifteen assistants, and therefore one doesn't know how much Foley put into making the statue. From the '98 Rebellion through the depression of the Catholic Church up to the 1916 Revolution all that was produced in any artistic sense was some interesting wood carvings, which were the Penal Crosses. This was the period before the foundation of the Abbey Theatre and the revival of Celtic culture, and before the foundation of the Irish State. At the time there was no real school of art or any powerful group interested in art. There were no patrons, therefore there were no artists. Patronage came from abroad, and the artists followed the patronage, so Ireland until then had few artists or sculptors — up to perhaps Jack B. Yeats — who were not under British Empire influence. For some reason, which I haven't always understood, many people get annoyed when you bring up Yeats. Some feel he's overdone, but most people would have to agree that Yeats was the starting point of the Celtic revival.

Going on from the Irish revival — or the Celtic revival, whichever you prefer — one finds a completely different approach to traditional landscape painting. That is a break from the really traditional scene when the artist painted exactly what he saw, no interpretation. Yeats painted in very powerful colors. His paintings of the Irish landscape of

Connemara are to me some of the finest of his work. Today Yeats is still the Irish artist most sought after by collectors. When there is an exhibition or sale or auction of his works, it always brings a crowd. He was the first Irish artist in whom people who otherwise had no interest in art invested money.

Another early landscape artist, well worth mentioning though less known and sought after, is Paul Henry. He painted great paintings, again of the West of Ireland. Places like Killary Harbour in the north of Galway, and the turf and bog landscape of Connemara. He has an interesting cool palette in comparison to Yeats. And he again is an artist who, I think, is slightly influenced by the French Impressionists. He is an artist of interest for anyone who wants to get a feeling of the beginnings of modern Irish painting.

Another is Charles Lamb, an important Irish painter who belonged to the Royal Hibernian Academy. In his younger years in the twenties he painted some fine portraits of the Connemara people. His wife runs a continuous exhibition of his work in his home in Carraroe, County Galway.

The break with the academic school began with Yeats, but one important thing happened in the forties that finally took the modern artists away from the traditional concept of the Royal Hibernian Academy. In 1943 Mainie Jellet, Louis le Broquy (who now lives in France) and Norah Maguinness formed the Irish Exhibition of Living Art, and that perhaps was the cradle of a new modern painting school in Ireland. That exhibition is still very much to the fore, though the older group has given over to the younger group. I wouldn't say it's improving the quality of Irish art, but it does give a cross section of what a number of Irish artists are painting.

Over the years there have been a number of Irish artists living and working in Paris. While I myself think that is fine, it has a disadvantage. The young artists who leave frequently have little contact with the threads of Celtic culture. I feel it's unfortunate to lose the influence of our ancient literature and art. I personally draw a lot of my influences from translations of early Irish writing, such as the Cuchulainn saga. I've done a series of paintings on this one tale. You can almost take a few lines from Yeats and turn it into a large sculpture. I remember these lines from *Countess Cathleen:*

> *The years like great black oxen*
> *Tread the world*
> *And God, the herdsman,*
> *Goads them on behind*
> *And I am broken by their passing feet.*

But there again I wouldn't say there's been a history of much exchange between artists and writers in Ireland. They've pretty much gone their separate ways. That's changing now. Irish poets today, like John Montague, Seamus Heaney, and Thomas Kinsella, have become involved with the artists. They are friends with the artist and know what the artists are doing. Even Samuel Beckett, who in the past has stayed away altogether from the visual arts, recently collaborated in a limited edition book, *Still,* with William Hayter, whom I consider one of the outstanding graphic artists of the century. This kind of thing is a breakthrough here.

The art education system here is very much to blame for the state of Irish art, particularly sculpture. It seems that the last thing the Irish government got around to doing something about after acquiring the twenty-six counties was art. Apparently art was not considered very important, and it was not taught in school. But things have progressed, and I'd say that looking back on the last ten or fifteen years there's a new technology coming into the visual arts in Ireland in all areas — painting, sculpture, tapestry, glass, and pottery.

It's important to keep bringing in new influences and exposures to Ireland. Over the past few years we had two *Rosc* exhibitions. These were the first real international exhibitions showing works of artists considered to be important artists of this period in the world. There was a great cross section — Europeans, Americans, Japanese and others. I think that this was the first time the Irish man on the street came in contact with art, because there was so much publicity about it.

There are now up to fifteen prominent galleries and a number of group exhibitions. To me one of the most interesting of these recently formed groups is the Project Arts Center in Dublin. There are continuous art shows, theatre workshops, poetry readings, and plays, everything from O'Casey to Pinter. It's a great place, where people can entertain themselves during intervals with art.

It's interesting how things have changed. The thing has swung to the extreme. Now everyone seems to be a hob art critic. I remember one time in Dublin after a statue of mine was unveiled. I was with a friend of mine, Liam Redmond, and this lady came up and said, "Do you like the statue?" And I said, "I don't think so." She said, "Well, whoever made it is capable of doing something great in art." "Well," I said, "who did it?" "I suppose some foreigner," she said. Redmond turned around, "This is the man, here, who did it!" She turned and said, "Look, don't be telling lies. He wouldn't have the hands."

◇ ◇ ◇

ART GALLERIES

These are a few of the art galleries around Dublin that exhibit the highest quality of Irish art — graphics, oils, and sculpture. They are open from 10 A.M. to 6 P.M. Monday through Friday, until 1:00 P.M. on Saturdays. Contemporary Irish art is centered in Dublin rather than spread around the country.

SETANTA GALLERY
37 Molesworth Street
Tel: 765338
Owner: John Maguire

DAVID HENDRICKS
  GALLERY
119 St. Stephen's Green
Tel: 756062
Owner: David Hendricks

DAWSON GALLERY
6 Dawson Street
Tel: 776089
Owner: John Taylor

PROJECT ARTS CENTER
39 East Essex Street
Tel: 781572

NEPTUNE GALLERY
122A St. Stephen's Green
Tel: 754190
Owner: Bruce Arnold

TOM CALDWELL
31 Upper Fitzwilliam Street
Tel: 688629
Owner: Tom Caldwell

DAVIS GALLERY
Capel Street
Tel: 748169
Owner: Gerald Davis

The *Irish Heritage Series* is a well done, knowledgeable collection of booklets for those who want a broader understanding of the Irish arts. Each booklet is authored by an expert in their field. A selection of titles—*Georgian Dublin, Irish Glass, Irish Bookbinding, Irish Coins & Medals, Roundtowers, Irish Furniture, Irish Silver* and many more. Available in most bookstores in Ireland.

Recently published is an excellent book by the Knight of Glin and Ann Crookshank, *The Painters of Ireland.* It is invaluable to anyone interested in collecting or appreciating the spectrum of Irish painting. The book has over 250 black-and-white plates and 65 color plates. Available at bookstores. Published by Barrie & Jenkins.

9. Music: Two Views

Hope, youth, love, home, each haunting tie
That binds, we know not how or why.
All! All that to the soul belongs
Is closely mingled with old songs!
                                        — Unknown

One evening in a pub in the Wicklow Hills during a music session
a gentleman came over to a friend of mine, Paddy Moloney, a
well-known piper and leader of the Chieftains, and asked him
would he play over a tune he had just finished. Paddy begged off,
saying, "It just won't be the same." Trying to set to words a
description of traditional Irish music will, I'm afraid, fall to the
same fate. All that is the essence of the Irish – elusive, capricious,
whimsical, and mournful – is in their music. It's their imagina-
tion set for the ear.

When you finally hear real traditional music, you realize that
the Irish, as hosts, have saved the good wine till last. Anyone who
has spent years avoiding "Mother Macree" and "MacNamara's
Band" sees the music as Ireland's best-kept secret. Only within
the past few years have the Irish allowed themselves to enjoy the
music outside their homes. A handful of people have been respon-
sible for the revival. One of these is Ciaran MacMathúna, who
tells of the history of the music. However, it is Ciaran's friends
who tell of his involvement, riding around the country with his
tape recorder, recording fiddlers, pipers, and other musicians
buried around the countryside, then playing their music back in
Dublin on Radio Eireánn. The Irish have a warranted reputation
for backbiting, but Ciaran is the exception. When you travel

around the country, everyone knows Ciaran, and they all have a story. "Ah, Ciaran, a man in his own class." Paddy Moloney, leader of the Chieftains, summed up Ciaran's work best. "Ciaran in a great way was responsible for the revival of Irish music when nobody else was interested. Through his radio programs he brought the musicians out of their homes. He made them feel they shouldn't be ashamed of this music. The attitude when Ciaran started was 'Awh...you're no playing that ole Molly.' Ciaran changed all that. Now, of course, it's all status."

Sadly, there have been brilliant music sessions all around the country for years, lost forever, like the fiddler's last note. But a little over ten years ago another Irishman, Garech Browne, came along with imagination and an eye for quality to set up Claddagh Records and capture the best of Ireland's music. Like all people of perception, he did not limit himself to his original plan to record only authentic Irish music. So Claddagh drew, like a sensitive magnet, poets Patrick Kavanagh and Austin Clarke to read their poetry, and actor Jack MacGowran reading Samuel Beckett – all dead now, but not lost. He also ranged to forgotten classical composers, living or dead, like John Field, buried in Leningrad, and Freddie May, who went deaf while waiting to hear his compositions played. Neither Ciaran nor Garech have a "note" themselves, so Paddy Moloney and Sean Potts of the Chieftains talk of the long lifeline of Irish music from the musicians' view.

◇ ◇ ◇

Reels of Infinity

with
Ciaran MacMathúna

Though we have a heritage of music and poetry, for various reasons we don't seem to know specifically what kind of music was played in ancient Ireland. Manuscripts refer to the harp and a type of pipes, and the Danes — our earliest invaders — refer to hearing the approach of the Irish armies from their music. The musicians in those days were charged with composing airs to excite the men to war. The bohran you hear today (a large tambourine of goatskin) echoes these early war chants. We do know that there were three styles of harp music among the ancients: *Geantraighe,* to incite merriment, dancing, and laughter; *Goltraighe,* which was the lamentation music to cause crying and weeping; and *Suantraighe,* which is described as lulling the people to sleep. This is about all we know.

In the thirteenth, fourteenth, and fifteenth centuries all the large houses of the Gaelic lords had resident musicians and poets. The two were linked together, and at the time music was for these families, not the populace. One of the few examples of this early harp is in the Trinity College Library, the Brian Boru Harp, and was the harp used for the national emblem. Harpers came in for their share of persecution because they were associated with the old Gaelic order. During Elizabeth I's time we have our first source of

names of the harpers in her *fiants* (legal documents) granting pardons to "so and so, harper." The harp, therefore,
was the great instrument up to the eighteenth century and
then began a rapid decline at the end of the century.

Turlogh O'Carolan is probably the best known and last
survivor of the bard-harpist tradition. His music seems to
be the only record of this ancient music. O'Carolan was
blinded at an early age from smallpox, as were many other
musicians, and he would travel to the large houses around
the country composing songs of praise for his host. His
visits were great events, and he was always an honored
guest. His verse compositions were always in Irish, and it
was Dean Swift who first translated O'Carolan's verse. His
talents as a composer were described in an essay by Oliver
Goldsmith. You see, Dublin at the time was attracting
many classical musicians such as Corelli, Vivaldi, Geminiani, and others, and Goldsmith wrote of a meeting in one
of the large houses of O'Carolan and Geminiani. Geminiani challenged O'Carolan to competition. First Geminiani played Vivaldi's Fifth Concerto on his violin, where-
upon O'Carolan took up his harp, played the whole piece
over, never having heard it before, and then proceeded to
compose himself a concerto that has been regarded as equal
to any Italian composition — O'Carolan's Concerto, which
we still have. O'Carolan died in 1738.

Just over fifty years later the last meeting of these harpists
took place in Belfast, and our first and only record of harp
music was written down. At this Belfast festival ten harpers
appeared, six of whom were blind. One, Denis Hempson,
was over ninety years old and played in the old style with
long crooked fingernails treated with chemicals to play the
brass strings. The average age of the gathering harpists was
over seventy, and, though it was hoped that the tradition
would survive, soon after the harp died out as a musical
instrument.

Only toward the beginning of the nineteenth century do we begin to have an idea of the tremendous popularity of the traditional Irish music we are talking about — folk music, music that is not composed by any one person. Though its sources may have been the ancient music, on the whole it was the spontaneous expression of the people, of their everyday life and experience. So many things affected the music. Some were words — poetry put to music; many were dances — jigs, reels, hornpipes. Airs and love songs seem to have been the most popular, but there are many others...lullabies, laments for separation and exile. The theme of emigration was very prominent during the nineteenth century. The transition from Irish to English songs followed the course of the language. As English began being used more, a new type of song emerged we still have today called macronic — verses alternating between English and Irish.

As I mentioned, by the nineteenth century the harp had vanished as a musical instrument and was replaced by the pipes. The whole situation in Ireland was very depressing, and music seemed the only source of entertainment. Accounts of travelers at this time always mention music. The tradition of the traveling musician continued, though it now transferred from the great houses to the small rural homes. Many of the musicians were blind during this time and took to music as a means of support. There was no welfare state then. The blind piper would arrive at a house and stay for about three weeks, and people would come to the house every evening for music and dancing, and then he would be taken to a house about thirty miles away. This is the way he would build up a yearly tour. A famous piper from County Clare, Garret Murphy, also blind, in his death notice at the hospital was referred to as a "traveling laborer."

At this time, side-by-side, was the fiddle. This was probably brought from the Continent for the classical music in

Dublin and the great houses. Wherever you find around the country an area where the fiddle was played, you can usually trace back to one fiddlemaster who came to the area, settled, and taught.

Music was more universal than any other Irish tradition and was taught in the home. Even today some of our great players learned from their parents or grandparents. By the end of the nineteenth century the tradition of the traveling musician had died out almost completely, due principally to emigration. Around this time another type of song was emerging as we became involved in nationalism, patriotic songs like "The Wearing of the Green." Once the Troubles came and the state was founded, there was neglect of music. People had other things on their minds — economics, political dissension. Even so, a few efforts were made to carry on the tradition; the Pipers Club in Thomas Street was one of them. Great pipers like John Potts, whose grandson, Sean Potts, plays with the Chieftains, worked at Guinness's and would go over and teach the youngsters how to play. The Pipers Club still meets every Saturday night, an unbroken tradition.

After the war there was a great revival of interest all over the world in folk music for various sociological reasons. In Ireland two things happened at the time. *Oireachtas* — meaning "gathering" in Irish — was promoting all-Irish events, and in 1953 the first *Fleadh Cheoil* was held, which was strictly for music. At a fleadh you would walk into a pub, and there would be, say, five or six people sitting around, and after a while someone would produce a fiddle, and then a little later a tin whistle, and more would drift in, and this would go on till you had a full band. The fleadh still goes on. This summer in Listowel there were two thousand entries in competitions; mostly youngsters who had learned to play from their parents.

Radio Eireánn was the second godfather of the music movement. In the early fifties a mobile unit was sent out around the country to record these hidden musicians. Seamus Ennis and I would travel around and record anywhere. For the first time it enabled the people from all over the country — Donegal, Galway, Kerry — to hear one another. Going out we found all sorts of people who had been hidden, partly because they were ashamed, and also because there had been no demand outside their own homes. All of a sudden people emerged out of nowhere. Musicians were given a status they had never thought of having. I remember fiddle players who told me that, in the beginning, they went to sessions in the country or in Dublin with their fiddle cases hidden under their coats because they were ashamed to have them seen. Now it's become a status symbol.

The tourist is only passing in the night and often hasn't the time to find the real thing. So castle nights and cabarets like New Jury's and the Abbey Tavern are laid on for them, and they are good; you get the idea, but the real traditional music by its nature is elusive and unpredictable. Given time the visitor can meet traditional musicians in their own setting around the country, just happening into a pub one evening. The problem for the tourist is that the real authentic thing can never be organized, it just happens. It's the music of the people, of individuals who may have gone to market or spent the day stacking hay.

O'Donoghue's Pub in Dublin on Merrion Row usually has musicians. Slattery's is another place in Dublin which has a music night twice a week. I mentioned the Pipers Club in Thomas Street, but there is no drink there, just music, so nothing gets started till after closing time in the pubs. If you go out to Clare, a great music area, many of the traditional musicians end up in Doolin in O'Connell's Pub. It's so unpredictable you'll just have to take a chance.

A Matter of Tradition

with
Garech Browne
Paddy Moloney
Sean Potts

The "right-time-people-place" maxim explains the most unimagined successes because it works. In the early sixties Sean O Riada returned to Dublin. He is now recognized, after his death, as one of Ireland's finest composers. He had come back from living on the Continent with the idea of investigating his native music. The long gestation period of an Irish traditional music culture ended. Garech, with Paddy and Sean, both members of the Chieftains and two of Ireland's finest traditional musicians, reminisce over the events of the renaissance of music. Its success seems so obvious now. The time was right.

◇ ◇ ◇

GARECH: I don't know when I first knew O Riada or how I met him or anything like that. He had been living in Paris and at a certain point we knew each other. He was living in Galloping Green and was in charge of the Abbey orchestra succeeding Freddie May. Of course, there is no Abbey orchestra now, but it kept two of Ireland's twentieth century composers going for a time. Somehow, like all of us, he became interested in Irish music.

PADDY: Sean was a great music scholar. When he was in Europe he was tremendously influenced by the Greek musician, Theodorakis, who wrote "Zorba the Greek." Theodorakis had been involved in the process of investigating Greek music for fifteen years, and Sean thought this could be done in Ireland.

GARECH: Every first or last Sunday of the month Sean had an evening of traditional music in Galloping Green. In the beginning he had no definite aim in mind. He may have been aiming to found an orchestra, which he eventually did, or maybe be was just trying to familiarize himself for his own interest in order to decide what to do. The traditional music was already in his blood, but he hadn't thought in terms of doing anything constructive with it. There was pretty well a steady nucleus. Sean would play the bohran and people would sing and dance. It was an evening for friends. One evening the dancing was so strenuous that the front sitting room window just disappeared onto the lawn. But there had been a great deal going on both in Dublin and around the country before these evenings that Paddy and Sean would remember.

SEAN: All my father's people played. Every one of them in the old house in the Coombe. I can go back as far as 1936. I can remember my grandfather's house, which was right in the heart of the Liberties, packed with people and music. There was one main room and a parlor with chairs all along the wall. There was special music going on in the parlor; my grandfather swopping tunes and talking about the pipes. They were completely engrossed. The crack would be going on in the other room. Sessions of fiddles and flutes going on together, and the dancing. This is how you learned most of the music, swopping tunes. Thousands of tunes. They come back. That was the life here.

PADDY: I used to go to a similar type of thing in Donnycarney. Every Wednesday night everyone — Willie Clancy, Seamus Ennis, and others — used to come to Peadar Flynn's. I was only fourteen then. "Here, put that on you, Moloney, and see what you can make of it," they used to say. They were very generous if you showed any enthusiasm at all.

SEAN: I remember seeing Paddy at that time still in short trousers. He had won a Feis playing the bag and chanter, and I was at the back of the hall looking up at this little boy. I was talking to another great musician from another musical family, John Keogh. He was a drummer in the Fintan Lawlor Pipe Band and had won two world championships. But I remember standing with Johnny at the back and every tune yer man Paddy played here — great! And Johnny turned to me and said, "Jaysus, that little shagger was on the world before us." You see at the age of fourteen he had that gimp. He played like an old man, a seasoned piper.

GARECH: Throughout the country the tradition of Irish music took place in people's houses. You ask anyone over thirty-five, and they will remember how they would go from house-to-house gathering, depending on the locality, with a singer and a couple of musicians. It was the social life of the village.

PADDY: My grandfather, who died at ninety-four, used to play the concert flute in his house up in the mountains. They used to do this thing every evening called "rambling." You rambled over to someone's house, went in and sat down. "Fine day," you said, and started off conversations that went on till two and three in the morning. They wouldn't be invited, and there was no drink, only tea and cake. They used to do this every night, and my grandfather would play tunes. Often the grandfather and I would ramble to Mr. Kelly's down the road. Old Kelly had a flute he kept in the river with a stone on top to keep it moist. My mother remembers how, when she was sixteen and seventeen, all the girls would go down to the crossroads where there was a fire burning, and there were lots of fiddles and flutes, and dancing and the swishing of skirts with the dust flying.

GARECH: This only really broke down after the war when the dance halls became popular. The local musicians lost their role and had nothing to do. Now this is a slight exaggeration, but it explains the evolution of the thing called the *ceili* band. Any number of musicians, up to twenty, would all start off together and end together, and the music of the ceili bands was suitable to dance to in the dance halls. With the ceili bands, the imagination of traditional music tended to be lost. Irish music lends itself to individual interpretation.

PADDY: It's very difficult for certain instruments to be played in groups. The first thing that was wrong with ceili bands was that they put in drums. Boom, boom, boom. Puncturing the music. And an accordion should never be used, because the moment you press the button it goes out of tune. To throw that into traditional music is the worst thing in the world. What most people know, who aren't aware of traditional music, is the inheritance of the ceili band.

GARECH: As things were breaking up, Sean came along. For once we were lucky we were backward, which we usually are! What happens in other countries doesn't happen here for fifty years. Sean came to the tradition while it was still alive. Music was given a new dignity by Ciaran. Most people who heard something on the radio were impressed. This was the modern world. If it was on the radio it must be good, just like if it's in the newspaper it must be true. They took a new interest as a result of Ciaran's programs.

What Sean did was go back to the basis of one musician playing his interpretation of any particular tune and then elaborating it to include other musicians, who would be expected to play together or separately, break apart or join up. But Sean went back also to the principle that to play a slow air you must know the words, so that with the words in mind you would make the singer's breaks instead of just playing a mechanical tune. He first of all got the tune from the musicians themselves. Besides that, he went to manuscript collections and resuscitated old tunes. In his arrangements he would use his broader musical knowledge, which was more classical. He was, after all, professor of Irish and Oriental Music at Cork. He was re-creating a mainstream of Irish music and at the same time making the music more widely accepted by the people who were in the mainstream of classical music.

One way he did this was with the film *Mise Eire*, which was considered an absolute and amazing breakthrough. When Sean produced the music for *Mise Eire*, this came as a complete revelation to people who were interested in traditional music, because for the first time they heard something that didn't sound to them like a country fiddle player. And also didn't sound like that awful maudlin type of Victorian arrangement. Sean's brilliant step was presenting Irish music that both sounds like Irish music for people who actually know and also sounds like what they think to be classical music. The music for *Mise Eire* brought Ireland up to date with the rest of the world. One great advantage was that our traditional musicians were still available.

After the evenings in Galloping Green Sean decided to form his own orchestra, *Ceoltóirí Chualann*. The musicians had been around for years in Dublin at the Pipers Club. There was a man in charge at the Pipers Club called Mr. Nolan. After every song he would say, "A bird never flew on one wing." Nobody ever performed less than two tunes and rarely more than two. We all used to go there for the music, myself, Ciaran, Brendan Behan, Sean, and the for-mer Minister for Labor, Michael O'Leary. All kinds of people were drawn to the music and knew the songs, even if they couldn't play.

One thing I particularly remember. Sean Potts was playing the tin whistle in my flat, which would be a couple of years later than we are talking about, and Brendan Behan was there and he had gone to sleep on the sofa. He had been lying there without a sound for about an hour. We thought we wouldn't hear from him until the next morning. But when Sean played a slow air that he particularly liked, suddenly a voice started singing, and it was Brendan, who would sing the song through from beginning to end, then lapse back into a complete and utter silence and continue to be asleep.

SEAN: Coming up to 1959 — that was the great year for me. Paddy and I were at a fleadh in Lisdoonvarna, and when I returned to Dublin I heard he had gone to Spiddal for a summer holiday. So I borrowed a motorbike and went down with my wife. I had known Paddy for years, but hadn't contacted him for the music. That for me was the start of combination playing. I realized that his style and mine could play. You know what it was — the sympathy that Paddy had for my playing and the sympathy I had for his. Now, if all musicians have that, then there's a great possibility for playing.

So, you see, when Sean came on the scene, he had a ready-made situation. Paddy had his own group going — the Church Street Quartet.

PADDY: Then Sean invited us to join *Ceoltóirí Chualann*. We had a natural sympathy for what he was trying to do. Sean would do the arrangement, but we would supply the tune and airs. Sean had a fantastic brain for sounds, and he knew all of us individually, as musicians, and our characters. When Sean left in 1963 for Cork, the Chieftains developed from this nucleus when Garech wanted to record the first record. We were experimenting then, moving away from the large orchestra to a small group.

GARECH: When we decided to record the first record, we wanted to preserve the tradition with a contemporary presentation. We got Edward Delaney to do the cover, and John Montague suggested the name "Chieftains." The most important thing that had happened then was that through Sean's work people began to realize there was such an animal as an Irish composer. So that having been established, people might at long last be willing to listen to other Irish composers such as Freddie May, Seoirse Bodley, Brian Boydell.

In the eighteenth century there were various composers, culminating in John Field, who invented the nocturne. He came along really when Dublin, as a musical city, went into a decline. He wasn't acknowledged as being Irish, but that wouldn't be unusual, since Ireland was no longer a separate entity after the Act of Union. Once I was playing Field's nocturnes for a French critic, and he thought it was Chopin. He was astonished to hear that it was Field, who had preceded Chopin "...It doesn't make Chopin any less great, but it certainly makes him less original." The odd thing is that Field's music is virtually not available. Had he come from any place else in the world he would have been promoted as a great national composer. He is probably more recognized in Russia where he lived than he is here.

For a composer to have the courage to continue, he must hear his work performed, and very often the work can only be realized in the performance. I must say that Radio Éireann Orchestra has been very good about getting performances of Irish composers.

◇ ◇ ◇

COMMENT

The suggestions for hearing true traditional music have already been given: Donoghue's Pub in Merrion Row, Slattery's in Dublin, the Abbey Tavern in Howth, and, for the real pursuer, the Pipers Club in Thomas Street. But remember there is no drink, and nothing begins before closing time. Later in Part Two there are a few suggestions for specific areas. Almost always in the Gaeltacht areas there are ceili dances weekly that are closest to the real music and are put on for the locals, not the tourists. There are also quite a few other traditional groups besides the Chieftains who are giving concerts in Dublin and around the country all year. Fleadh are held all during the year à la Woodstock, with thousands of musicians and drinks, but be sure to make reservations and arrive at the hotel before your room disappears. The Local Tourist Board will always help if you tell them what you are looking for and insist upon the real traditional music.

The finest in traditional music has been recorded on two labels—*Claddagh* and *Gael Linn*. Their recordings are available in all record stores.

10. Geology:

The Great Non-Gold Rush

with
George Madden

> *Qu'est-ce que c'est la différence entre l'Angleterre riche et florissante et l'Irlande pauvre et imbécile? Le savoir industriel.*
>
> — Briavonne, 1845

The Irish have always been wary of stealing the leprechauns' pot of gold, which is one explanation for Ireland's recent economic dilemma. Over the last century or so, while other nations were building their economies on natural resources, Ireland was left to determine its livelihood on the export of her people and produce. In all but a few books written in the last hundred years is the curious assertion that Ireland was a cursed land with no natural resources, only vast grazing tracts separated by desolate granite plains. Suddenly, Ireland finds its ministers in moss-colored headdress negotiating with multinational conglomerates for its mineral and drilling rights. The story of the recent discovery of the rich deposits is far less interesting than the story of the nondiscovery for centuries.

A friend in Dublin, George Madden, long interested in the subject, shares some of the history of this relatively new industry.

The turning point in Ireland's arrested geological development was the arrival of Sir Roderick Murchison in the mid-1860's. Murchison was director general of Britain's Geological Survey and director of the Royal School of Mines. He was sent over to determine the possibility of setting up a mining industry in the country. After preliminary investigations, applicable to English geological patterns, Murchison determined that there were not sufficient resources to make continued exploration worthwhile. This fortunate misevaluation enabled the Irish to keep what natural wealth they had; from then until only recently they continued to believe Murchison's assessment.

Museums all over the world are filled with ancient Celtic goldwork, yet no one seemed to connect the fact that to produce these works the source of this metal must have been in Ireland. The *Annals of the Four Masters* mentioned gold discovered in the reign of Tighearnmas MacFolliagh, one of the early Milesian kings of Erin, around 1600 B.C. Eugene O'Curry, a great scholar on ancient Ireland, writes of MacFollaigh:

> And this king is everywhere recorded as having been the first to discover gold and to work gold mines in this country. The precise location is not laid down for us, but it is recorded that it was in the forests standing on the east side of the River Liffey that the ore was smelted for Tighearnmas and that it was smelted by a worker in metals of the name Iuchadan.

O'Curry goes on to mention Muinemon, of the race of Eber, who introduced gold neck chains to be worn by chieftains. Later, in 3882 B.C., Fail-dearg-doid (man of the red-fingered hands) first caused gold rings to be worn on the fingers of nobles.

If anyone had bothered to pay attention, the ancient Irish literally left treasure maps in their tracts called *Dinnshenchas* — the ancients' etymological history of the mountains, hills, valleys, lakes, and rivers of Ireland. In these, through their Irish place names, were the clues to the locations of the vast minerals they used in their society, which was not limited to gold alone.

O'Curry relates the story of the Irish place name for the celebrated Lake of Killarney, Loch Lein, which he found in *Dinnshenchas:*

> In this article we are told that Len Lin was Cerd (goldsmith) to Chieftain Bodhah Derg's noble mansion at Sliabh na-mBan in Tipperary, that he went to this lake to make splendid vessels for Fand, the daughter of Flidas, and that Len met his death at this lake, hence the name Loch Lein or Len's Lake.

> *I have heard of Len with his many hammers*
> *Having been upon the margin of its yellow strand*
> *Where he fashioned without mishap or flaw*
> *Splendid vessels for Fand, daughter of Flidas.*

The Bog of Cullen in County Tipperary has for centuries produced vast amounts of ancient gold in all forms of preparation, from the primitive ore to the most delicate works of art. O'Curry's research into the ancient tribes offers an explanation of these artifacts:

> It is not unreasonable to assume that this bog was anciently a wooded valley resorted to by a party or parties of gold smelters and smiths on account perhaps of its contiguity to a gold mine, as well as convenient to charcoal. There is extant an historical reference to this precise location which I believe identifies it with a family and a race of workers in the finer metals.

> There was in this ancient district a small chieftaincy called *Cerdraighe,* that is, the territory of the Goldsmiths; and this territory, as well as the tribe who owned and occupied it, had received the name from a man who bore it as his distinctive title in right of his profession as *Cerd* or goldsmith.

> The pedigree of the Cerdraighe of Tulach Gossa, that is, they

were called *Cerdraighe* because every man of them was called
Cerd for seven generations... According to genealogical com-
putations the years of the seven generations were two
hundred ten. The last of the seven generations come down to
500 A.D.

And so we find that the trade and art of gold manufacture if not
of gold smelting and mining was carried on in this district
probably in this very spot during the long period of two
hundred years.... It is a singular fact that there still exists some
five miles west of Cullen, but in the County of Limerick, a
well-known townland bearing the name Baile na gCeard or the
Town of Goldsmiths.

Though they were entitled to some privileges, according
to Brehon law, the Cerds were placed among the base
professions (Daer Menidh), which included: Saer (carpen-
ters); Gobha (blacksmiths); Umhaide (bronze workers);
and Rennaidhe (engravers). These were considered in the
Gaelic order to be base because they were the work of
hands or fists.

Though the Geological Survey Office is skeptical today
about the possibility of finding the "mother lode" of gold,
its prospecting history is interesting to follow. Because of
the ancients' records and legends handed down, the activity of prospecting has centered in the Wicklow Hills. Toward the end of the eighteenth century gold in quantity
was found in the gravel and sands of the Gold Mines River
near Croghan Kinshelagh, near the town of Woodenbridge. The Geological Survey records show that since then
the deposit has been worked at least on fourteen occasions
and has produced between 7,400 and 9,000 ounces of gold.
The earliest prospecting in this area is reported to have
been by a local schoolmaster, Dunaghoo, in 1770, and from
then until 1795 a Dublin jeweler bought four to five ounces
of gold each year from another person in that area. It was
about this time that it became known that gold was to be
found in the sand and gravel, and immediately the local

work stopped and J. Lloyd reported that "about 300 women at one time, besides great numbers of men and children" worked the area. This continued until October of that year, when the Kildare militia were dispatched to the area to take possession and disperse the diggers. It is estimated that the work yielded up to 10,000 ounces. G. H. Kinahan wrote that a commission was empowered "to collect all the gold deposited and thereby remove every temptation for the assembling of mobs, whose numbers had, before that time, increased to a very alarming number." It was kind Providence that the British were not available to keep "order" during the American gold rush!

Various mining companies were set up in this area during the nineteenth century and failed to find significant gold or any other mineral. Sir Robert Kane in 1845 wrote in *Industrial Resources of Ireland* explaining the failure:

> Numerous companies from time to time have been formed in England for the purpose of developing branches of the industrial resources in Ireland, especially our mines. They have been almost universal failures, and Ireland as a field of enterprise has been hence at a discount in the English market.
>
> It is not difficult to see why they failed; the causes were ignorance and lack of economy. Thus, to work a coal mine in Ireland an overseer and miners are employed who perfectly know how coals are worked in Newcastle and who bring over their steam engines on a scale proportionate to English beds.

Their chauvinism defeated them, and while they refused to see it was possible that Ireland contained glaciations completely different from England's, their operations failed. This generally was the history of mining in Ireland until recently.

The work that is the fascinating link between the ancients and modern mining in Ireland is George Henry Kinahan's *Manual of the Geology of Ireland* written in 1878. Kinahan's work is the last treasure map to modern mines. Nothing has been found in the last few years that is not in Kinahan's work, and it lay in the libraries and geological offices for decades. He not only projected the locations of precious metals, but also the industrial resources that have proved more vast.

The first "modern" mine, as the industry and the government refers to it, was located at Tynagh, which has become, in the last ten years, the largest single producer of silver in Europe. Unfortunately, it has not been the Irish who have benefited by this and other vast discoveries. Canadians were invited by the government to do the preliminary explorations and were granted the mining licenses.

A boom followed the discovery of Tynagh, and soon other mines were prospected and developed. The largest underground zinc mine in Europe is Silvermines in County Tipperary; the finest barite deposit in the world is Ballynoe, and the largest mercury by-products mine in the world is located at Gortdrum. The revenue figures on all this tends to make everyone nervous, especially the Irish. And if they're not nervous, they simply don't believe it. At the moment the boon is owned by foreigners, and these finds deal only in the mineral resources. Only very recently have the offshore gas and oil fields been realized. Unfortunately, in the sixties the drilling rights, on and off shore, were sold to an American exploration company, Marathon, for £500! Marathon's stock, before a drop of oil has been taken from the beds, has gone to £300 million. The granting of the rights was a naive gesture by a failing economy that didn't have the facilities to imagine such wealth.

The situation for Ireland now is very different from even twenty years ago. With anything so volatile the solutions range in extremes. There is a segment demanding immediate nationalization, as they did in Algeria; the other extreme comes from the few Irishmen who are making money out of the operation. They would naturally want everything to remain as it is, with the government getting a percentage of the companies' profits and taxation on the export of raw material.

Some problem developed from the system of land distribution after the Free State was established in 1921. A landowner could purchase the land, but not necessarily the mining right. It became more complicated with the Minerals Development Act of 1940, which empowered the Minister for Industry and Commerce with the right to confiscate any land he determined was not being used to its fullest potential, so that mining rights and their acquisition can become very complicated.

Historically, the development of natural resources has affected countries in two ways: England, Canada, and the United States based their economies on natural mineral wealth. For countries like Indonesia, the Congo, and other Third World countries, the existence of mining operations has made little difference to the welfare of the native people. In such countries mining operations take place as an *enclave* in the economy. That is, there is the least possible integration in the national economy. The resources are "developed" by internal interests, which export the wealth produced, thus destroying the possibility of developing the local company.

This is the situation the shrewdest of the Irish wish to avoid. The Resources Study Groups, a volunteer civilian organization, opts for the most sensible proposal, though protests from board rooms are assured. Their first and most immediate proposal is the control of the extraction amount allowed per year to prolong the lifetime of any given mine. In order to obtain maximum revenues from the wealth, the mining operations must involve the country in all three stages: extraction, smelting, and the establishment of a metallurgical industry. It is only within the ancillary aspects of mining that the country can benefit in the long term. Much of the present mining operations promise to leave hollow craters around the country in less than a decade, with the familiar ghost towns that follow every burnt-out boom. The potential oil and gas industry is still in the preliminary stages, though the one exclusive license has been issued. A petrol industry is more than possible if the Irish are willing to meet and maneuver the multinationals on equal terms. Ireland, for a change, finds itself in an unusual position with a new dilemma — the possibility of vast wealth in a country with the two basic industries of the world, agriculture and mining.

11. The North:

Silent Awarenesses

with
Seamus Heaney

Though I have spent over two years in Ireland, I experienced nothing of the North and its devastation. When I first arrived, people offered to take me there to see for myself what was happening. But I hesitated for two reasons. The first was my revulsion to war. The closest I was willing to come to it was a television news clip. Also, I was certain a visit could only give me an experience of the horror of the situation, without the texture of the life it was destroying on both sides. I knew that one could not write about Ireland without the North, yet I also believed that no one should try to describe the North who hasn't been a part of all that has happened there.

Almost everyone I met had an opinion on the North: the reasons, the causes, the hatreds, the oppressions. But few people ever told me anything of the way it was to live there. One day I was down in Wicklow visiting friends, Maire and Seamus Heaney, and I asked Seamus if I could reprint one of his poems, "The Grauballe Man," from his yet unpublished book, North. *We had almost no talk that day of the North, nor during the many times I spent with the Heaneys. However, when the time came a year later to include something on the separate six counties that still belonged to Britain, I rang Seamus. He is Northern, and his collection of poems had by now been published, and to date has sold more copies than any other volume of poetry in the history of Ireland or Great Britain. Rather awesome, although Seamus himself is anything but awesome. One good friend describes him as a "practical mystic." The day I rang Seamus to ask for help he had just returned from a few days in London, having received the W. H. Smith award for "the most outstanding contribution to English literature during the year." He had also moved that week from the cottage in Wicklow to a house along Dublin Bay. Ever generous Seamus asked me to come around that evening. So we sat for a few hours in the new house in front of the fireplace by candlelight (no electricity yet, and the furniture hadn't been delivered) talking about a place that is known to the world as "The North," which is where he grew up, and about people and friends we've heard about only as statistics. There are two regrets I have about this interview. One is that it is impossible to let you hear Seamus's low deep laugh, recalling the experiences. There is something else missing too, Maire, his wife, who was in the North packing for the move. Maire is a rare person with a unique perception and fiery opinions and would have given quite a different view. But that is really the essence of this thing called the North...so many views.*

◇ ◇ ◇

Dublin has only been my home since 1972. I was born in County Derry in a village half way between Belfast and Derry City, and grew up there at the end of a world in some ways. I say that because the poems I have written, in one way or another, are all related to growing up at that time. When I say the end of a world, I mean first of all a way of life that was traditional and rural and unmechanized, and contained a lot of experiences that were essentially archetypal. For example, I remember seeing my father sowing seed out of an apron round his loins. Mowing...I learned to mow with a scythe. Haymaking with forks. Plowing with horses, and so on. All that lost pastoral order was there. Then suddenly in the fifties, through mechanization and the arrival of the tractor and many other things, it all changed. I grew up on a farm called "Mossbawn," which appears in my book, *North*. It was at one end of the parish of Bellaghy. When I was about fourteen, we moved five or six miles away to the other end of the parish. I have often thought lately that maybe that move away, at the end of childhood, even if it was only six miles, was a move from one world to another, a different place, different friends.

I lost contact with all the people I had grown up with. When I started writing in the sixties, I jumped straight back into that place. In terms of experience of the North, that place was, I suppose, what they call a "mixed community." Although we were Catholic, the people across the road from us were Protestant. Castledown would be a kind of predominantly Protestant/Orange village. But a place called Newbridge and Bellaghy village itself would be predominantly Green. So you grew up in an atmosphere that was full of the silent awarenesses of the division. You were conscious of that; not politically aware of it. Still, the texture of one's life and the posture of one's consciousness, if there is such a thing, were determined by what was there. To the Catholics the police were figures of fear. They were a paramilitary force. They carried arms then. No police in Britain did. It was an Orange-Green thing. You were on one side or the other. It was a caste system, really, I suppose. You belonged to one caste, or tribe, and you breathed in the attitudes.

My parents weren't politically active in any way. I draw a distinction between two classes of Catholic homes in the North. There's a Papish house, definitely nationalistic in their approach. They thought of themselves as Irish. They were against the Unionist majority and against the British connection, but had no active political Sinn Fein ideology. The other kind of house belonged to the Republican, or Sinn Fein, tradition. There are, and were, families who maintained that tradition from the 1920's. Our household fell into the Papish rather than the Republican class. I never had any hint of blistering Republican dogma. For example, I knew very little about 1916. On the other hand, I knew a lot about 1798. When people met in the house, they would sing songs or recite poems about '98.

Our schools were under the British education system. The Catholics and the Protestants were in different schools, though we had at our school a number of Protestant kids. I suppose it was handy for them, and they left at catechism time. The texture of the division was even in children's rhymes. We would say:

> *Red, white, and blue*
> *Should be torn up in two,*
> *And sent to the Devil*
> *At half-past two.*

and

> *Up the long ladder*
> *Down the short rope*
> *To hell with King Billy*
> *And God bless the Pope.*

That was all part of the subculture of the North. And plenty more. I remember a fellow, Jacky Dixon, who was on the road with us. He was a Protestant chap. I guess his age would have been nine or ten. The Catholics were called Fenians. I remember Jacky, when he'd get inside the gates of his own house would shout, "I could beat every f...ing Fenian at Anahorish school."

I've been remembering and questing within myself lately, because of what's been happening. "In what way did we feel it, know it?" Well, we knew it from a very early age. There's a cottage garden flower called Sweet William. A lovely flower, strong crimson and white. I'm certain that my response to Sweet William was affected by the William thing and the Orange element. In other words, it wasn't a matter of getting into the crevices. It affected the whole constitution of your sensibility and consciousness. Even in the way people spoke. A too proper "Englishy" accent would be regarded as a Unionist overbearance.

The whole pageantry of the Orange and Green affected you. The Orange drums in July. That was a kind of purple memory. Not necessarily menacing, but obviously unforgettable. On the first of July the Orangemen started the "wee 12th." They would practice drumming in the evening. There were drumming matches in the summer. Down the field from us was the Hibernian Hall, run by the Ancient Order of Hibernians, and they practiced too. So you had the air full of the music of division. I wouldn't like to be melodramatic and say that you were scared. We weren't scared, but we knew the meaning of the Orange drums.

I think what tends to happen in the North are those tribal tendencies. The world is divided into "goodies" and "baddies." What happened was that that world was ratified as you grew up. People's tolerance was excellent, I think, usually on a person-to-person level. In other words, it is possible to have a community life on a civil basis, on an accepting basis. But there was no society for which either part of the community would give a cent.

As for socializing, "having meals together" is a phrase from a different world. You don't have dinner parties in that sense. There would be a ceili in the Gaelic hall or parochial hall, and there would be a "dance" in the Orange hall. This separateness was true in sports. The GAA (Gaelic Athletic Association) was our crowd, and we went to football matches on a Sunday. Whereas the Protestants would go to a soccer match on a Saturday, because they wouldn't break the Sabbath.

The Protestants would padlock the parks on Sundays, and that made me a little uneasy. It's a way of exercising their authority and bigotry. It's a way of defeating the Papishes. I think what you say is right; there is of course a strong Puritanical streak. But there is also, say, in working-class Belfast or throughout the country a strong streak of rascality and pleasure in Protestants too. If you see the Orange bands on the Twelfth, you see a kind of fatality and wildness about them. I'm generalizing from my own district, but the Catholics in the North aren't the "typical Irish." Some noble wild-eyed figure with a great flow of eloquence and wit, with a kind of primitive energy about him, untrammeled in some way. My people were not like that at all. They were quiet, watchful, oblique, sly. There was a great element of respectability. I think whatever they had been in the early days, they had been debilitated by a certain "churchiness." I think that the dominant Protestant ethos affected them. The other was the clerical influence tending toward respectability. On the other hand, my wife Maire could give you a completely different version of life in Arboe, where there is a different independent Gaelic life. A different kind of fatality and different kind of reckless-ness and fecklessness. Arboe, in County Tyrone, is only fifteen miles away from me. The Plantations stopped at the Ballinderry River, and Maire's district has much more of a Gaelic feel to it. They are fishermen, who are men with a mystery of their own, you know.

Being at Queen's University, I suppose, was a good time. It was hard work. Seamus Deane, the poet, and Austin Clarke, the political leader, were there. We were the first generation of "11+" Catholics. That was the examination that qualified you for school and a scholarship. It was the beginning of free education. In a sense the Civil Rights movement of 1969 was in some ways related to this "11+" program. The Catholics became more articulate and confi-dent. Or maybe there were just more of them with an idiom of abstract thought about their own condition.

On October 5, 1968, there was a Civil Rights march. I

remember the week after that. I was teaching in Queen's University in Belfast. I had to write an article for Carl Miller. I was publishing poems in the *Listener* and Carl was editing it. Conor Cruise O'Brien had been to Queen's just that week. He had been talking about civil disobedience as a mode of resistance and a political weapon. He talked about Antigone. And about Creon being opposed to Antigone. On the whole, he was identifying with Antigone's stand, her refusal. Since then he has recanted on that. At the time it was an exhilarating moment, because here was an intellectual, a speaker of persuasion and eloquence and distinction, drawing the exalted Greek analogies. We had just had an example of the crassness of police power. There was a feeling that things were on the move. Well, things *were* on the move, with the Liberal Unionist oligarchy in command and this feeling that we would not tolerate it, that things were going to change. So I was involved, not as a member of any civil rights organization, but I was on the marches. There was an energy and excitement and righteousness in the air at that time, by people like myself who hadn't always been political.

Then in 1969 I got a thing called the Somerset Maugham Prize for travel, and I was in France and Spain when the pogroms started and the Falls were invaded and supported by the police. I remember coming back kind of exhilarated because the Army had come in and was protecting the Catholics. Lynch (the Prime Minister) was not about to "stand idly by." I thought everything was coming to some kind of head. When I got off the boat at Rosslare with Maire and the kids, we drove to Dublin and called in to John Horgan's house. Two friends of mine from Belfast had been down the night before and were still there. I was all excited, and they were very depressed. Of course, they're Protestant and I'm Catholic. But they had seen the smoking ruins and the bricked-up houses. Funny, it's all I remember about it, them being depressed and me being exhilarated and me being rebuked for my exhilaration. But I thought that things were productively breaking up or breaking down. Because I think that was the main thing, that the old blocks were breaking. The heraldic, definite world I mentioned had always seemed unshakable. Somehow intelligence and possibility were now penetrating it.

It was a spectacle like everything else. Everybody was exhilarated by it, excited or menaced by it. The North is so compact. You blow on one string, and the whole harp begins to whisper. It's so compact that it produces a very compact animal. The self is not for a long time free of what produced it. In fact, it never is, I suppose. But in the North for anybody coming out of it, Catholic or Protestant, it takes effort and intention to achieve a state of freedom in the self. And if it's worth attaining I don't know. But if you break any strong and tender bonds, you feel unfaithful. In the North it's the sense of self growing up with the sense of being Protestant or Catholic and being on one side or the other.

I remember all of us saying, "This is all right until somebody gets killed." I remember that time when everyone was terrified of the first death. Civil rights was a stick to beat the English with, of course. But the English always saw it as a cover for subversives and Communists and Sinn Feiners and rebels. That was partly true too. So that there was, on the one hand, one's exhilaration at the modernity of the occasion and, on the other hand, there was the old, cute slyness that it was a Papish action and an antipartitionist movement too. Then, as things progressed, you had the original blueprint of the society and the psyches that made up the society. It just reestablished itself. I don't think people were really shocked at the violence, because it was as if that fundamental blueprint was being ratified again, that this was the shaped reality. I think that a number of middle-class Protestants were genuinely shocked. When I say that I mean intimately distressed in the privacy of their own hearts and heads. Again it was inevitable. That was the way it was understood. I think that by now that has been cauterized. I think there are a lot of people now alienated. This is again from my own experience. You always felt that you were responsible for what happened, and you couldn't honestly withdraw from it, because it was a part of you that was happening. You think that because you withdraw yourself, you have stopped. And yet now it has a new generation of activists.

But there is still no future until there is a political structure to allow dignity and self-respect for both sides. My position is that the Protestants could live with dignity and self-respect in a United Ireland. Now, their position is that there will be no power sharing, of course. But that's not very satisfying.

I've always thought, and still think, of the North that people have to live there after, whatever happens. They're going to have to maintain or reestablish some kind of community. So I suppose that I've always thought of it as an isolated condition. That is partly the victory of the Unionist way of life.

I wrote a poem called "Bogland" in '68 or '69. The allusion was that the bog was a kind of Jungian ground or landscape in that it preserved traces of everything that had occurred before. It had layers of memory. The objects, the material culture by which the nation identifies itself, were mostly found in the bogs and are now in museums. I remember when we were children, they used to tell us not to go near the bog because there was no bottom to it.

In 1968 a book came out called *The Bog People* by a Danish archaeologist, P. V. Glob. In 1969 the killings started. The bog people fascinated me, amazingly enough, not because of any political reason at all. There were photographs of these victims cast into bogs in Jutland in the early Iron Age. One man in particular, the Tollund Man, from a place called Tollund, entranced everyone who looked at him. I've thought since that he looked like every old country man, every great uncle at home, that I had ever seen coffined, with that kind of gentleness on the face that is partly a product of rigor mortis. The photograph of that man moved me at just that subconscious level. So the bog then, when I moved to Wicklow in 1972, was my fascination. At the time I was established as a writer with three books out, and I was thought of as a Northern writer. I was trying to clear my head to become a *writer*. I'm not really political, and I can't think politically, but in a sense I can feel the meaning of the politics in these things.

Around the time of the move to Wicklow, I had a chance to go to Jutland, after which I wrote "The Grauballe Man." During that trip girls were being tarred and feathered in Derry. I wrote a poem called "Punishment," which is maybe the most explicit poem, where the connections are made. It moves more uneasily, but I hope through the tack of the words it works. From a girl, an adulteress, who has had her head shaved and who was buried in the bog to the girls whose faces are black, not because of this inhumation in the bog, but because of the tar on them, to the girls in Derry. Both victims, the adulteress and the girls; both supposed to have betrayed their community; both punished by their own community. Also both viewed from the outside with some civilized outrage. The *Daily Telegraph* was writing about the punishment of the girls by tar and feathering, very righteously and "how inhumane" it was, and "in violation," and so on. Well this is true enough. On the other hand the British armies were using brutal and much more efficient methods. So connections like that came up. I suppose that that was what was in the poems and the reason I was able to do them was that the bogs were a part of a chain, part of one's own psyche. It was the irrational symbol, and I was trying to harness the dynamo of the irrational with the politics and problems of the moment. The book ends up in Wicklow in December '73. It's in some ways the book all books were leading to. You end up with nothing but your vocation, with words and your own free choice. Isolated but not dispossessed of what produced you. Having left a context, stepped away, you can't really go back. It ends up with just the responsibility of the artist, whatever that is, and that responsibility has no solutions.

I would say that I am a product of that isolation we were talking about before. And for me now it's just the usual middle-age coasting toward extinction, but trying to define the self. I'm not interested in my poetry canvassing public events deliberately any more. I would like to write poems of myself at this age. Poems, so far, have been fueled by a world that is gone or a world that is too much with us — public events. Just through accident and all the things we've been talking about, I've ended up with myself, and I have to start there, you know.

◇ ◇ ◇

THE GRAUBALLE MAN

As if he had been poured
in tar, he lies
on a pillow of turf
and seems to weep

the black river of himself.
The grain of his wrists
is like bog oak,
the ball of his heel

like a basalt egg.
His instep has shrunk
cold as a swan's foot
or a wet swamp root.

His hips are the ridge
and purse of a mussel,
his spine an eel arrested
under a glisten of mud.

The head lifts,
the chin is a visor
raised above the vent
of his slashed throat

that has tanned and toughened.
The cured wound
opens inwards to a dark
elderberry place.

Who will say 'corpse'
to his vivid cast?
Who will say 'body'
to his opaque repose?

And his rusted hair,
a mat unlikely
as a foetus's.
I first saw his twisted face

in a photograph,
a head and shoulder
out of the peat,
bruised like a forceps baby,

but now he lies
perfected in my memory,
down to the red horn
of his nails,

hung in the scales
with beauty and atrocity:
with the Dying Gaul
too strictly compassed

on his shield,
with the actual weight
of each hooded victim,
slashed and dumped.

12. Sports:

The Sporting Life

with
Tony O'Riordan

The Irish are a sporting people, loving chance and challenge, whether coming up to Dublin for their "matches" or returning to the country – their lush lands and cobalt blue lakes – for their ancient pastimes of hunting, fishing, and shooting. My friend Tony O'Riordan, always a generous source of fascinating anecdotes, tells of Ireland's "sporting life."

◇ ◇ ◇

Hurling is among the oldest games in the world; it has its place firmly in Celtic mythology, and as far as one can trace, it is the game with the oldest international contests in the world. It is also one of the only games to be banned by law. In 1367 the Statute of Kilkenny stated: "It is ordained and established that the English do not henceforth use the plays, which men call hurling, with great sticks and a ball on the ground."

In the oldest Irish mythological saga of Cuchulainn, the hero, Setanta, sets off from his home with a hurley and a ball to play on the way to shorten his journey. En route he was invited to the home of the smith, Culann, to a huge

feast for Conor the King. He arrived late for the feast and
was met by a huge hound guarding Culann's door. Setanta
rammed the hurling ball down the throat of the dog, who
had never been defeated. Culann was so surprised he
asked Setanta to stay on to be his guard, literally the hound
of Culann, Cuchulainn. In the Fianna series Grainne tells
Diarmuid that she fell in love with him as she watched him
"drive" into the ranks of the game, winning the goal three
times upon the men of Tara.

Hurling became a landlords' game with landlords vying
with one another for the best players. Games were frequently arranged between the various provinces in the
Phoenix Park before the "presence of Her Excellency, the
Countess of Westmoreland, and several of the nobility and
gentry, besides a vast concourse of spectators." The landlord in Wexford, the Colclough family, took a team of forty
in the eighteenth century to Bristol, England, to play the
gentlemen of Cornwall. They carried a yellow sash around
their waist to identify them, and to this day the Wexford
team is referred to as the "Yellow-bellies." In the eighteenth century Robert Devereaux sent an account of a hurling match to his son on the Continent in the form of a poem:

> Thus by an effort was the goal put out
> Instant the ear is deafened by a shout
> Hats, wigs, shoes, stockings, quickly fly in air
> Victors to the beer barrel repair
> Where huntsmen the games played o'er again
> And bagpipes drone – while all rejoice in twain.

Joseph Strutt writes: "Hurling to the goals was fre-
quently played by Irishmen in the fields at the back of the
British Museum." And the headquarters of the English
Polo Club outside London is called Hurlingham, from hurl-
ing originally played there. Hurling traveled as far as
Argentina, but died out there in the 1914-18 war.

Ireland had its equivalent of the Olympic Games, the *Tailteann Games*, which are older than the Olympic Games, dating back to the Bronze Age and lasting until A.D. 1168, although their Greek counterparts came to an end in A.D. 394. The site of the games, which has been anglicized to *Teltown*, is about thirty-five miles from Dublin near Tara. It is not as impressive as the excavated sites in Olympia; however, the place where the chariot races and mock naval battles were held, and the viewing area, can still be seen. Like the Olympic Games, they were great literary and social events, but unlike those games, women were allowed to attend. There was one curious happening at the games, which is still referred to in local tradition. It was the Teltown marriage, which lasted for "a year and a day." Upon the ending of that period, the married couple came together at *Rath Dubh* (Black Ford) and stood back-to-back — one facing south, the other facing north. Their walking away from one another was a signal that the marriage was ended.

Irishmen have made a name for themselves in and out of contests. The father of Princess Grace of Monaco — John Brendan Kelly — was the first man in Olympic rowing history to win three gold medals. He had been refused permission to take part in the Henley Royal Regatta on the Thames because he was a man who "worked with his hands." King Edward VII likewise refused to shake hands with Boss Croaker when he won the Epsom Derby with Orby. This Tammany Hall boss had come to Ireland and, with his Irish-trained horse, had won England's premier racing event.

The first political protest, long before the black clenched fists at the Olympic Games in Mexico, was made by an Irishman, Peter O'Connor, at Athens in 1906. He, with two other Irishmen, Con Leahy and John McGough, had to enter under the British flag. When "God Save the King" was played, O'Connor climbed the two-hundred-foot flag-staff and placed the Irish flag at the top.

From 1900 to 1932, with the exception of one Olympic, the Hammer Event has been won by an Irishman, usually representing the United States. In Limerick there is a monument to John O'Grady, who was a world champion weight thrower. It is curious that these winners were not only all born in Ireland, but also that they were born within a score of miles of one another in the Limerick-Tipperary region.

Irishmen were also inventive sportsmen. Rugby football was founded when Roscrea-born William Webb Ellis ran with the ball instead of kicking it at Rugby School in 1823. Roger Bresnihan, one of the leading baseball players of his time, came from Tralee, County Kerry, and was known as the "Duke of Tralee" in his playing days. He was the inventor of shin guards and the first to wear them in 1907.

One of the most unusual facts is that the earliest known yacht club in the world — the Cork Harbour Water Club (now the Royal Cork Yacht Club) — was founded in 1720.

One would expect sport in Ireland to have its humor, and so it has. The first post-war Rugby International against France was in 1946. Irish newspapers had been full of accounts of the grim conditions in France and Europe regarding food shortages while Ireland itself had all the food it required. The French team's arrival was awaited with great interest, almost like looking at people from another world. We had been cut off from Europe for seven years. As the French team came onto the field, all eyes fell on two of the biggest men we had ever seen; they looked like great oaks that had grown outward instead of upward. They bore the extraordinary names of Moga and Soro. Someone in the crowd turned from looking at these giants where he had expected wraiths and said: "They must have been f...ing collaborators."

· Mick English playing for Ireland failed to stop Brian Horrocks-Taylor scoring. "What happened?" he was asked. "Well," he said, "he came toward me with the ball and I had him covered, but then Horrocks went one way and Taylor the other and I was left tackling the bloody hyphen."

Ireland's record at sport is a creditable one. This year the Republic of Ireland beat the Soviet Union in soccer football three goals to none, an almost incredible feat when you compare the population of the two countries. Ireland was the current rugby football champion in the five-nations tournament representing France, England, Scotland, Wales. The two most popular games are Gaelic football and hurling, which have drawn crowds of 85,000 and 50,000 from provincial centres.

Ireland's rugby teams represent their thirty-two counties, with Orangemen cheerfully donning the green jersey to play for Ireland.

RACING

An Irish horse trader is said to have sold a mare as sound in wind and limb and "without fault." It afterward appeared that the poor beast could not see at all out of one eye and was almost blind in the other. The purchaser, finding this, made heavy complaints to the dealer and reminded him that he engaged the mare to be "without fault." "To be sure, to be sure I did," said the dealer, "but then, my dear, the poor crater's blindness is not her fault, but her misfortune."

In the lean days roguery was the poor man's revenge. Today, however, Ireland's bloodstock is the envy of international traders, "the Race" every Irishman's passion. In a single year there are more than two hundred race fixtures around the country at thirty courses. Dublin alone has Phoenix Park, Leopardstown, and thirty miles away the Curragh. The Curragh sits on 5,000 acres of rolling Irish countryside and is the home of the National Stud. Today there are over 350 registered stud farms spreading over the fertile counties of Kildare, Meath, and Tipperary. Two of Ireland's trainers are legends in their lifetime — Vincent O'Brien and Paddy Prendergast — and between them have won almost every international prize a few times over.

The three- and four-day meets at Galway, Listowel, and Tralee go from dawn to dawn devoted only to "the Race" and "the Drink." At Laytown races the horses take their post positions along the sandy beach. There are three ways of betting the race. The famous Irish bookies travel around to each meet changing their odds in the last seconds before the starting bell. Others prefer the "Tote" of the racecourse, and some don't even bother going to the races at all and just pay a visit to the local turf accountant in the town (there's usually more than one).

The races with the largest purses are the Irish Derby at the Curragh on the last Saturday in June and the Irish Grand National at Fairyhouse on Easter Monday. International colors parade, and top racing jockeys from all over the world, such as Lester Piggott and Willie Carson, compete. The race is a part of Irish life not to be missed.

Tickets for the Irish Sweepstakes, begun in 1962, are available *everywhere*, with prizes up to a quarter of a million pounds each draw, made a few weeks before the race. The only complaint the Irish have against the Sweeps is that the winner is usually a tourist or someone off in Canada or Australia.

COMMENT

Flat racing: Usually begins on St. Patrick's Day in March and continues through November.

Steeplechasing: All year round

Point to Point: Spring

RACE MAP

HUNTING

Oscar Wilde described the English gentlemen riding to the hounds as "the unspeakable in full pursuit of the uneatable." The Irish themselves are more endeared to the hunt than Wilde, as it's not the exclusive pastime it is in England. *Everyone* — country ladies and gentlemen, farmers, locals, visitors and foreigners — gather in the local pub to warm at the open fires, swap stories, swill Irish whiskey...and then the hunt. As you drive near Galway between November and March, you're likely to see a flash of the Galway Blazers in their blazing red vests, or further up toward Tuam you may pass Ireland's most famous horsewoman, Lady Cusack-Smith, Master of the Bermingham Hunt. Ask the locals in the area for the story of Lady Cusack-Smith's reply to a local when she returned a borrowed horse after a particularly strenuous ride.

Ireland has always been regarded as the most magnificent land for hunts — the West for its stone walls, the East for its streams and ditches, and the South for its double banks. There are more than eighty-five hunts — fox, harriers, and stag — spread over the country, and with some packs meeting on Sundays hunting is available seven days a week.

When you decide to come for an Irish hunt holiday, contact the Tourist Board for making arrangements to stay at some of the country houses, such as Lady Cusack-Smith's Bermingham House, in the hunting season. Come join the Scarteen (Black and Tans) Hunt of Tipperary, the Harriers Hunt of Dublin, the South Union Hunt of Cork, and many others.

(For detailed information contact direct: Joe Lynam, Irish Tourist Board, Baggot Street Bridge, Dublin 4.)

SHOOTING

Seasons

August 12 — September 30   Grouse in all counties

September 1 — January 31   Mallard, pigeon, teal,
white-fronted geese,
plover, snipe, woodcock

November 1 — November 15   Partridge

November 1 — January 31   Cock pheasant

The Irish *by custom* do not shoot the following birds: black-birds, thrushes, larks, swans, finches, herons, and others.
   Certain birds, such as hooded crows and magpies, are regarded as pests and may be shot, though there doesn't seem much gamesmanship in that. Irish shooting laws protect some species by law or custom.

GOLFING

Ireland has won the amateur golfing championships more often than any other country, and it is no surprise, with over two hundred courses around the country. Ireland was also one of the few countries, other than the States, to have won the World Cup at professional golf. Dan Sheehan is one of the few world amateurs to have beaten professionals in a major tournament since the heyday of Bobby Jones. Irishman Jimmy Bruen, with his unique loop style, was the world's greatest draw at golfing tournaments in the thirties and forties. It's possible to do nothing else in Ireland but a

round-the-coast tour, and you will still have every variation of the Irish landscape and enjoy your sport.

The clubs listed below are only the beginning of those
available, and the Tourist Board will give you a full list of
those other 190 clubs:

COUNTY DUBLIN

PORTMARNOCK GOLF CLUB: Portmarnock, Tel: 323050
Secretary: Captain R. L. Gregan. Tel: 323082
Par: 72. Professional Harry Bradshaw.
Facilities: Showers, towels, car park, bar, meals, caddy car
   and caddy service, shop, map of course.

ROYAL DUBLIN GOLF CLUB. Dollymount, Dublin 3.
   Tel: 337153
Secretary: D. Beglin. Tel: 336346
Par: 73. Professional Christy O'Connor.
Facilities: Showers, towels, car park, bar, meals, caddy car
   service, shop, map of course.

COUNTY CLARE

LAHINCH GOLF CLUB: Lahinch.
Secretary: Austin Slattery. Tel: Lahinch 3.
Par: 72. Professional William McCavery. Tel: Lahinch 3
Facilities: Showers, towels, car park, bar, meals, caddy car
   and caddy service, shop, map of course.

COUNTY KERRY

BALLYBUNION GOLF CLUB: Ballybunion.
Secretary: Sean Walsh. Tel: 20
Par: 71. Professional Brendan Houlihan
Facilities: Showers, towels, car park, bar, caddy car and
   caddy service, shop, map of course.

DOOKS & CARAGH GOLF CLUB: Glenbeigh. Tel: Glenbeigh 5.
Secretary: Declan Mangan. Tel: Killorglin 125.
Par: 70.
Facilities: Showers, towels, car park, bar, caddy car and caddy service, map of course.

KILLARNEY GOLF CLUB: Mahony's Point, Killarney and Kileen, Killarney
Secretary: Captain D. D. O'Connell. Tel: (064) 31034
Par: 72. Professional Tony Coveney.
Facilities: Showers, towels, car park, bar, meals, caddy car and caddy service, shop, map of course.

WATERVILLE GOLF CLUB: Waterville. Tel: Waterville 22
Secretary: Sean Power
Par: 74. Professional Liam Higgins.
Facilities: Showers, towels, car park, bar, meals, caddy car and caddy service, shop.

COUNTY MAYO

WESTPORT GOLF CLUB: Westport.
Secretary: Michael J. Moran. Tel: Kilmeena 614
Par: 73.
Facilities: Showers, towels, car park, bar, meals, map of course available.

COUNTY SLIGO

CO. SLIGO GOLF CLUB: Rosses Point. Tel: (071) 3042
Secretary: Mr. H. Roughan. Tel: (071) 3520
Par: 71. Professional John McGonigle.
Facilities: Showers, towels, car park, bar, meals, caddy car and caddy service, shop, map of course.

COUNTY WICKLOW

WOODBROOK GOLF CLUB: Bray. Tel: 862073
Secretary: Lt. Comdr. F. G. Bambrick. Tel: 863155
Par: 74. Professional William J. Kinsella.
Facilities: Showers, towels, car park, bar, meals, caddy car
   and caddy service, shop, map of course. Green fees
   average £1.00. Check with the club.

DUBLIN HORSE SHOW WEEK

The Irish have a way of reversing patterns...and as most
European cities become ghost towns for the August holiday, Dublin rears its horsey head for one of Europe's last
elegant gatherings — *Dublin Horse Show Week.* The city
swells with international visitors arriving as early as a week
before to settle in with friends in nearby country houses
while others head for the Shelbourne (headquarters for the
riders) or the Hibernian or the Gresham Hotels to relax
before the whirling week of parties and hunt balls till dawn
with only a few hours sleep till the opening trumpet of the
day's events. By ten in the morning traffic jams as the
high-stepping thoroughbreds hoof across Merrion Road
heading for the rings in the Royal Dublin Society show
grounds. Glistening Rolls Royces, state cars, sleek
limousines, and Mini Minors roll to a halt at the entrance as
the grounds fill with spectators...the President, the Prime
Minister, Ministers, Ambassadors...all of Dublin and their
friends.

The excitement intoxicates. Strolling the grounds are
Irishmen wrapped in nobby tweeds...men capped in
tweeds, bowlers, top hats, and even a few in cowboy
hats...the ladies in everything from layers of chiffon to
durable denim. Since early morning the stable hands have

been darting from stall to stall polishing, braiding the horses, and calming the riders. Children struggle with oversized tack for their Connemara ponies they'll show during the day. Almost two thousand of Ireland's envious bloodstock will be shown and sold at Ballsbridge during the week.

Aga Khan Day...3:00 P.M. The President arrives flanked by the military honor guard and the dozen judges in gray morning suits, top hats, and red carnations to review the Parade of Nations. The faint notes of the Pipers Band fill the air as they approach, leading the international teams of four horses and riders around the jumping enclosure. For one week gasps and cheers break the hush in the arena while these riders compete for the Nations Cup, the Aga Khan Trophy, donated by His Highness in 1926 and awarded to the country winning three years in succession. Riders such as Eddie Macken and Captain Raimondo D'Inzeo make their aristocratic flights over doubles, trebles, and water jumps challenging last year's records. There are others, too, who'll compete during the week, including those elegant ladies riding sidesaddle in their black veils and silk hats. It all seems some other lovely era...not quite lost.

◇ ◇ ◇

COMMENT

Horse Show Week, usually the second week in August, is the most popular gathering in Ireland. Be sure to make your reservations well in advance through the Irish Tourist Board. Or write:

The Secretary
Royal Dublin Society
Ballsbridge, Dublin

ANGLING

With 950 miles of fresh water lakes, 2,000 miles of coastline, and —

salmon	bass
sea trout	pollock
brown trout	wrasse
pike	conger
perch	shark
bream	mullet
roach	haddock
dace	skate
carp	swordfish

that's only the beginning of the fishing stories.

Whether it's game fishing, coarse fishing, or sea angling, you're warned ahead to bring extra strong gear to cope with the oversized fishes with strong fighting ability. Before your trip the Tourist Board can help you plan the best holiday for fishing since many of the finest runs for game fishing are operated by private owners and hoteliers.

POLO

The "game of playboys and kings" is played in the Phoenix Park from May to the end of August, Tuesday, Thursday, and Saturday afternoons.

International games are played during Spring Show (May) and the Dublin Horse Show Week (August).

John McCormack

Willie McCormack (the photographer's uncle), talking to Monie at his Sligo home, dates the disappearance of the fairies and banshees "when they brought in the Angelus."

Jeffrey Craig/Claddagh Records

Playwright Samuel Beckett recording one of his works with Irish actor Jack MacGowran (1918-73).

Liam Redmond, internationally known Abbey Theatre actor and founder of the Players Theatre in Dublin.

Brendan Behan (1923-64)
with his wife Beatrice.

The bells of hell
Go ting-a-ling-a-ling
For you but not for me.
— from *The Hostage*

John Barry

Irish Times

Alan Simpson, the Abbey's
Artistic Director, says of the
Irish theatre: "It's been dying
almost as long as it's
existed...and if it hasn't already been finished you
should have seen it fifteen,
twenty, fifty years ago."

Patrick Kavanagh (1905-67), Irish poet.

"Go into a pub and listen well
If my voice still echoes there."

Novelist and raconteur Benedict Kiely comments on the Censorship Board: "The only way to settle it was to laugh it out of existence."

Irish poet Austin Clarke
(1896-1974).

"Awake or in my sleep, I
have no peace now...
...in this land, where every
woman's son
Must carry his own cof-
fin...."

Sean O'Sullivan's portrait of
the poet William Butler Yeats
in the National Gallery.

"Cast a cold eye
On life, on death..."

Garech Browne, patron of Irish music and founder of Claddagh Records, at home in County Wicklow.

Fiddle player Mairtáin Byrnes. "Music to the Irish is a living delight. A mysterious key to a host of undiscovered emotions hoarded in the secrets of the soul."

Paddy Moloney (foreground) and Sean Potts of the Chieftains playing tin whistles by the black lake at Luggula.

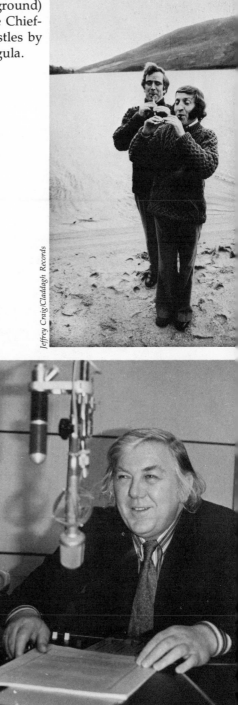

Jeffrey Craig/Claddagh Records

Ciaran MacMathúna, Radio Télefis Eireánn music broadcaster, traveled the countryside taping traditional music.

John McCormack

Sculptor Edward Delaney by his statue in St. Stephen's Green in Dublin of 18th-century Irish hero Wolfe Tone, founder of the Society of United Irishmen.

Children at a Fleadh Cheoil (music festival) at Listowel.

"We are the music-makers

And we are the dreamers of dreams."

John McCormack

Dublin monument to Charles Stewart Parnell. "No man has the right to fix the boundary to the march of a nation."

Seamus Heaney, Northern poet. "You grew up in an atmosphere full of the silent awarenesses of the division."

Skellig Michael, 6th-century home of hermits off the Kerry coast. Bernard Shaw said of this granite island: "No experience that conventional tourist travel can bring you will stick in your memory so strangely, for Skellig Michael is not after the fashion of this world."

The country look. The new varies little from the old.

Old water-powered corn mill at Foulksmill, Co. Wexford, built in 1851.

The late President of Ireland, Erskine Childers, presents the Aga Khan Trophy at the annual Dublin Horse Show to the British team.

The Meath Hunt at Dunsany Castle. *"Everyone*—country ladies and gentlemen, farmers, locals, visitors and foreigners" ride with the more than eighty-five hunts in Ireland.

John McCormack

The country publican practicing the art of drawing a pint of Guinness.

PART TWO

Along the Roads

Introduction

Over the months I've met travelers who breathlessly told me they had just returned from a few days' spin around Ireland, having seen Dublin, Blarney Castle, the Lakes of Killarney, Galway Bay, Donegal, and stopped at Shannon on their way home. Others were embarking on the same breakneck itinerary. They seemed to be describing some race. With one such couple who seemed to be traveling like nervous birds I had the urge to stroll out to the car park and let the air out of their tires so they could stay *somewhere* for a few minutes longer than they had "planned." First of all, for a very practical reason, Ireland is not suited for such a reeling tour. The roads are narrow and winding and cluttered daily with cattle, sheep, and the odd ass and cart. Second, such a pace is out of time with Irish rhythm and insures that you'll be running alongside, not *within*, Irish life.

Ireland is a place to linger and lull a while, to discover unknown pleasures or rediscover lost ones. If you have a passion or obsessive pursuit — hunting, fishing, riding, boating, archaeology, music, theatre, art, or just conversation, eating and drinking — the Irish encourage indulgence in any pleasure.

"Along the Roads" has been separated into four areas, Shannon Circle, Cork/Kerry Circle, Galway Circle, and Dublin Circle, in an attempt to slow the traveler down. When you've traveled over the different counties, you'll realize that each area is a separate trip. Each is really a small pocket civilization with a few consistent Irish qualities and a few hundred inconsistent ones. Some of the differences are quite subtle, others more obvious. Even the accents vary from county to county.

The descriptions and suggestions in "Along the Roads" are an effort to offer *only* the best and the most unusual during your stay. The hotels, country houses, and farmhouses recommended are of the highest quality, and in almost all cases have a proprietor in residence.

Ireland also offers three other unique, well-organized schemes for accommodation that are less expensive and very successful: *Bed and Breakfast; Farmhouse Holiday,* and *Rent-a-Cottage.* Though a few have been recommended in this book, more extensive listings are available through the Irish Tourist Board. The other areas — Restaurants, Antiques Trails, Buyers' Markets, Entertainment, and Diversions — are all limited to what seems particularly unique for your tour.

Thackeray wrote an introduction to the Irish well over a century ago in his *Irish Sketchbook* (1842) which has yet to be improved upon:

> In a couple of hours' talk an Englishman will give you his notions on trade, politics, the crops; the last run with the hounds or the weather; it requires a long sitting and a bottle of wine at least to induce him to laugh cordially or to speak unreservedly; and if you joke with him he will surely set you down as an impertinent fellow. In two hours over a pipe, a German will be quite ready to let loose the easy flood gates of his sentiment and confide to you many of the secrets of his soft

heart. In two hours a Frenchman will say a hundred and twenty smart, witty, brilliant, fake things and will care for you as much then as he would if you saw him every day for twenty years, that is, not one single straw; and in two hours an Irishman will have allowed his jovial humour to unbutton, and gamboled and frolicked to his heart's content. Which of these, putting Monsieur out of the question, will stand by his friend with the most constancy and maintain his steady wish to serve him? That is the question the Englishman (and I think with a little cool assumption) is disposed to decide in his own favour; but it is clear that for the stranger the Irish ways are the pleasantest, for here he is at once made happy and at home.

◇ ◇ ◇

BEFORE YOU GO

Life can be made easy just once in a while — and when you've decided to travel to Ireland, the Irish Tourist Board and Aer Lingus (Irish International Airlines) will be your "patrons and protectors."

The Irish Tourist Board will help you plan your trip before you go, and with their computerized reservations system all your hotel and ground reservations will be taken care of well in advance. They will help you finally decide whether to rent a cottage, travel from castle to castle, stay in a farmhouse, or cruise the Shannon. In usual Irish style they make *everything* easy.

I've made over a dozen Atlantic crossings with Aer Lingus, some on overnight notice and others long planned, and having now become old friends, I'm still waiting for the flaws to surface. The Aer Lingus staff may be your first introduction to the Irish, and you won't be disappointed — they're generous, helpful, efficient, *and* seem to remember the old days when passengers were supposed to enjoy their flight. Traveling with Aer Lingus, you begin to feel you're in Ireland before you've left Kennedy.

IRISH TOURIST BOARD OFFICES

NEW YORK:
590 Fifth Avenue
Tel: 212/246-7400

CHICAGO:
230 North Michigan Ave.
Tel: 312/726-9356

LOS ANGELES:
510 West Sixth St.
Suite 317
Tel: 213/624-8961

SAN FRANCISCO:
681 Market St.
Tel: 415/781-5688

Tourist Offices are located in almost every town across Ireland and can be recognized by the green-and-white TIO signs. They will help you with hotel reservations and advise local entertainment and interest. Summer hours: 9:30 A.M. to 6:00 P.M.

AER LINGUS OFFICES

NEW YORK:
590 Fifth Avenue
Tel: 212/557-1110

CHICAGO:
230 North Michigan Avenue
Tel: 800/223-6292

DALLAS:
7701 Stemmons Freeway
Tel: 800/223-6537

PHILADELPHIA:
2000 Market Street
Tel: 800/223-6006

BOSTON:
Dunfey Parker House Hotel
Tel: 800/223-6006

CLEVELAND:
1422 Euclid Avenue
Tel: 800/223-6270

LOS ANGELES:
510 West Sixth St.
Tel: 800/223-6537

SAN FRANCISCO:
681 Market St.
Tel. 800/223-6537

GENERAL INFORMATION

The Constitution of Ireland was adopted in 1937, creating a sovereign independent democratic republic of twenty-six counties, ruled by *Oireachtas* (Irish Parliament). The six northeastern counties that form the area known as Northern Ireland are governed separately as part of the United Kingdom.

AREA: 32,524 sq. miles (all Ireland)

POPULATION: 3 million (approximately) Republic of Ireland
CAPITAL: Dublin *(Baile Atha Cliath)*
NATIONAL FLAG: Tricolor of green, white, and orange. Green
  represents the old Gaelic order, orange represents the
  followers of William of Orange, and "the white in the
  center signifies a lasting truce between the 'Green' and
  the 'Orange.'"

CLIMATE: Moderate Gulf Stream
  High: July and August, 58°F — 70°F
  Low: January and February, 40°F — 45°F
  During summer months daylight until 10:30 P.M.

HOLIDAYS:
  January 1
  March 17 (St. Patrick's Day)
  Good Friday
  Easter Monday
  June Bank Holiday (1st Monday)
  August Bank Holiday (1st Monday)
  Christmas
  St. Stephen's Day (December 26)

BANKING:
  10:00 A.M. - 12:30 P.M.; 1:30 - 3:00 P.M. (Weekdays)
  to 5:00 P.M. Thursdays
  Banks are open extra hours at all airports — Shannon,
  Dublin, Cork — to accommodate passengers.

CURRENCY:
  Rate fluctuates daily.

Coins	*Notes*
New half pence	£1
New penny	£5
Two new pence	£10

Five new pence	£20
Ten new pence	£50
Fifty new pence	£100

    100 new pennies per Pound.
    Rate approximately: $2.00 to £1

PUB HOURS: 10 A.M.-11 P.M. (Winter)
    10 A.M.-11:30 P.M. (Summer)

    Sundays: 12:30-2:00 P.M.; 4:00-10:00 P.M.

    Dublin & Cork: Pubs close for "Holy Hour"
    2:30-3:30 P.M.

SHOPPING HOURS: Generally 9 A.M.-5:30 P.M. Most shops have
an early closing day. Wednesday is early closing day in
Dublin. Saturdays most businesses close at 1:00 P.M. in
Dublin.

POST OFFICES: 9 A.M.-5:30 P.M.
    Luncheon closing 1-2 P.M.

POLICE: Known as the *Garda Siochana,* these are civic guards
and carry no guns. For emergency dial 999 in the city
and 10 in the smaller towns.

TIPPING: This may vary from 10-12½% depending on the
establishment, and usually is included in the bill. Tipping in pubs is not customary unless you are served in
a lounge by a waiter or waitress.

ELECTRICAL CURRENT: Standard is 220 volts. Hotels usually are
equipped with dual 220/110 voltage. As a general rule
leave most electrical appliances at home unless they
are *really* necessary.

CLOTHING: The weather is the most unpredictable part of your trip, so be prepared for a full range ... a few warm sweaters, some rain gear, *and* a bathing suit. It's hard to say which you'll use more, just make sure they're comfortable ... the Irish are less interested in haute couture than almost anywhere you'll visit.

USEFUL ADDRESSES

AMERICAN EMBASSY   42 Elgin Road
Ballsbridge
Tel: 688777

AMERICAN EXPRESS   116 Grafton Street
Dublin
Tel: 772874
Hours: Mon. - Fri. 9 A.M.-5 P.M.
     Sat. 9 A.M.-1 P.M.

DUBLIN TOURISM   51 Dawson Street
Dublin
Tel: 747733

14 Upper O'Connell Street
Dublin
Tel: 747733

Hours: 9:15 A.M.-5:30 P.M.

C.I.E.
(Irish Transport
    Company)   Passenger Information Booth
Upper O'Connell Street
Tel. 746301

IRISH TOURIST
BOARD   Baggot Street Bridge
Dublin
Tel: 765871

AER LINGUS   40 Upper O'Connell Street
                             and
                             42 Grafton Street
                             Tel: (International) 377747
                             (Ireland and U.K.) 377777

AUTOMOBILE RENTALS

Avis Rent A Car   1 Hanover Street
                             Dublin
                             Tel: 776971

Murray- Europcar   Baggot Street Bridge
                             Dublin
                             Tel: 681777

Hertz   19-21 Pearse Street
                             Dublin
                             Tel: 772971

Dan Ryan Rent A Car   2 Fitzwilliam Place
                             Dublin
                             Tel: 765594

Though there are many other car rental agencies in Ireland,
    these have been chosen because they accept all major
    credit cards and have offices across the country which
    can assist you if there is any difficulty. For those who
    wish, each of these firms offers chauffeur-driven cars.
    REMEMBER ... Driving in Ireland is on the lefthand
    side. GO SLOWLY.

(Parking: Double yellow line indicates parking is prohib-
    ited.)

ADDITIONAL NAMES AND ADDRESSES

SHANNON CIRCLE

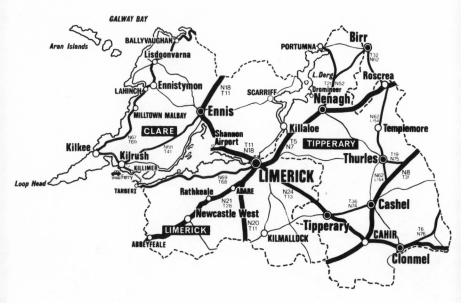

COUNTY CLARE

HOTELS   COUNTRY HOUSES   FARMS

ENNIS

*OLD GROUND HOTEL (H)
(065-21127)

When you approach the Old Ground, it appears as though the hotel has grown up in the middle of an oversized topiary. The hotel was the home of an old Clare clan, the O'Gorman Mahons. The story goes that a nephew in London inherited the mansion, and on the evening of his return to take up residence the old retainer met him at the entrance taking his hand, "You are welcome back to the ould ground." Hence the name. Warm receptions are still the tone set for visitors by manager Brian Oldfield and his staff. The hotel extended the facilities with a modern addition a few years ago, but it hasn't diminished the Old World atmosphere. A meal at the Old Ground alone is worth a journey to Clare — the superb continental cuisine and excellent wine list mellow the evening after a day of golfing, fishing, or touring the Clare coast.

Season: All year round   AE, CB, DC
Luncheon: 12:30 - 2:30
Dinner: 7:00 - 9:00

KEY
H - Hotel
CH - Country House
C - Castle
F - Farm
* - Indicates a hotel with an
   outstanding restaurant,
   should be visited.
( ) - Telephone number

CREDIT CARDS
AE - American Express
CB - Carte Blanche
DC - Diners Club
V - Visa/BankAmericard
   (Many places have begun
   to use *Visa*, though they
   have not listed it officially.
   Check in advance.)

LAHINCH

*ABERDEEN ARMS (H)
(Lahinch 20)

Some visitors before they come to Ireland have imagined the perfect stay — a hotel set nearby roaring Atlantic, bleached white beaches, challenging golf courses, fresh homemade meals, a place to meet the Irish, and an embullient host-patron brimming with Irish wit and hospitality. All those expectations and more are standard offerings at Michael Vaughan's Aberdeen Arms. The Vaughan family took over the hotel ten years ago and renovated all the rooms in modern, tasteful décor. The dining room has the advantage of the best Atlantic "catch," "Burren" lamb, and "Clare" beef. And the wine list is good and moderately priced. The "crack" in the bars always seems to linger on till the wee hours. Michael Vaughan and his brother Eamon run one of the envied hotels in the country ... it has everything.

Season: Easter — October 30   AE, DC,
Luncheon: 1:00-2:30
Dinner: 7:00-8:45

KILLALOE

LAKESIDE HOTEL (H)
(061-76122)

One advantage of the Lakeside Hotel is that it happens to be located in one of the prettiest villages in Ireland on the banks of Lough Derg. There's no pretense to elegance, but perfect for the traveling family holiday. There's a swimming pool, riding school, and waterskiing on the hotel grounds. The food is simple and well prepared if unexciting. In the evening the hotel's Nautical Bar along the waterside is packed with guests and locals. Saturday evening entertainment.

Season: All year round   AE, DC,
Luncheon: 1:00 - 2:30
Dinner: 7:00 - 9:00

NEWMARKET
on FERGUS

*DROMOLAND CASTLE (C)
(061-71144)

Everyone's dreamt of a night in a castle, though a hundred years ago an Irish emigrant passing Dromoland on his way to America would hardly have dreamt that his grandson, Bernard McDonagh, would return to Ireland and turn this Gothic castle into one of the most elegant resort hotels in the world. Mr. McDonagh spared nothing when he bought the residence and its 1500 acres from the descendants of the ancient O'Brien clan. The temptation after a few hours at Dromoland would be to never move from the castle grounds during your stay in Ireland. Everything you can imagine is within the castle walls — riding, fishing, wild goose and duck shooting, boating, tennis, and an 18-hole golf course. The halls and lounges are crowded with rare antique Irish furniture, and oversized portraits of the O'Brien clan line the foyer. The chef of Dromoland has won well-deserved international awards, and the wine lists rare and extensive. The only hint of the modern world beyond the gates is in the beautifully renovated rooms filled with floral prints. The grande dame of the castle is Miss Barry, who will look after you and seems to be able to arrange any whim. A visit is passing through past elegance.

Season: April 1 - November 1   AE, DC,
Luncheon: 1:00 - 2:30
Dinner: 7:00 - 9:00

QUIN

BALLAKILTY MANOR (CH)
(065-25627)

For those who prefer the country house atmosphere the Tom Conroys' Georgian manor set back from the main Shannon thoroughfare is relaxed and sporting. Ballakilty is the former homestead of the infamous Blood family since 1614, one of whom stole the British Crown jewels during the reign of Charles II. The kitchen, coach houses, and stables are all part of the original building. The rooms are spacious, cheerful, and light, and the food fresh local produce.

Season: All year round
Luncheon: 1:00 - 2:30
Dinner: 6:00 - 7:30

RESTAURANTS AND PUBS

BUNRATTY
DURTY NELLY'S

There's no particular time of day or evening when you're passing Roger Porrit's white-thatched pub up on the grounds of Bunratty Castle that you won't find something going on, and it will be packed. Pat Sheehey is the resident host, serving up luscious smoked salmon, fresh brown bread, and frothy pints of Guinness. Around 8 P.M. the piano player arrives for the roaring ballad sessions. The pub's been a watering hole since 1620, and Pat searched the country to find all the old fittings and furnishings to restore it to its original look. Be sure to make at least one stop ... and you'll find yourself going back again and again.

Open: 11:00 A.M. - 11:30 P.M. daily
Pub lunches served all day and evening

DOOLIN
O'CONNELL'S PUB

Even if you can spend only an evening or a few hours in this solitary pub along the Clare coast, it will be one Irish night you'll always remember. One of the half dozen pubs in Ireland where you'll always find a cluster of musicians — fiddlers, pipers, tin whistle players — gathering for the music. And it's not geared for tourists, and nothing is put on.

Reels, jigs, and slow airs fill the night air. Be sure to drop in for awhile if you are in Clare.

ANTIQUES TRAIL

ENNIS

HONAN BROTHERS
(21137)
Tony Honan

SIX MILE BRIDGE

THISS 'n THATT
(72213)
John and Nancy Hawkshaw

ENTERTAINMENT

BUNRATTY

BUNRATTY CASTLE BANQUET

When the 17th century Gaelic poets lamented the death of the Gaelic order with all its gaiety and sybaritic pleasures, they couldn't have foreseen the plans at Shannon for their castle banquet nights — a rollicking return to medieval Ireland. You're welcomed at the door with a jug of mead — the ancient brew of honey and apple — and then invited in to the Great Hall for the banquet itself — sumptuous *removues*...and no silverware, as the old days. Throughout the evening castle wenches entertain with songs and music and recitations. It's fair to warn that if you don't like crowds and intervals of raucous entertainment, perhaps you'd better choose another castle banquet and visit Bunratty Castle during the day. Bunratty stands on the island of Tradraighe on the banks of the Shannon, and was built in the mid-15th century. The castle was a stronghold of the O'Briens, kings of Thomond. Rinnuccini, the Papal Nuncio, wrote of Bunratty during a visit in 1646: "Bunratty is the most beautiful spot I have ever seen. In Italy there is nothing like the grounds and palaces of Lord Thomond." The castle was restored to its medieval magnificence, with all its 15th-century furnishings, by the late Lord Gort, who bequeathed it to the Irish nation.

Open: All year round   AE, DC,
Banquets: Twice nightly 6:00 and 9:00
Reservations: Shannon Castle Tours (061-61788)
Castle: Open daily — 9:30 A.M.-5:00 P.M.
Be sure to make reservations well in advance during the summer season.

BUNRATTY

SHANNON CEILI
Bunratty Folk Park

A perfect way to end the day in this 19th-century folk village at an Irish *ceili* (meaning dance in Irish). In the early evening fiddlers, pipers, tin whistle players, other musicians begin to arrive in the park for the village dance, but first a traditional dinner. The food is not as grand as the castle fare next door (it never was), but still there are those who prefer a plate filled with Irish stew, and fresh brown bread and homemade apple tarts. The girls make all the jigs and reels seem so easy, but don't be fooled ... the art of Irish dance is something in the blood. An Irish evening is never complete without the town shanachie — he'll sit by the fireside entertaining you, as shanachies have done for hundreds of years.

Season: April 15 - October 31   AE, DC,
Ceilis: Twice nightly 6:00 and 9:00
Reservations: Shannon Castle Tours (061-61788)

QUIN

KNAPPOGUE CASTLE BANQUET

The MacNamaras (meaning, in Gaelic, Son of the Hound of

the Sea) were for centuries one of the most powerful warrior tribes in Clare and by 1580 had built over forty castles in the territory of Clancullen, including Knappogue between Limerick and Ennis. Each evening after the luscious banquet of Clare salmon, spicy beef, fruits, cheeses, and jugs of wine, the Knappogue players take their guests back to visit the castle's medieval lords. For the next few hours their poignant historical pageant, written by Kerryman Bryan MacMahon, traces the castle life of the medieval stronghold, laced with love ballads, drinking songs, and warrior chants, through the broken spirit of the years of Cromwellian confiscation to the stormy days of the Troubles. The evening ends with the patriot's song, "A Nation Once Again" — a reminder that Ireland's sad days continue. It's an evening not to be missed, and the memory will linger on for days.

Banquets: April 1 - October 31 AE, DC,
    Twice nightly 6:00 and 9:00
Reservations: Shannon Castle Tours (061-61788)
Castle: Open daily all year 10:00 A.M. - 5:00 P.M.

DIVERSIONS

BUNRATTY

BUNRATTY FOLK PARK
(061-61511)

Before the jet age eclipsed all traces of rural Irish life, John Hunt, a leading Irish art historian, and some people at Shannon began to collect and reconstruct various Irish homes across the Shannon Circle — from humble one-room cottages to the grander farmhouses. Not only architecture, but the sounds and smells of rural life in the Folk Park carry you back a century — the clanking of the blacksmith's hammer, the thud of the maid churning the butter, the scent of soda bread baking over the turf fire. Refreshments in the cottage Tearoom and Crafts Shop.

Open: All year round 10:00 A.M. - 5:30 P.M.

KILRUSH

SCATTERY ISLAND

This tiny island off the coast of Kilrush is filled with relics of
the beginning centuries of Christianity in Ireland. Saint
Senan founded the monastery in the beginning of the 6th
century, and like Saint Kevin in Glendolough was notorious
for his antipathy toward women. In the small chapel is his
gravestone inscribed in Irish. The monastery was continu-
ally assaulted by invaders, and as protection one of the
largest Round Towers in the country is extant on the island.
It rises over 120 feet and has the unusual feature of a
ground-floor entrance.

LAHINCH

THE CLIFFS OF MOHER

These eerie ancient cliffs along the Clare coast rising over 700
feet above the roaring Atlantic are one of the most glorious
views in Ireland. Not far in the distance from the
19th-century O'Brien's Tower are the Aran Islands and Galway Bay. The cliffs were named after the ancient fort
"Mothair" on Hag's Head, which disappeared in the last
century. The nearby village of Liscannor was the birthplace
of John Holland, who invented the submarine, hoping by his
invention to defeat the British Navy and free his country.

THE BURREN

These strange limestone fields in the Barony of Burren
spread over fifty miles along the azure Atlantic. Hundreds of
rare species of flora and fauna of distant origin — from the
Arctic to the Mediterranean — dig into its craggy surface.
During Cromwell's days an officer described this westerly
coast: "Not a tree whereon to hang a man; not water in which
to drown him; no soil in which to bury him." Popular round
for the botanist and hiker.

QUIN

QUIN ABBEY

This old monastery takes its name from the Irish *Cuinche,* meaning arbutus grove. An unknown religious community is believed to have established a spiritual center on the site about the 11th century. The Abbey over the years has been a Franciscan Friary, a station for Elizabethan troops, and a home among the ruins for the last known friar in 1820. The Abbey architecture is Irish Romanesque, and five of the altars remain in perfect condition. Also of interest are the tombs of the MacNamaras of Knappogue.

CRAGGAUNOWEN PROJECT

This wonderful "living museum" was begun a few years ago by John Hunt, who also oversaw the restoration of Bunratty Castle. Mr. Hunt bought the castle to house his vast collection of Irish antiquities, considered the most comprehensive outside the National Museum of Ireland and the Ulster Museum. Last year he added a 300-foot replica of a *crannog* to the project. The *crannog* was an Irish lake dwelling — man made — used in the late Bronze Age as a defense fort. Craggauowen Crannog was built with 15-foot larch poles from the local forest, and 8,000 wattles were woven around the circumference. The circular house took ten tons of mud to cover its walls and 3,600 bales of rushes to thatch its roof. The crannog huts are furnished with tools, weapons, and utensils.

Open: Daily 9:30 A.M. -5:00 P.M.

COUNTY LIMERICK

HOTELS   COUNTRY HOUSES   FARMS

ADARE
DUNRAVEN ARMS (H)
(061-94209)

Adare is one of the most beautiful villages in Ireland, and the ivy-covered inn along the main street caters to the sporting life enthusiasts — hunting, shooting, and fishing in season. The inn belongs to the Earl of Dunraven, who resides across the road in Adare Manor.

Dinner is served in an elegant small period dining room filled with the Earl's antiques. Meals are simple and well prepared. Wine list limited.

Season: All year round   AE
Luncheon: 1:00 - 2:30
Dinner: 7:30 - 9:00

RESTAURANTS and PUBS

GLIN
GLIN CASTLE GATE SHOP
(068-34188)

Along the banks of the Shannon the present Knight of Glin has opened the Georgian Gothic folly at the edge of his estate, serving lovely luncheons prepared by his manageress, Joan Stack. If you call ahead she'll be more than happy to prepare a dinner if you're in the area in the evening, but give her warning by noon the same day. Joan is an excellent cook *and* full of local information of this ancient area.

Season: May - September
Open: 10:00 A.M. - 7:30 P.M.
Meals served throughout the day including dinner

ANTIQUES TRAIL

LIMERICK

THOMOND ANTIQUES
George Stacpoole
35 Cecil Street
(061-45433)

BUYERS MARKET

GLIN

GLIN CASTLE GATE SHOP
(068-34188)

Madam Fitzgerald and Joan Stack have searched the country for the highest quality of Irish goods. They've found something for everyone — elegant ladies, traditional cloaks, brightly colored crocheted skirts and dresses, unusual sweaters, and tweeds in every form. They also have an excellent selection of Irish books. As they say, "well worth the journey."

PALLASKENRY
(near Askeaton)

MICHELINA STACPOOLE LTD.
(061-93119)

Michelina Stacpoole came to Ireland from Italy a few years ago, met and married an Irishman, and then decided to open her own knitting mill in this tiny Limerick village. The result is a boutique filled with some of the most beautiful fashions available, not only in Ireland but any couturier center. And the prices for her lovely knits are so reasonable! Call ahead to make sure Michelina will be there.

Open: Monday — Friday

SHANNON

SHANNON AIRPORT DUTY-FREE CENTER
Airport Terminal

Something to look forward to with your shrunken purse as you depart Ireland. This compact department store has both Irish and international merchandise *all* duty free. Because of Shannon's popularity, difficult-to-find Irish goods around the country are usually well stocked in the center, so don't worry if you arrive for your flight home having forgotten a gift for someone Stateside. Only be sure to arrive at the airport well in advance of your flight — you need time to wander through the stalls, since some buys are better than others.

ENTERTAINMENT

LIMERICK

FESTIVAL OF THEATRE

This summertime festival began only in 1974 as the West Coast complement to Dublin's Theatre Festival in the fall. It draws on much of Ireland's talent involved in the theatre — playwrights, producers, and the various theatre companies — the Abbey Theatre Company, the Lyric Players Company of Belfast, National Theatre Company, and, last season, the visiting London Theatre Company. The Festival goes on for six weeks, from mid-August to the end of September. Tickets are available through the local tourist office.

DIVERSIONS

ADARE

ADARE MANOR
(061-94119)

This Gothic mansion has been the ancestral home of the Earls of Dunraven since the 17th century. However, the history of the estate is recorded back to the Desmond clan of the 13th century, and the ruins of their towers and keeps are scattered around the grounds. The original home was a small Georgian house built by Vincent Quin in 1720, a descendant of the O'Quins of Inchquin, one of the ancient Gaelic families. The present mansion was built as an extension to the manor by the 2nd Earl of Dunraven in 1832 and took over thirty years to complete. No fewer than three architects were involved in the plans. The house is full of treasures collected by the Earl during his travels. The exquisite tapestries were done by the locals during the Famine. The geometrical box garden was designed by Hardwicke. The present Earl of Dunraven and his family occupy a wing of Adare Manor.

Season: March 24-October 31
Monday - Friday: 10:00 A.M. - 5:30 P.M.
Closed Saturday
Sunday: 2:00 - 5:30 P.M.

LOUGH GUR

This small lake south of Limerick is a find for antiquarians. Many ancient artifacts were found at the bottom of the lake when it was dredged in the late 19th century. Located near the lake at Grange is the largest pagan stone circle in Ireland, a megalithic tomb dating back to the Bronze Age, and two stone forts calculated to have been constructed during the Viking period. Also located at the lake are two crannogs — man-made islands popular with the ancients as fortified forts.

GLIN

GLIN CASTLE
(068-34173)

By special advance arrangements, selected groups such as those affiliated with museums, art galleries and garden clubs may have organized a guided tour of the Castle. Glin Castle has long been regarded as containing one of the finest collections of Irish paintings and furniture.
Please make all requests in writing to:
>   Madam Fitz-Gerald
>   Glin Castle
>   Glin, Co. Limerick

◇ ◇ ◇

When traveling from the Tarbert area in Limerick across to County Clare, 100 miles can be cut from the journey by taking the car ferry that runs between Tarbert and Kilrush. It departs every three hours in the summer. It's an inexpensive shortcut and enables a tour of Clare's southern peninsula.

COUNTY TIPPERARY

HOTELS   COUNTRY HOUSES   FARMS

CASHEL

CASHEL PALACE HOTEL (H)
(062-61253)

Travelers tended to race from Dublin to Kerry or the West and ignore the mid-country until recently, when the Cashel Palace Hotel was renovated, and ever since hardly anyone passes without a stop. The hotel was formerly built for the Archbishop in the 18th century and reflects all the opulence due those gentlemen in olden days. Up the sweeping front hall stairs are enormous rooms decorated in regal splendor looking out on the famous Rock of Cashel. The staff is one of the most efficient and friendly in the country. Below the main floor is the Derby Kitchen, with an excellent grill menu and an atmosphere geared toward the horsey set. (One of the directors is Vincent O'Brien, among Ireland's most prestigious horse trainers.) The dining room upstairs is more elegant, with a Continental menu and substantial wine list.

Season: All year round
Luncheon: 12:30-2:30
Dinner: 7:00 - 9:30
AE, DC,

Derby Kitchen
Luncheon: 12:30 - 2:30
Dinner: 6:30 - 9:30
Sunday: Noon - 9:30

RESTAURANTS

CASHEL

CHEZ HANS
(062-61177)

In 1967 Hans Peter Matthaie and his Irish wife, Derry, bought this tiny Gothic chapel in the shadow of the Rock of Cashel and transformed it almost overnight into one of Ireland's most acclaimed restaurants. As can be imagined, the chapel was not Catholic, but built by a rebel Wesleyan, James Morton, in 1852, hoping to establish a sect in the community. Hans was born in Mainz and traveled across the Continent honing his culinary talent in such cuisine capitals as Lugano and Paris. Derry is the greeter and oversees the guests, and it's unlikely you'll even meet Hans during your stop — from early afternoon till late evening he disappears into the kitchen preparing his daily *specialités*. The only mistake you may make visiting Chez Hans is to eat *anything* within twenty-four hours before your meal...the courses are many, and the portions enough for two.

Luncheon: 12:30-2:00
Dinner: 6:30-9:30
Reservations advised
Closed Monday

ANTIQUES TRAIL

CASHEL

CASHEL ANTIQUES
Joseph & Nora Barry
(Cashel 278)

TIPPERARY

COURTVILLE ANTIQUES
Catherine Pierse
(062-51249)

DIVERSIONS

CASHEL

ROCK OF CASHEL

Patrick's Rock is a limestone mound swelling 300 feet about the low Tipperary countryside and has been used as a fortification of power since the first invasions of Ireland. In the 5th century it was built as a stone fort by the King of Munster, who at the time refused to recognize the overking of Ireland at Tara. Legend says that Saint Patrick explained the Trinity by the leaves of the shamrock at Cashel. He baptized King Aengus, and from that time on the kings of Cashel were often both kings and ecclesiastics. In 1101 Murtough O'Brien gave the fort to the Church as a gift. The Round Tower is believed to have been constructed in the 10th century; it is 85 feet in height, and the walls are four feet thick. The doorway into the tower is 14 feet overhead. The small Romanesque Cormac's Chapel to the side of the cathedral was built by Cormac MacCarthy, King of Desmond in 1127. Forty years later Donal Mor O'Brien, King of Thormond, built a newer, larger cathedral. This was destroyed and replaced by what presently stands in ruins. In 1495 Gerald, the great Earl of Kildare, set fire to the cathedral. When asked by King Henry the VII why he had done this, he replied, "Because I thought the Archbishop was inside." When the Archbishop heard this, he said, "All Ireland cannot rule this man." The King answered, "Then he shall rule all Ireland." For the next few hundred years it was repeatedly vandalized and rebuilt, until 1874, when the ruins were given to the country.

GOLDEN

ATHASSAL

Along the River Suir off the main road from the village stand the ruins of what was once the largest and wealthiest Norman monastery in Ireland. At one time the Prior was a lord in Parliament. This Augustinian monastery was founded by William de Burgo in 1193, who had been granted lands from here through Connacht by King John. The style of architecture is Early English. The town that surrounded the monastery was destroyed by the O'Briens in the 14th century, and in 1447 the monastery itself was sacked and became the property of the Earl of Ormond. Today it sits still by the river as a large granite crow's nest.

NEWTOWN

GLEN OF AHERLOW

This lush green valley in South Tipperary — so peaceful and secluded — was for hundreds of years the site of battles among the Irish and later with the English. Bordering the Glen are the Galtee Mountains, the highest range in Ireland, climbing to 3,000 feet. The Fitzpatricks and O'Briens fought here over landownership, but the O'Briens were able to maintain their stronghold for 300 years. The caves in the Galtee hills were used as hiding places during the battles. A perfect place to spend a lazy day walking the hills. Take the road to Bansha and on to Rosswoodbog. Park the car and take the path into the lakes. For a drink along the way stop into P. Condon's country pub.

THOMASTOWN
THOMASTOWN CASTLE

The ruined 18th-century castle was once the home of the Mathews, the Earls of Llandall. The mansion was built by the last Earl for the purpose of accommodating forty guests, whom he would invite free of charge, and they were expected to stay as long as they wished, enjoying the hospitality of their eccentric host. Dean Swift stayed on for nearly four months. Another Mathew descendant, Father Mathew, born in 1790, abhored the sybaritic atmosphere and traveled the country preaching abstinence — he later became known as the Apostle of Temperance. A statue of Father Mathew stands in the town square.

CRUISING THE SHANNON

It's very near impossible to slow people down to a lazy holiday, especially if they want to try a bit of everything — fishing, swimming, water-skiing, touring ancient ruins, visiting local pubs and restaurants, *and* relaxing, all while trying to avoid a lot of traveling. But there is a way...cruising the Shannon aboard your own private cabin cruiser. Whether for two days or two weeks, you'll drift along this ancient river winding through over one hundred miles of verdant Irish countryside, changeless for hundreds of years. You're the captain of your own ship and can linger or move on from dozens of tiny port villages, such as Killaloe, Portumna, Athlone, according to your whim. The Shannon swells into larger lakes — Loch Allen, Loch Ree, and Loch Derg, with their ancient crannogs and scattered islands to investigate. Some days there may be a rally or sailing regatta and others your only company may be a passing swan or two.

In typical Irish spirit it doesn't matter whether you know about boating. The captains will teach you in the morning or till you feel secure, and then you're on your own. (But don't worry, there is always help nearby.)

If you're feeling adventurous, there are two popular rallies during the season: Shannon Harbor Canal Boat Rally from Shannon bridge the third week in June and the Shannon Boat Rally the last week in July. If you're sailing the Shannon during the first two weeks of July, plan on a stop at Carrick-on-Shannon for the Festival of the Shannon, a chance to hear traditional music, see a football match or canoe races, and other festivities.

There are many firms renting cruisers along the Shannon, ranging from two to eight berths. If you let them know in advance, they'll stock your boat with plenty of delicious Irish food and booze. They will also arrange to collect you at Shannon when you arrive. *The Shannon Guide* is a must during the trip, filled with navigational maps even a novice can understand, descriptions of ports and ancient ruins, wildlife and fishing. Ask ahead of time to reserve a copy. These are a few suggestions:

CORMACRUISERS LTD.
The Marina
Killaloe, Co. Clare
        (Limerick 49485)   2 to 6 berths

CARRICK CRAFT
Carrick-on-Shannon
Co. Leitrim
        (Carrick-on-Shannon 236)   2 to 8 berths

EMERALD STAR LINE
Carrick-on-Shannon
Co. Leitrim
    (Carrick-on-Shannon 234)   4 to 8 berths

FLAG LINE
Carrick-on-Shannon
Co. Leitrim
    (Carrick-on-Shannon 172)   4 to 8 berths

ATHLONE CRUISERS
Shanourragh
Athlone
Co. Westmeath
    (Athlone 2892)   3 to 8 berths

All boats are equipped with refrigerator, hot and cold water, gas cooker, toilet, electric lighting, life jackets, and others on request have shower, central heating, and other extras.

Additional names of firms, rates, and varieties of boats may be obtained from:

Irish Hire Boat Operators Ltd.
23 Clyde Road
Ballsbridge, Dublin 4
(680674)

CORK/KERRY CIRCLE

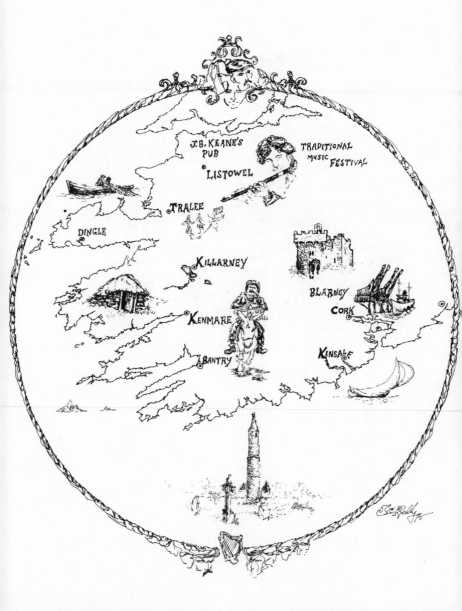

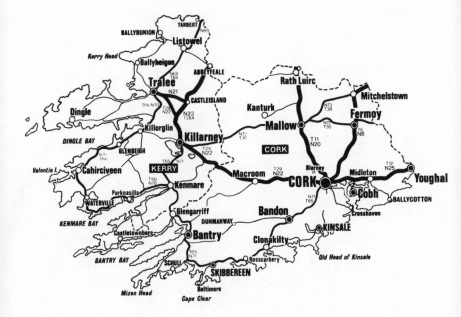

COUNTY CORK

HOTELS   COUNTRY HOUSES   FARM

BALLINASCARTY
ARDNAVAHA HOUSE HOTEL (CH)
(023-49135)

This 18th-century country house combines the luxuries of three centuries. The rolling forty acres of wooded land have remained untouched and may be enjoyed on horseback from the hotel's stable. A few years ago the hotel added a modern wing and a swimming pool in the center courtyard, with an adjacent sauna and solarium. Also on the grounds are tennis and croquet, and only a mile away a lawn tennis club. Nearby is the harbor town of Courtmacsherry, where fishing and boating may be arranged. All twenty-four bedrooms are with bath and telephone. The cuisine is Continental.

Season: Easter, April-November

BALLYLICKEY
*BALLYLICKEY HOUSE HOTEL (CH)
(Bantry 71)

Mr. and Mrs. Christian Graves have created one of the most elegant stays in Ireland. Originally built as a shooting lodge for Lord Kenmare in 1650, each room has been decorated with delicate French fabrics, some with canopied beds, and touched with fresh flowers each day from the garden. Modern chalets surround the swimming pool and are ideal for families. Though a cold buffet is served daily around the pool, weather permitting, the real fame of Ballylickey is centered in the main house. Few restaurants in Ireland can rival their haute cuisine or their wine cellar. Depending on the whim of the chef, a soufflé may appear in the first course of fish or later tempt the diner in rich chocolate or fresh fruit.

Each day the menu changes, making the only effort of the day to choose among the dozen specialities. Mr. Graves requests that you make your choice of wine well in advance in order that it may be served at the correct temperature. If you plan to have a meal only at Ballylickey, be sure to book in advance.

Season: April - mid-May   AE
Luncheon: 1:00 - 2:45
Dinner: 7:30 - 9:00 (High season: 7:15 *or* 8:30)

KANTURK
ASSOLAS HOUSE (CH)
(Kanturk 15)

Though the ivy-covered Queen Anne facade is that of a stately residence, the atmosphere in the Bourkes' house is geared to easy relaxation. Mrs. Bourke oversees the kitchen with the help of her daughters, and preference is given to residents. But if you call in advance, you may be able to book a reservation. A light buffet luncheon is served, but in the evening the menu offers freshly caught fish from the local Blackwater River, or veal, which is rare in Ireland, or local lamb. The desserts are always homemade, usually of berries out of the garden. Eating is not the only pastime at Assolas.... fishing, hunting in season, riding, and tennis are all part of the activity when you are with the Bourkes.

Season: April 15-October 15
Luncheon: 1:00
Dinner: 7:30

KINSALE
ACTON'S (H)
(021-72135)

Along the waterfront of one of Ireland's most historic harbors. The hotel is one of the Trust House Forte group, which also runs the Shelbourne Hotel in Dublin. The only way to describe the hotel is comfortable and clean and the food banal. But Kinsale itself is one of the most beautiful resort towns in the country, and most of your time should be spent *outside* the hotel. There are at least a half-dozen excellent restaurants in the town, so don't waste precious gourmet moments on the hotel's dinner menu.

Season: All year round   AE, CB, DC, V

TRIDENT (H)
(021-72301)

Modern glass hotel set among the boat quays. All rooms available with baths, and the décor is like most every other modern hotel in the world. It is comfortable and clean with each room having a lovely sea view. Excellent angling center, and hotel will make all arrangements. Very active nautical bar on the first floor. The hotel restaurant is average fare.

Season: All year round

KINSALE
*THE MONASTERY (CH)
(021-72664)

This tiny renovated monastery is a jewel for anyone who prefers intimate unusual surroundings. Situated on seven wooded acres overlooking the River Bandon, only a few minutes walk from the harbor town. The proprietors, Anne and Dick Burmby, have a rare sense of detail for the finest they can offer their guests. The rooms are delightful and all with baths. The meals are full of originality and high quality, and nonresidents are welcome. A stay here is not to be missed, but be sure to make reservations well in advance, since there are only ten rooms.

Open: All year round   AE, DC,
Dinner: 7:30-10:00

KNOCKRAHA

ASHTON GROVE (F)
(021-821537)

This Georgian farmhouse is the residence of Mrs. Nancy Fitzgerald, who is president of the Farmhouse Association. Mrs. Fitzgerald told us that she has one couple who returned for their ninth visit last summer, which is a tribute to her home cooking and warm hospitality. Ashton Grove is remote, but riding and golfing are available locally, along with fishing in the Blackwater River.

Season: All year round

MALLOW
*LONGUEVILLE HOUSE (CH)
(022-27156)

There's a temptation every once in a while to try and keep a place a private find for awhile ... but, unfortunately, Michael and Jane O'Callaghan's Georgian manor gets more popular *and* more well known each year. Every aspect of the 500-acre estate belongs to another era ... a roaring fire in the sitting room after dinner, billiards in the game room, and in the cellar one of the most vast wine collections in the country (and one of the most reasonable). The mistress of the house, Jane O'Callaghan, however, is anything but "Old World." She seems to be going 26 hours a day. With the help of a few local girls, she prepares every feast, and when the house closes down for the winter months she takes a "vacation" in London at the Cordon Bleu to gather a few new recipes for the next season. *Everything* on the table is grown on the farm, from the freshly killed lamb or beef to the day's catch of salmon or trout. The excesses come with dessert...flans, gateaux, fromages of all varieties. Luncheon is reserved for residents.

Eighteen elegantly decorated Georgian rooms, only eight with bath.

Season: end March to mid-October
Dinner: 7:00-8:45 (closed on Sundays and Mondays to non-residents). Reservations advised

SHANAGARRY
*BALLYMALOE HOUSE (CH)
(021) 62531

It's difficult to imagine so many sybaritic delights in one household. Ivan and Myrtle Allen's 400-acre country house farm was originally an old Geraldine castle, which, over the centuries, became extended and modernized, though a 14th-century keep still stands on the grounds. No one should go to Ballymaloe who has not a few days to spend. Each of the fifteen rooms in the main house has been decorated in an individual theme, and works of well-known Irish artists are enjoyed throughout the house. Across the old cobblestone courtyard in the 16th-century gatehouse are rooms the Allens have renovated for children or less expensive accommodation for guests. They've even thought of the couple on the wedding trip — secluded in a one-bedroom gatehouse. Every possible recreation is available on the grounds, with a swimming pool, tennis court, 9-hole golf course, and horses and ponies and fishing. Ballymaloe is a family enterprise...their son has just returned from farming in Australia for a few years to help his father and eventually to take over Ballymaloe, while last year his sister Wendy opened one of the finest craft and gift shops in the country. Her choices and finds are most .unusual, and, inventive herself, she has gotten local craftsmen to produce some of her ideas. The Yeats Rooms are a maze of intimate candlelit rooms that have won almost every international award for cuisine. Some of the finest of Jack B. Yeats's paintings hang on the walls when they are not out on loan to museums and galleries for exhibition. With hundreds of acres of working farmland, *everything* at Ballymaloe is home produced. Each day Mrs. Allen's culinary genius presents a limited but unusual menu. One of the most popular restaurants in the country, it is always necessary to book. Closed on Sundays and Mondays to nonresidents.

Season: All year round
Luncheon: 1:00 - 2:30
Dinner: 7:00 - 11:30 Must book

SCHULL
*ARD na GREINE INN (CH)
(028-28181)

West Cork has always offered the most breathtaking hours of pleasure with its scenery and antiquities. However, much less could be said for its accommodations. Finally, an absolute treasure has appeared. Frank and Rhoda O'Sullivan, after returning from living in Africa, took over this first-class inn. The 18th-century converted farm sits high on a hill, a little way out from Schull, overlooking the magnificent Cork coast. During their first season the O'Sullivans filled many of the rooms with African mementoes, but this fall they closed to do renovations and hopefully the new rooms will have a more Irish theme. Rhoda is usually found in the kitchen, or trekking to the local market to find the freshest fish and vegetables available that day. The results are simply, quite impressive. The desserts are homemade and accompanied by the best coffee outside Bewley's. The wine list is good. A memorable stay is assured.

Season: March 31-October 30
Lunch: 12:30-2:30 (Pub style)
Dinner: 8:00-10:00

RESTAURANTS and PUBS

BALLYDEHOB
BASIL BUSH
(Ballydehob 59)

If you are traveling too quickly you might very well pass not only this wonderful restaurant but the town itself. West Cork seems to specialize in tiny towns, saving grandeur for vistas and coastlines. Alfie Lyons has created a restaurant proving "less is more." In this bright, charming stone room only twenty can dine, seated on glossy white park benches at tables covered with green-and-white checkered cloths and small vases of fresh flowers. Each course is served on clay pottery made locally. The food is as unusual as the presentation. One evening the menu offered: marinated mackerel in a white wine and herb sauce, smoked eel, homemade paté, and French onion soup. For the main course there was: pan-fried trout, fresh salmon with an airy hollandaise sauce and an unusually spicy Chicken Marengo. Each meal is accompanied with an individual loaf of homemade sour dough bread. There was a choice of four desserts and an excellent cheese tray. The wine list is small but appealing.

Lunch: 12:00-2:00
Dinner: 7:00-10:00 (Reservations)
Closed Sunday and Winter

CASTLETOWNSHEND
MARY ANN'S BAR
(Castletownshend 15)

A strange find tucked in the harbor town of Castletownshend along the Cork coastline. It seems to be merely another Irish pub on the outside, but once you can secure a reservation for dinner you can rely on the most delicious seafare and French cusine from Norman Davis and his wife. The menu is seasonal and depends on the local catch of the day, but if you let them know in advance of a particular preference, they'll see what they can do. Very popular with the locals and doesn't particularly care to cater to tourist trade, so book in advance.

Luncheon: 12:30
Dinner: 7:30

CROOKHAVEN
JOURNEY'S END
(028-35183)

If you pleasure in the unexpected, then an evening at Ina Manahan's is a necessity. This attractive woman, who is also a very good chef, runs a very popular restaurant in this gorgeous harbor village. Her menu changes on a whim, and just about everything is homemade — from soup and bread to profiteroles. While you're eating you may hear someone singing in the kitchen . . . it's Mrs. Manahan. The phone doesn't always work, so she suggests you come out during the day and make a reservation or just take your chances and come in the evening.

Open: June-early September
Dinner: 7:30-9:00

KILLBRITTAIN
THE PINK ELEPHANT
(023-49608)

Bill and Betty Weafer took over this former coast guard cottage overlooking Courtmacsherry Bay about three years ago. The food is good, solid fare, though sometimes unimaginative, but it's a good stop along the way touring the coastline out of Kinsale. You can sit and have a drink in their outdoor garden and stay on for dinner.

Dinner: 5:30-9:30

KINSALE
GINO'S
Market Square
(021-72374)

One of the disappearing host-patrons, Gino Gaio emerges from the kitchen at intervals to be sure you had enough of his creamy pasta creations or if you'd like more of any course ... and will finish up insulted if you haven't room for one of his specialties for dessert. Like all fine Italians, he has no sense of excess. Almost every entrée is sure to arrive with a special sauce. If you're a plain meat-and-potatoes diner, stay far away from Gino. Without any question one of the finest restaurants in the country and worth a journey. Be sure to book a reservation in advance, since Gino can accommodate only thirty people at a time.

Dinner: 7:30-9:45
Closed Sunday & Monday
December-March

MAN FRIDAY
(021-72260)

It's believed that the real Robinson Crusoe, Alexander Selkirk, sailed from Kinsale on the *Cinque Ports* on September 14, 1703 ... hence the name of this nautical restaurant set above the harbor in Scilly. Man Friday specializes in seafood, and their steaks are better than the average you find around Ireland. Vegetables are not always fresh. The wine list is average. You should book before 2 P.M. or after 6 P.M.

Dinner: 7:00-10:15
Closed Sunday

LE BISTRO
Guardswell
(021-72470)

Breton cooking is appearing all over Ireland. The newest Breton restaurant was opened last year by Heidi Roche. Though the menu seems almost too extensive at first glance to be first-class, the delight was in finding each course equally well prepared. Every seafood available in the area seems to appear somewhere — mussels, river trout, sea trout, salmon, lobster and crawfish and prawns. The atmosphere is informal. Good wine list.

Dinner: 7:00-10:00
Closed Monday

THE VINTAGE
Main Street
(021-72502)

A few seasons ago the Gavins dared to open another restaurant in this ambitious gourmet center, and their efforts have accomplished overwhelming results (including some awards). The menu is decidedly French, and its preparation and presentation are so unsparing that even the chauvinistic French couldn't scoff. The fish dishes are particularly imaginative — try the soufflé aux fruits de mer. The prices are surprisingly reasonable (unless they've increased since this writing). Be sure to book in advance.

Dinner: 7:00-10:30
Closed Tuesday
        Tuesday and Wednesday (October-May)
        January and February

THE SPANIARD
Scilly

This white stucco pub overlooking Kinsale Harbor in Scilly is one of the best pubs in the South, and if you're looking for a good pub lunch, grilled sandwiches or fresh salmon and brown bread are always on. In the evenings there's usually great crack, with lots of ballad singing, either professional or impromptu. Don't travel to Kinsale without at least stopping in for a pint.

HOLE IN THE WALL
off Market Street

Denis and Nora Nash returned from forty years of running a pub in England to open this pub two years ago. Mrs. Nash is an excellent guide to Kinsale and serves very good pub lunches, both hot and cold.
Closed Sunday

SCHULL

THE O'KEEFE
(Schull 7)

Along the road out of Skibbereen, the O'Keefe pub is a good stop for a midday meal. It's hidden down a lane off the main street, which leads into a courtyard where you can order your lunch al fresco or, if you prefer, sitting in front of the open hearth fire indoors, something that is getting rarer and rarer to find in the country. There's an excellent pub lunch offered, which includes toasted sandwiches of crab, salmon, ham, cheese, and other specialties.

Open: Mid-March - September 30
Closed Sunday

YOUGHAL

AHERNE'S SEAFOOD PUB
163 N. Main Street
(024-2424)

An excellent stop for a first-class pub lunch. Specializing in fresh, fresh seafood — lobster, prawns, crabs, and so on. Served with home-baked Irish brown bread.

Daily: 10:30 A.M.-11:30 P.M.   AE
Sunday: 12:30-2:00
         4:00-10:00

BUYERS MARKET

SHANAGARRY

THE BALLYMALOE SHOP
Ballymaloe House

None of the usual tourist goods. Tweeds you won't see around the country. Glassware from Kilkenny Design Center. Bed quilts made by the locals. Fine dinnerware from the Shanagarry Potters. You could safely do all your shopping in Ireland here, with prices reasonable for the quality. New merchandise arriving often. Be careful, though, the shop is open well into the evening, and it's very tempting after a luscious dinner and bottles of wine in the main house to stroll over to the shop and spend extravagantly.

CROOKHAVEN
ANNIE'S (and SOMETIMES TONI)

There's a bright mustard-colored renovated cottage in this sleepy village at the tip of Ireland that has some of the best goods in the country. Annie and, as the name says, sometimes Toni travel all over to find their interesting stock. Annie designs some of the clothes in the shop, which are very attractive and expensive, but very unusual. Open all year round; if closed, just go around the back to the pink house or down to the Crookhaven Inn to find them.

ANTIQUES TRAIL

CORK
THE ANTIQUE SHOP LTD.
17 Academy Street
(021-22950)

MARLBORO ANTIQUES AND CURIOS
11 Marlboro Street

KINSALE
ANTIQUES and BYGONES
Main Street

MALLOW
THE OLD CURIOSITY SHOP
Main Street
(022-21871)

ENTERTAINMENT

CORK

BLACKROCK CASTLE
(33737)

If you are unable to enjoy one of the castle evenings arranged near Shannon, then Cork's equivalent will be well spent. Situated along the River Lee a few miles to the east of Cork city, the castle was originally built in 1605 by Lord Mountjoy to defend the city's harbor. You have your choice of merely enjoying a drink or staying on for the banquet evening, which takes place every Sunday during the season. You may make reservations through the Tourist Board or by telephone. Unfortunately, the production isn't quite as professional as that in Shannon, nor the food as good.

Banquet: 7:30

THEATRE of the SOUTH
Opera House
Emmet Street
(22637)

Probably the best entertainment evening to be spent in the Cork area. Today there's less fascination for some Irish actors and actresses to travel to Dublin to join the Abbey, and more incentive to remain in Cork. The productions of the theatre tend to concentrate on plays by contemporary Irish writers such as John B. Keane. Tickets may be reserved by calling the theatre directly.

GROUP THEATRE
South Main Street
(22637)

An evening at the Group Theatre is a little difficult to explain, since it really is more or less an artists, commune — writers, actors, photographers, painters, with all taking turns with the hundred-odd-seat theatre.

DIVERSIONS

BANTRY
BANTRY HOUSE

One of the few remaining grand homes of Ireland where a member of the original family still lives. Mrs. Clodagh Shelswell-White is the last Earl's great-grandaughter, and has lived in the house since she was a child. The Whites purchased the residence in Bantry over two hundred years ago. However, the palatial estate was built around the time of the Union, when George III made Richard White first a baron, then a viscount, and finally Earl of Bantry. He received his title for attempting to defend Bantry Harbor from an invasion of the French fleet, which never materialized, though White captured a few French soldiers.

The house is surrounded by elaborate Italian gardens, and the interior collection contains vast Continental acquisitions — Aubusson tapestries, a variety of French period furniture, Flemish tapestries, Italian pictures, Roman mosaics, and both Chippendale and Sheraton furniture. The house remains exactly as it was when the last Earl died. Overlooking Bantry Bay.

Open: March 17-end October
Daily: 10:00 A.M.-12:30 P.M.; 2:00-6:00 P.M.
Sunday: 2:30-6:00 P.M.
Closed Saturday

BLARNEY
BLARNEY CASTLE

Probably the most well-known castle in the world next to Windsor, though all that remains of the original 15th-century castle is the keep with the "Blarney Stone" just below the battlement. Queen Elizabeth I is credited with saying to Cormac MacDermott MacCarthy in exasperation, "That is all Blarney; what he says he never means." Hence legend has come down that if you kiss the Blarney Stone you'll gain the gift of eloquence. However, kissing the stone is not all that easy. You have to turn upside down and hold on to the railings. It all seems to take a great deal of belief in legends. Nearby are the Groves of Blarney, where some of the trees are believed to be over three thousand years old. Another legend at Blarney is that when the castle was being attacked, MacCarthy dumped all his treasures into the lake, though none have been found.

Open daily: 9:00 A.M.-8:00 P.M.

DONERAILE

KILCOLMAN

For those who prefer tracing literary trails the ruins of Edmund Spenser's Kilcolman Castle and its surrounding woods and streams will recall verses of his *Faerie Queen* and *Colin Clouts Come Home Again,* both written at Doneraile. After the Desmond rebellion in 1586 Spenser was given Kilcolman and 3,000 acres. He lived on and off in Ireland for the next decade until 1598, when the castle was attacked and set afire. Though he and his wife escaped to London, their infant son was burned. Another of Ireland's literary figures, Canon Sheehan, lived and wrote in Doneraile in the late 19th century, and a statue commemorating him stands in the town square.

EYERIES

Standing on the outskirts of this tiny village on the Beare Peninsula along Coulagh Bay is the highest known Ogham stone in Ireland — 17½ feet tall. These ancient pagan stones were erected as commemoration, and the inscriptions of dissecting lines were the writing forms of the ancient Irish before Christianity translated their script into a Latin alphabet. Also nearby are an ancient stone fort and *souterrain* (underground chamber).

GLANDORE

DROMBEG
Recurrent Stone Circle

Ancient pagan stone circles in Ireland are smaller than those found in England, such as Stonehenge. However, they are numerous, and indigenous to West Cork. These circles are constructed of freestanding, upright stones, which vary in number from five to fifteen, and the diameter of the circle may be as wide as 30 feet. These monuments were for some form of ritual and may enclose a burial mound. What is of interest in these finds is the "recurrent stone" in the center, lying flat opposite a pair of matched stones. The meaning and particular purpose of these pagan sites is unknown.

GLANMIRE

RIVERSTOWN HOUSE

Though a small house by Georgian standards, the former home of Jemmet Browne, Bishop of Cork, with plasterwork by the Francini brothers, makes Riverstown a worthwhile visit. The Francinis arrived in Ireland about mid-18th century, and only two other Irish houses — Castletown and Carton — are known to have engaged these brilliant Italian stuccodores.

Open: May 1-September 30
Thursday-Sunday: 2:00-6:00 P.M.

GLENGARRIFF

GARINISH ISLAND

This small island guarding the harbor of Glengarriff in the Gulf Stream waters has one of the most beautiful gardens in Ireland. The Bryce family in the beginning of the century brought plants, trees, and shrubs from all over the world to the once barren island, and later gave it to the government.

This was the place where George Bernard Shaw wrote *Saint Joan*. Garinish Island is reached by a ferry service from Glengarriff, a town so lovely and lush that Thackeray wrote of it: "Were such a bay lying upon English shore, it would be a world's wonder. Perhaps if it were on the Mediterranean or Baltic, English travelers would flock to it in hundreds."

Weekdays: 10:00 A.M.-5:30 P.M.

KINSALE

This lazy southern fishing village, with its harbor crowded with yachts and fishing boats, has a sad memory for the Irish. It was here in 1601 that the Spanish fleet, with 4,000 men, sailed into the harbor to defend the town from the English. The Earls of Tyrone and Tirconnell — Red Hugh O'Donnell and Hugh O'Neill — came from the North, but all were defeated. The "Flight of the Earls" to the Continent from Kinsale marked the end of the Gaelic Order in Ireland forever. Later, from Kinsale James II made his failed attempt to recover the country and his crown. The architecture along the narrow streets of Compass Hill shows the remnants of the various occupations — French, Spanish, and English. The Church of St. Multose was built in the 12th century and houses the old town stocks. Outside the town is a tip of land called the Old Head of Kinsale, where the Norman de Courcys built their castle over an existing ancient three-ringed stone fort, which was common to do in those days. The view from the cliffs overlooks the location where the Lusitania was torpedoed in May, 1915. It's rare to find anyone in Ireland wearing traditional clothing. However, the Kinsale cloak has survived and is often a popular purchase for both travelers and the Irish.

MIZEN HEAD

Past Crookhaven and Barley Cove, these ancient 700-foot cliffs tower against the Atlantic at Ireland's most southerly tip. Named in Irish Cairn Neid, since legend is that an Irish chieftain is buried in a cairn at the tip.

YOUGHAL

Few places can trace an ongoing industry backward two thousand years. However, documents show that a pottery industry was established by the Phoenicians with the rich clay from Youghal Bay. The town has been an active port for invaders and pirates since the 12th century. As a beneficiary of the Desmond Rebellion Sir Walter Raleigh was given 42,000 acres of confiscated land. His home, *Myrtle Grove,* of unusually good Elizabethan architecture, still stands in the town center. (Unfortunately, it is still a private residence and not open to the public.) Within the old town walls above Main Street is the old Clock Gate erected in 1777, from time to time used as a prison, but now a museum. There is also Cromwell's Arch, a remembrance of his landing in Ireland at Youghal in 1649. In 1955 John Huston used Youghal as the setting for the fishing village of New Bedford in his version of *Moby Dick.*

COUNTY KERRY

HOTELS   COUNTRY HOUSES   FARMS

GLENBEIGH

*TOWERS HOTEL (H)
(Glenbeigh 12)

It's hard to imagine *anyone* visiting Ireland without stopping at Ernie Evans's inn. This small hotel in the seaside village of Glenbeigh belonged to Ernie's father, and Ernie went off to the Continent to be trained at Ecole Hotelière Lausanne. The place exudes Ernie's personality and sense of perfection. There's no particular feature that draws you to the Towers ... it's *everything*. His wife Miriam has decorated each room individually and in great taste. But the few hours you're not outdoors riding from the hotel's stables, fishing and shooting in season, hiking or swimming along the beaches, you'll be drawn into the bar where something is always going on. Guests range to every nationality, but the test is that it's the favorite of the Irish themselves, and more likely than not you'll be dining alongside the President or the Taoiseach (Prime Minister). Speaking of dining, this is where Ernie's Swiss training shines. He prepares and oversees everything in the kitchen, and the menu is the most imaginative in the country. *Everything* is fresh, from paté to peach flan. After a few days with the Evanses you're reminded of something Samuel Johnson said a few hundred years ago: "There is nothing which has yet been contrived by man by which so much happiness is produced as by a good inn." If the Towers is booked, don't be discouraged ... down the road a few hundred yards is the Glenbeigh Hotel run by Ernie Evans's mother, which has equally attractive décor. And you can still dine at the Towers.

Season: January 1-October 1   AE, DC,
Luncheon: 1:00-2:30
Dinner: 7:00-9:30

KILGARVAN

HAWTHORN FARM (F)
(Kilgarvan 26)

The most Irish of Irish farmhouses. The family is Gaelic speaking, and Mrs. Dineen is a well-known cook and television personality. The farmhouse is modern, and the main activity is fishing for the plump local salmon and trout. Accommodations for twenty persons — a good-sized house party. Very popular during the summer season, so book in advance.

Open: All year round

KILLARNEY

AGADOE HEIGHTS HOTEL (H)
(064-31766)

There's an old hotelier maxim that the tone of the hotel comes down from the management, and Agadoe's manager, Louis O'Hara, is one of the best in the country. This modern hotel commands one of the most beautiful views of the Killarney countryside and lakes, and the dining room looks out over the ruins of the Agadoe Abbey and Round Tower. The menu is Continental and well prepared, and the service throughout the hotel is excellent. Dancing in the evening during the summer season. One of the best-run hotels in the country.

Season: All year round
Luncheon: 1:00-2:30
Dinner: 7:00-9:30

DUNLOE CASTLE HOTEL (H)
(064-32223)

EUROPE HOTEL (H)
(064-31900)

These sister hotels were built along the finest Continental lines for resort hotels. However, they are recommended with reservation. They are owned and run by Germans and are devoid of any Irish spirit for your visit. Every facility is available at both hotels. They have their own riding stables with palominos, tennis courts, rowboats for the lake, putting green, saunas, heated indoor Olympic pools, gymnasium, billiard rooms, hair salons, and a bath and telephone in each room. Food is of good quality.

Season: Dunloe Castle Hotel: May 1-October 15
Europe: All year round
Luncheon: 1:00-2:30
Dinner: 7:00-9:30

GREAT SOUTHERN HOTEL (H)
(064-31262)

One of the last relics of the grand Victorian days in Kerry. The center of activity in Killarney. It has become two hotels in recent years after the addition of a modern wing that includes a swimming pool and sauna baths. The rooms have all been renovated, and baths are attached to all. Beautiful lush gardens and walkways. Food in the Great Southern hotels is always well prepared, if not elaborate. Fine hotel in the old tradition with an excellent friendly staff. During the summer season the hotel presents one of the most authentic Irish traditional evenings.

Season: All year round   AE, CB, DC
Luncheon: 12:30-2:30
Dinner: 6:30-8:30

PARKNASILLA
GREAT SOUTHERN HOTEL (H)
(Sneem 3)

Winding along the fuchsia-bordered drive toward the old gray granite mansion is a path backward to the luxury of another era. The hotel is set along the banks where the

Kenmare River flows into the ocean in an overgrown sub-tropical garden. The doorman, Tom, bounds forward to introduce himself and welcome you for your stay. Past the opulent foyer are three floors of comfortable, simply decorated rooms. The activities of Parknasilla are all outdoors — waterskiing, riding, boating, fishing, and swimming along the sandy beaches or in the new heated indoor pool with its adjacent sauna baths. In the evening there's always entertainment after dinner ... either traditional music or a cabaret. Another favorite vacation spot for the Irish. The food is generally well prepared and the wine list extensive.

Season: Easter to end October   AE, CB, DC
Luncheon: 1:00-2:30
Dinner: 7:00-9:30

VALENTIA

VALENTIA HEIGHTS HOTEL (H)
(Valentia 38)

If you prefer breathtaking views and a home atmosphere, the Allens' hotel perched on the heights of Valentia Island is a find with its sweeping views of the Kerry mountains in the distance, the glistening Atlantic below. Deep-sea fishing is particularly popular from Valentia Harbor. The hotel is small, and the décor is simple and straightforward. Mrs. Allen is an excellent cook, who prepares a limited menu each day of homemade soups and fresh bread, fresh daily caught fish, and local lamb, beef, and vegetables. Limited wine menu. Off the worn tourist track.

Season: Easter to October
Luncheon: 1:00-2:30
Dinner: 7:00-9:30

WATERVILLE

WATERVILLE LAKE HOTEL (H)
(Waterville 7)

Without question the most luxurious modern hotel in Ireland ... a complete resort ... at the tip of Kerry along the Gulf Stream currents of the Atlantic. Situated on the shores of Lough Currane, the hotel has one of the largest golf courses in Europe (Par 74). Bright, plushly decorated lounges and rooms. Gourmet cuisine with an extensive menu and wine list. All resort activities — riding, tennis, fishing, swimming. The hotel-owned luxury cruiser, *Anna Maria*, takes hotel guests for picnic cruises around the Kerry coast. Other amenities are billiard room, sauna baths, and room service. Caters to international clientele with highest standards.

Season: March 15-December 31   AE
Luncheon: 1:00-2:30
Dinner: 7:00-9:45

RESTAURANTS and PUBS

DINGLE

DOYLES SEAFOOD BAR & RESTAURANT
(Dingle 144)

Stella and John Doyle opened two seasons ago one of the few seafood restaurants in the country — amazing considering Ireland's vast coastline. They've renovated an old town pub, retaining the cobblestone walls, gray flagged floor, and pot-bellied stove. Along the walls are photos of old Dingle in the 1900's. The atmosphere is informal, and you eat off butcher block tables. The menu depends on the day's catch, and the dinner menu is the same as luncheon with a fish stew added in the evening and more elaborate desserts.

Open: Easter-October   AE
Luncheon: 12:30-2:15
Dinner: 6:00-9:00
Closed Sunday

SNEEM

THE BLUE BULL
(Sneem 76)

Practically everyone who comes to Kerry spends a day driving around the Ring. Unfortunately there has always been a dearth of good eating places. Now Michael and Niall Scott have opened this delightful, country-style restaurant. Since Mr. Scott is a well-known Dublin architect and patron of the arts, the works of modern Irish artists line the walls. Peter Robinson, the former owner of the much acclaimed Armstrong's Barn in Wicklow, has joined the Scotts here and the menu reflects Peter's imaginative, first-rate style.

Open: April-September
Luncheon: 12:00-2:00
Dinner: 6:30-10:30
Closed Monday

BUYERS MARKET

KILLARNEY

LADIES VIEW INDUSTRIES
Ladies View

Though Killarney is one of the most popular tourist centers, after hours in and out of every craft and gift shop Ladies View has the best variety and quality of Irish goods in the area. Even if you don't find anything to take home, Ladies View is one of the best locations for viewing the Killarney Lakes. Refreshments available.

Open during summer season 9 A.M.-7 P.M.

ENTERTAINMENT

TRALEE

"SIAMSA"
Ashe Theatre

When Father Ahern began this Folk Theatre Company, he merely intended to extend the activities of the church choir. However today *Siamsa* (meaning merrymaking in Irish) is one of the most popular traditional evenings in the country. The pageant is a few hours' visit into the rural life of Ireland through song in the Irish language, dance, and mime.

Summer Season: Mondays and Thursdays
Reservations through any tourist office

LISTOWEL
WRITERS WEEK

Since 1971, toward the last weekend in May and the first week in June, writers, playwrights, actors, shanachies, and publishers converge on this North Kerry town for workshops, seminars, and competitions. Two of Ireland's most well-known contemporary writers — John B. Keane and Bryan McMahon — are natives of Listowel and the anchormen of the project. More than likely, while Bryan McMahon oversees the competitions, John B. commutes between the theatre workshops and his pub on William Street. The concept of the week is to give special attention to young, unestablished writers.

For information and reservations:
  Frank Lewis
  54 Church Street
  Listowel

FLEADH CHEOIL

Later in the summer, about mid-August, the tiny village swells its population by about 2,000 for Ireland's traditional music gathering. The streets and pubs overflow with pipers, fiddlers, tin whistle players, amateurs and professionals, old and young. Pubs are allowed extended hours, and like every other Irish gathering you never know who'll turn up. It's one of the most popular festivals in the country, and it's wise to make hotel reservations well in advance *and* arrive on time or they'll be given away.

DIVERSIONS

CAHERDANIEL
DERRYNANE

Home of the ancient Gaelic family of O'Connell who made their fortune during the English oppression smuggling the "Wild Geese" to Continental armies from their harbor site. The birthplace of Daniel O'Connell, "The Great Liberator" and the organizer of the "monster rallies" of the Irish poor. Balzac regarded O'Connell, with Napoleon and Couvier, one of the greatest 19th-century figures, because he "incarnated in himself a whole people." Also known as "King of the Beggars," he worked for Catholic Emancipation, which he achieved, and for dissolution of the Union, which he failed to see come about.

Open: Daily and Sunday
Summer season: 9 A.M.-1 P.M.; 2 P.M.-7 P.M.
October-April: 1 P.M.-5 P.M.

DINGLE PENINSULA
While the tour buses wear out the Ring of Kerry, this westerly peninsula sits calm and untrampled with its roads winding around layered slopes of heather and gorse and walls of wild fuchsia. Approaching from Glenbeigh around to Anascaul to the left is Inch Strand, an endless strip of white sand bordering the silver Atlantic. Dingle is one of the oldest ports in Ireland, with close trading history with ancient Spain. Along the road to the left out of town the Atlantic swirls against the massive sea cliffs of Slea Head, looking out onto the Blasket Islands, the last earth mounds before the coast of America — though it is believed that somewhere between the two lies the island of Tir na nOg, the Land of Eternal Youth. These islands were inhabited by an Irish-speaking community until 1953, when the islanders moved to the mainland or emigrated to America. Three unusual, moving books were written in the 20's and 30's by islanders retelling folk stories and describing Blasket life. At

least one should be read before visiting the area, or even Ireland, for that matter. The first was *An   tOileanach (The Islandman)* by Thomas Crohan, translated by Dr. Robin Flower, who spent many years on Blasket and whom the islanders called "bláthín," meaning "little flower." The next was *Twenty Years a Growing* by Muris O'Suilleabhain, describing his youth on the Blaskets. Finally, the woman's version of island life from Peig Sayers, the most famous shanachie on Blasket, whose stories were captured in *Peig*, before she died. A curragh may be hired at Dunquin to row over to the islands if the weather is safe. Fahan — sometimes called the ancient city — contains vast quantities of structures from the ancient pagan world and early Christianity. Over 400 *clochans* (beehive-shaped cells and huts), a dozen *souterrains* (underground chambers), and many inscribed standing stones and ringed forts. One of Ireland's popular contemporary artists, Maria Simmonds-Gooding, came to the area a decade ago, and much of her work is influenced by the mysterious blending of this ancient untampered piece of Ireland and the relics of the old orders. Her work is interesting and unusual, and you may meet her in the area. Stopping in the local pubs along the way, you are as apt to hear an ancient legend as the morning's local news. Ventry is remembered for *Cath Fionntragha* — the Battle of Ventry Strand — recorded in a 15th-century manuscript. Daire Don — King of the World — landed with his forces to invade Ireland and was defeated in the harbor by Fionn MacCumhaill (Finn MacCool). The most unusual early Christian building in the area is outside Ballyferriter, Gallerus Oratory, a corbelled structure, which, though over 1,200 years old, remains in perfect condition. This aesthetic structure represents a period in Christianity before excessive demonstrations of ornamentation were introduced. The path over the Brandon mountain range — Conor Pass from Dingle to Brandon Bay — is one of the most scenic in the country, with a vista of all Kerry. Brandon Mountain in the distance, usually covered with soft, white clouds, is the fifth highest in Ireland at 3,127 feet. As you descend the pass, the glen is a boulder-strewn moonscape.

KILLARNEY

The lakes of Killarney have been described by almost everyone — Tennyson, Wordsworth, Thackeray, to yesterday's travel journalist. But though the lakes remain as beautiful, the town and atmosphere have changed a great deal since those Victorian writers. It's become a cul-de-sac of tourist vendors, so now, as a visitor, you're forewarned. The best view of the lakes is from the Queen's Walk or Agadoe Heights. The only thing of interest in the town is Seamus Murphy's sculpture of the Irish muse — *The Sky Woman of Kerry* — in memorium to the 17th- and 18th-century Gaelic poets, Peirce Ferriter, Geoffrey O'Donahue, Aodhgan O'Rahilly, and Eoghan Ruadh O'Suilleabhain. She's the symbol of the *aisling*, a vision poem for these saddened poets of the declining Gaelic order. In their poetry she appears unexpectedly as a young lady whom they realize is the spirit of Ireland, burdened and shamed, to announce the coming of the great king, her lover, to restore Ireland to her old order. Muckross House on the outskirts of Killarney is a 19th-century mansion and folk museum run by Ned Meyers and well worth visiting. All the old crafts are demonstrated in a maze of rooms below the main house — harvesting, cobbling, printing, stone carving, along with demonstrations by a blacksmith, potter, weaver, and harness maker. On the second floor of the mansion is a display of the housing of rural Ireland, popular from the time of the Famine to the present. There is a craft shop and refreshments.

Open: All year round daily (ex. Monday) 11 A.M.-5 P.M.
Season hours: Easter-June 30 and September 1-October 30
Daily: 10:00 A.M.-7:00 P.M.
July and August: 9:00 A.M.-9:00 P.M.

LEACANABUAILE
(near Cahirciveen)

This archaeological excavation is one of the best cashel structures to survive in the country. Believed to date back to early Christian times. Housing and encircled fort in almost complete original structure.

STAIGUE FORT
(near Caherdaniel)

Considered the best-preserved example of an ancient Irish ringed fort, with architectural plan dating back to the Iron Age. The homestead plan is the precursor of more modern thatched structures. The circular stone wall, made of local grit stone, is 13 feet thick, and was placed around the homestead to protect the livestock from wolves (which are now extinct). Unusual stone staircase climbing the wall ten feet used for defense of the farm.

SKELLIG ISLANDS
(off Bolus Head)

These twin solid granite islands rising in the Atlantic were the 6th-century homes of hermits and aesthetics until the Danes arrived, destroying their curraghs, and eventually the inhabitants died of starvation. Little Skellig appears snow covered from the shoreline, but is the home of 22,000 pairs of gannets during their mating season. Skellig Michael (named after the Archangel Michael) is used as an Atlantic lighthouse station, and, besides the lighthouse keeper — Teddy O'Sullivan — the only other natives are wild black rabbits. Perched over 800 feet above the Atlantic are the remains of the early Christian monastic life — dry stone beehives, an oratory, and a graveyard. These may be reached up the path over worn stone steps. George Bernard Shaw wrote of Skellig: "No experience that the conventional tourist travel can bring you will stick in your memory so strangely; for Skellig Michael is not after the fashion of this world."

Fishing boats depart daily from Derrynane (Sean O'Brien) and Valentia (Des Lavelle), weather permitting. Plan to spend a lazy day. The boat out is three hours and back three hours, and be sure to have the hotel prepare you a picnic basket for the trip.

VALENTIA ISLAND

This sweeping island in the Atlantic off the Ring of Kerry was recently connected to the mainland by a bridge at Portmagee. From the heights of Jeokaun Mount is a view of the Skellig Islands to the South, the MacGillicuddy Reeks of Killarney in the North, and in the distance the deserted Blasket Islands off Dingle. In 1866 the first Atlantic cable was placed off Valentia. A hundred years later it was discontinued after communications improved. Des Lavelle runs an excellent deep-sea diving and fishing service, as well as the boat to Skellig daily at Kingstown. For boat reservations phone Valentia Island 24.

GALWAY CIRCLE

Courtesy of Irish Tourist Board

COUNTY GALWAY

HOTELS   COUNTRY HOUSES   FARMS

ARAN ISLANDS
Inishmore

Only in the past few years have the islanders welcomed overnight guests, and accommodations are limited to a few farmhouses and a few guesthouses. Two of the most popular on the island are set side by side at the rock base of Dun Aengus overlooking the Atlantic and only a few hundred yards from sandy beaches.

JOHNSON HERNON'S (F)
(Kilronan 10)

CONNEELY'S (F)
(Kilronan 35)

Both offer full board with substantial, if unimaginative, food. Open: May 1-September 30. Located in Kilmurvey (2½ miles from Kilronan). Transportation by island taxi or jaunting car.

BALLYNAHINCH

BALLYNAHINCH CASTLE (C)
(Clifden 135)

Formerly the ancestral home of the O'Flaherties, Chieftains of Connacht. Standing on its own private demesne on the shore of Ballynahinch Lake, the castle was renovated after World War I by the Maharajah Jam Sahib, the famous cricketer. He spent enormous sums of money developing the surrounding fisheries. More a rustic sportsman's residence than an elegant castle dwelling. Each evening the chef features the day's catch. Sportsman's holiday resort.

Season: June 1-mid-October
Luncheon: 1:30-2:30
Dinner: 7:00-9:00

CASHEL

*CASHEL HOUSE HOTEL (CH)
(Cashel 9)

Dermot and Kay MacEvilly's small white country house is set along the wild rock shoreline of Connemara's coast. If you arrive in the morning, you're more than likely to see dozens of wicker picnic baskets piled in the entranceway for the guests to take along during their day's outing ... all the activity is outdoors. Fresh water fishing, sea fishing, horseback riding, mountain climbing, and just about anything else you can think of. Its most famous visitor was General de Gaulle and his wife; he chose Cashel House as the place to begin his memoirs. Nothing is more regarded and feared than French chauvinism toward cuisine, but Cashel's chef kept the General enthusiastic for over a month. The wine list is full of rare surprises. The house is small with only eighteen rooms, all cheerfully decorated.

Season: Easter-end of October
Open Christmas holidays
Luncheon: 12:30-2:30
Dinner: 7:00-9:00

Be sure to make reservations for dinner if not a guest at the hotel.

CLIFDEN

*ABBEY GLEN HOTEL (H)
(Clifden 138)

Situated on the Sky Road leaving Clifden, the hotel rises a few hundred feet above the roaring Atlantic. The main interest of the proprietor, Paul Hughes, is his cuisine, which he prepares himself daily, specializing in local seafare — salmon, lobster, prawns, mussels, and scallops. It's all delicious, especially after a day of touring the Connemara countryside. Mr. Hughes's second pet interest is wine, and his cellar is filled with unusual Bordeaux, Burgundies, Hocks, and Ports.

The hotel has its own swimming pool, and it is also near to many sandy beaches along the coast. The rooms are simply decorated.

Season: Easter-September 30
Open Christmas holidays
Luncheon: 1:30-2:30
Dinner: 7:30

GALWAY

ARDILAUN HOUSE HOTEL (H)
(091-65452)

The hotel's countrystyle setting in the middle of Galway is preferred by those who steer away from large city hotels. You're about a ten-minute walk from the city center, or, if you prefer, there are always taxis and buses close by. The rooms of the Ardilaun have all been recently renovated, combining a country house atmosphere with all the modern facilities. The dining room carries on the country house spirit with oak-beamed ceilings, chintz table cloths, and candlelight. Fresh seafood is the house specialty, but the chef also prepares French dishes, some more successful than others. Very good wine list.

Season: All year round   AE, DC,
Luncheon: 1:00-2:30
Dinner: 6:30-9:00

GLENLO ABBEY (F)

Mrs. Palmer's elegant Georgian house, three miles out of Galway City, is a treasure for the traveler, but it is difficult to make reservations, since there are only six bedrooms. She's decorated all the rooms in lovely English prints, and both bedrooms and bathrooms are aristocratically huge. She serves no meals except breakfast.

Season: May-September

*GREAT SOUTHERN HOTEL (H)
(091-4041)

This grande old dame of Ireland's railroad hotels has had a recent face lift — modernizing her rooms but retaining her elegant old atmosphere. *Everyone* stops at the Great Southern on Galway's Eyre Square green, whether for a few drinks, a meal, or a few days' visit. The Claddagh Room Rooftop restaurant overlooks Galway Bay and the Aran Islands and offers a luxurious meal while visiting the rugged Connemara countryside. The chef uses plenty of local vegetables, beef, and, of course, the fresh fish from the Bay. The staff is one of the best in the country, and Tom — the head porter, who's been with the hotel over two decades — can help you find or arrange almost anything in the area.

Season: All year round
Luncheon: 1:00-2:30
Dinner: 6:30-10:30

AE, CB, DC
Coffee Shop: 10:00 A.M.-
11:00 P.M.

HEADFORD

LISDONAGH MANOR (F)
(093-21428)

Valda Palmer's early Georgian country house is particularly for those who would like to travel back a hundred years into the past. The ivy-covered manor standing on the edge of its private lake has belonged to Miss Palmer's family for many generations and is filled with rare antiques and paintings handed down over the years. Miss Palmer advises, "Americans do too much traveling to cover too much area." This is a wonderful place to settle for a while and enjoy the fishing, shooting, and hunting paradise of the area. (By the way, Miss Palmer is a crack shot.) During your stay Miss Palmer will more than likely have a dinner party inviting her local friends so you have a chance to meet the Irish.

Season: All year round
Dinner: 7:30

LEENANE

LEENANE HOTEL (H)
(Leenane 4)

This century-old coaching inn surrounded by lush gardens of fuchsia and rhododendron sits along the silent glistening fiord, Killary Bay, at Leenane. Definitely one of the most romantic settings in Ireland. Angling is one of the most important activities at the hotel — both deep sea and coarse — but there's also sailing and water skiing in the harbor. Leenane has a tennis court and croquet lawn. The dining room has been modernized, and the fare is straightforward Irish cooking.

Season: June 1-September 30
  Easter holidays
Luncheon: 1:30-2:30
Dinner: 7:30-9:00

LETTERFRACK

ROSLEAGUE MANOR (CH)
(Moyard 7)

The Foyle family have welcomed guests to their Georgian manor on the edge of Clifden for over half a century. Over forty acres of woodland to roam. Salmon and trout fishing available in private streams. For the golfer a private putting green, and a heated swimming pool located on the grounds. The rooms have all been renovated, but should you be traveling with the family or a group of friends, "The Old Stables" are renovated cottages with open fireplaces in the living room, double bedrooms, and private kitchens should you prefer to do your own cooking. Son William Foyle is the chef in the main house, nightly preparing quality Irish and French cuisine.

Season: Easter - October 1
Dinner: 7:30-9:00

OUGHTERARD

*CURRAREVAGH HOUSE (CH)
(091-82313)

Trying to write about Currarevagh is like trying to describe your first love, you're afraid the magic will disappear when set to paper. It was the first place I visited in Ireland many trips ago. Winding up the half-mile drive, the ivy-covered Georgian manor house is nearly hidden in its 140-acre private forest surrounded by oversized rhododendron and fuchsia high above the silent shore of Lough Corrib. The manor has belonged to the same family for over six generations. A few years ago Harry Hodgson brought home his lovely bride June to take over Currarevagh. Unlike most country houses, the restoration of Currarevagh did not entail clashing modernizations. Currarevagh's Old World atmosphere hasn't been tampered with, and the rooms seem as though they haven't been touched since it was a private residence.

June is an imaginative cook and is usually tucked away in the kitchen during the day preparing her unusual menus, which change daily. Since the Hodgsons welcome their guests as if it were a relaxed house party, nonresidents are discouraged from intruding on dinner. However, once in a while Mr. Hodgson makes an exception. When you have a chance to engage Mr. Hodgson in a conversation, he'll share an incredible range of knowledge about the Connemara area. Currarevagh is a special stay for a traveler who prefers a private, peaceful, and totally relaxing holiday.

Season: Easter - October
Luncheon: 1:15
Dinner: 8:00

SWEENEY'S
OUGHTERARD HOUSE HOTEL (H)
(091-82207)

If you've dreamt of a small Irish village with thatched cottages, a river rushing along the edge of town, all unchanged for a few hundred years, Oughterard is ideal. Thackeray wrote in his *Irish Sketchbook* in 1842: "A more beautiful village can scarcely be seen than Oughterard. It stands upon Lough Corrib, the banks of which are here ... picturesque and romantic ..." Moira and Patric Higgins' country inn is set across the road from the Owenriff river, a few doors down from the center of the village, surrounded by lush gardens. The atmosphere at Sweeney's is cozy and welcoming, with open fires blazing even in the summer months. The food is solid Irish cooking, with special emphasis on the day's catch from Lough Corrib, and fresh vegetables and fruits from Moira's garden. Wine list good and well priced.

Season: All year round
Luncheon: 1:00-2:30
Dinner: 7:30-9:00

RENVYLE

*RENVYLE HOUSE (H)
(Renvyle 3)

Of his home, Renvyle, Dr. Oliver St. John Gogarty, the brilliant Irish wit, once wrote:
"My house too stands on a lake, but it also stands on the sea. Water lilies meet the golden seaweed. It is as if the faery land of Connemara at the extreme end of Europe, the incongruous flowed together at last; and the sweet and bitter blended. Behind me islands and mountainous mainland share in a final reconciliation at this, the world's end."
Set on its craggy Atlantic nest, Renvyle is one of the most breathtaking sites in Ireland. The house where Gogarty entertained Yeats, Lady Gregory, and others of the Literary Revival burned, but in its place an equally beautiful country hotel has been built.
Hugh Coyle manages the family-run hotel and has seen that every modern convenience is available. The dining room overlooks the rolling Atlantic. The restaurant serves

only home-grown vegetables, local seafood, and local Connemara beef and lamb.

During the day all the activities you can imagine for a holiday are available on the grounds: boating and fishing on Renvyle's private lake, swimming on the hotel's sandy beach, tennis, croquet and putting on the hotel's green. Horseback riding available nearby. In the evening you can usually depend on some traditional music and dancing provided by the Irish guests.

Season: Easter - November 1
Luncheon: 1:30-2:30
Dinner: 7:30-9:00

RESTAURANTS and PUBS

BARNA

TY AR MOR
(091-5031)

Off the coast road on a pier overlooking the ocean in the tiny village of Barna, near Galway, is Hervé Mahé's *Ty Ar Mor* (House of the Sea), one of the finest restaurants in the country. The restaurant happens to be Breton (but that's not unusual, since Brittany and Ireland have ancient ties).

For luncheon the restaurant specializes in crepes, those thin pancakes filled with seafood, vegetables, or cheese. For dessert more crepes: banana flambé, rich dark chocolate, fresh fruit, a dozen selections.

Being a Breton, Hervé has spent all his life by the sea. During the day he's out in one of his fishing boats or along the beaches searching for the plentiful seafare of the Western coastal waters — scallops, mussels, periwinkles, oysters, sole, turbot, and crab. When he returns in the afternoon Chef Jean Chevalier, a native of Nice, decides on his specialties for the evening. There's always a variety. The specialties include Jean's homemade paté or fish soup. For your main course try his scallops on skewers with bacon and peppers, or mussels Provencal with baked tomatoes, a touch of garlic, breadcrumbs and cheese, or the tournedos of local beef in a rich creamy herb sauce. Being French, Jean insists on only fresh vegetables and fruits. The rich crepes reappear to tempt after your meal or, if you prefer, heaps of fresh strawberries in season.

The restaurant has no liquor license, but can offer you an apéritif or sherry. Hervé imports his own wines on his trips to Brittany, and they're excellent. Be sure to try his Muscadet.

The dining room is small and intimate, and in the evening candles flicker against the all-white interior.

Season: March-December
Luncheon: 12:00-2:00 (July-September only)
Dinner: 7:00-11:00
Be sure to make reservations in advance. Closed Sunday.

BEALADANGAN
THE HOOKER
(091-92120)

Looking back, there are only a few places where you can sense Ireland unchanged for hundreds of years. One of them is John and Lucy O'Toole's pub in Bealadangan, a tiny island village in the heart of the wild rocky landscape of Connemara. Bealadangan was the home of the Connemara hookers, the sailing boats that carried peat to the Aran Islands. The pub is surrounded by thousands of tiny silver pools of water and clumps of wild yellow gorse, with the Twelve Bens mountain range rising in the distance.

Lucy serves a pub luncheon by the open hearth fire all afternoon, of fresh smoked salmon, Limerick ham, and sandwiches. The wood carving behind the bar was a gift from one of Johnny's neighbors, John Huston.

Across the road are three cottages clustered together that Johnny has renovated and rents to visitors. He's kept a keen eye in renovating them to include all the modern conveniences while preserving the traditional atmosphere. He received Ireland's architectural award, *An Taisce,* for the cottages.

Bealadangan is in the Gaeltacht, and you'll rarely hear English spoken except to the visitor. Whether you spend an afternoon or your entire holiday with the O'Tooles, you'll find a disappearing Ireland.

(Directions: Take the coast road from Galway city to Costelloe, then follow the road to Lettermore.)

CLARENBRIDGE
PADDY BURKE'S

Another pub stop for enjoying the oversized Galway Bay oysters in season. A favorite haunt over the years for visiting celebrities, and their photos line the walls. Burke's was taken over by the Lydon family, who have kept both the spirit and the cozy atmosphere of the old pub. Besides oysters in season, Burke's serves an unusual soup of cream of scampi, smoked salmon, prawns, and sandwiches. Meals served all during pub hours.

AE

KILCOLGAN
MORAN'S ON THE WEIR

The old thatched cottage on the Weir has been in the Moran family for over 200 years and is one of the most popular stops in Ireland for the plump luscious Galway Bay oysters. Moran's is a perfect place to spend a lazy day or evening. During the summer months you can sit outdoors lying on the grass, swilling Chablis or a frothy pint with your smoked salmon or fresh crab, and watch the rushing river and the tides reverse. In the fall and winter months warm yourself by the aga cooker or by the open turf fire in what used to be the cottage kitchen. The young Morans — Willy, Doreen, and Martáin — are busy with the customers from midday to late evening serving the food and drink, and exchanging local news, sports reports, and "travelers' tips." Later in the evening you may meet grandfather Moran back from the day of fishing or combing their oyster beds for the day's catch. Especially delicious is the home-made mussel soup with Mrs. Moran's fresh-baked brown bread.

Even if it means a 20-mile detour, you shouldn't leave Ireland without a stop. (It's a little difficult to find — watch for the sign a half mile out of Clarenbridge on the road to Limerick from Galway.)

ENTERTAINMENT

GALWAY

"SEODA"
Taibhdhearc na Galliimhe
Middle Street
(091-2024)

Seoda, meaning "merrymaking" in Irish, is one of the few traditional evenings in *any country* that doesn't seem as though conceived by the "Department of Folklore." Risteard O'Broin, the director, gathers the finest actors, musicians, and dancers to present one of the most authentic of Irish entertainment. Celine Hession and her troupe high-step to the music of Ceoltoiri Chonnacht. There's a one-act play in Irish, and then more music and dancing. Don't miss the evening if you're near Galway.

The theatre was founded in 1928 by Michael MacLiammoir and Hilton Edwards as a center for drama in the Irish language. The tradition is still carried on, and during the rest of the year productions continue to be presented in the Irish language.

Performances: Monday, Wednesday, and Friday 8:30 P.M. Bookings: Daily 2 P.M.-6 P.M.

KINVARA

DUN GUAIRE CASTLE EVENING

Every evening during the summer months, in the fishing village of Kinvara, 17 miles south of Galway, the Dun Guaire players wine, dine, and entertain in the castle's keep on the Atlantic's edge. You're welcomed with a mug of claret and plump Dublin Bay prawns. The banquet is Irish food at its best — a rich lobster soup, fresh smoked salmon, roasted hen, oven-baked brown bread, and creamy Irish pud. Then settle back for an all too brief encounter with "Literary Ireland," with readings from Yeats, O'Casey, Synge, and others, rollicking barbs and anecdotes from Dublin's premier wit, Oliver St. John Gogarty, all laced with Irish songs and ballads you're not likely to hear along the usual tourist trail. Dun Guaire is a small intimate evening gathering and regarded as the finest of castle banquets.

Season: May through September　　　　　　　　AE, DC,
　　Twice nightly: 6 and 8
For reservations:
Shannon Castle Tours (061-61788) or the local tourist office where you're staying.

ANTIQUES TRAIL

CLIFDEN

PHOENIX ANTIQUES
Market Street
(Clifden 10)

GALWAY

MALCOLM ALEXANDER
Eglington Street
(091-62693)

COBWEBS
Nives O'Sullivan
Phyllis Lydon
7 Quay Lane

HEASLIPS ANTIQUE FURNITURE
Cross Street
(091-3095)

BUYERS MARKET

CLIFDEN

MILLAR'S
(Clifden 32)

If you're looking for handwoven Irish tweeds, caps, hats, capes, jackets, skirts, shirts, bedspreads or just bolts of material, Millar's is *the* source in Ireland. The prices are lower than what you'll pay around the country. They also handle Waterford glass and Galway crystal.

Open: 6 days a week 9:00 A.M.-6:00 P.M.

GALWAY

KENNY'S BOOKSHOPS
High Street
(091-2739)

The Kennys really have three locations brimming with their antiquarian finds. Maureen Kenny runs the bookshop filled with rare editions, but be prepared to spend money, they're collector's items. Son Tomas is down the street with thousands of old maps, drawings, and prints he's found around the country. Desmond Kenny is the most difficult to locate, buried in the third floor loft sorting the overflow of another few thousand books. A perfect way to spend a few hours.

Open: Six days a week 10 A.M. — 6 P.M.

LETTERFRACK

CONNEMARA HANDCRAFTS LIMITED
(Letterfrack 6)

The Bennetts and the Plemings seem to have a knack for finding the most unusual and unique of Irish handcrafts, all of particularly high quality. Besides hundreds of varying tweeds, the shop carries much of the Kilkenny Design Center work — glassware, pottery, and silver jewelry.

There's a fantastic range of Irish books, records, and maps, as well as the best of the Aran knitwear. If there were an award for taste and quality, the Bennetts and Plemings are well deserving. A must visit for shopping.

Open: Six days a week 10:00 A.M.-6:00 P.M.

DIVERSIONS

ARAN ISLANDS

These strange three chips of land off the Connemara coast still retain an eerie continuance of their ancient past. On Inishmore, the largest island, is Dun Aengus, the fort of the Fir Bolg, who inhabited mythical ancient Ireland. Dun Aengus has guarded the ragged coastline since 200 B.C., rising 300 feet above the roaring sea and described as "the most magnificent barbaric monument in Europe." Eventually paganism partially yielded to Christianity, and relics by the hundred are scattered on the landscape. At one time, around A.D. 483, over 3,000 students resided at the monastery of St. Enda. Teampall an Cheathrair Alainn, one of the island's churches, shows the curious blending of the two faiths in the "Church of the Four Beautiful People." The graveyard of St. Enda in Killeany contains the worn grave slabs of over 127 saints during that time.

When you arrive, you may not understand the islanders, nor will you know them any better when you leave. Unless you're born on the island — an islander — you'll never know them. But that's not unusual. All islanders *everywhere* have inborn suspicion and fear of strangers to their island and will keep their distance. They won't seem particularly Irish either. They're islanders with little connection to the mainland except to do business. They've survived a bleak, meager, and often desolate existence for centuries, surviving on their fishing. It's been their main source of income and over the years their source of tragedy.

When you go over to the islands, plan to spend at least a night. It's a haunting solitary visit, like no other place you've ever traveled. To walk or bicycle the roads, mere strips winding and slicing the stonescape, or wander through the ancient relics, or just sit hundreds of feet above the howling Atlantic as the wild sea birds circle the lonely island is an experience unimaginable.

If you go just for the day, the islanders will take you for a tour in the jaunting cars, but it won't be the same as an overnight stay.

The boats from Galway Bay land at the Kilronan Pier on the big island, Inishmore. To get to the smaller islands you can hire a currach, the tarred and lathed fishing boats of the islands, to take you across. On the middle island of Inishmaan is the finest stone fort remaining in Ireland, Conors Fort, and Cil Ceannanaigh (Church of the Fair-Headed One) is regarded as the most perfect primitive church standing in Ireland. The smallest of the three islands, Inisheer, is only 1,400 acres looking out onto the Clare coast.

The islanders are Irish-speaking, but many speak English today. Many of the islanders have English surnames, such as Piggott and Harrington, all of whose ancestors were Cromwellian soldiers.

There are two ways to travel to the islands. By boat the journey is three hours. The two ships — *Naomh Eanna* and *Galway Bay* — sail daily from Galway Pier to weather permitting.

Tickets may be purchased at: Dockside Booking Office prior to departure *or*

Kelly Shipping Ltd.
Commercial Docks
(091-2347)

Galway Railroad Station
(091-2141)

Be sure to make reservations well in advance.

By air: Aer Arann
66 Dominick Street
Galway
(091-65110, - 65119)

Daily flights: 10 A.M., 11 A.M., and 6 P.M.

(This twenty-minute ride is an ideal way to view Galway Bay, Connemara, and the Clare Coast.)

CLIFDEN

This small Connemara village is an ideal start for a tour of the countryside of Europe's edge. Start a few miles south of Clifden at Derrygimlagh Bog. Along the edge of the bog are the foundations and masts of the first transatlantic wireless station set up by the Marconi Company. Close by is the spot where Alcock and Brown landed at the end of the first nonstop transatlantic flight in June, 1914.

When you pass through Clifden, take the Sky Road north, winding along the golden gorse-covered hillsides as they slope into the Atlantic. Below are miles of sandy, bleached beaches. Sky Road is one of the most breathtaking drives in Ireland.

In the lush Kylemore Valley is Kylemore Abbey, sunken between the Twelve Bens in the south and the Dooaugh Mountains in the north. The Abbey is a 19th-century stone mansion in the Elizabethan style. Kylemore was built by an Englishman, Mitchell Henry, who planted thousands of ferns and plants in the surrounding barren bog. It is now a convent for the Benedictine nuns. The flag in the great hall was captured by the Irish Brigade at the Battle of Fontenoy and given to the nuns for safe keeping.

As you turn toward Leenane, the still fiord of Killary Bay comes into view. The harbor travels inward for ten miles and is sheltered from disturbance by the mountain banks of the Mweelrea range. The fiord is 13 fathoms deep.

As you head back toward Galway you pass through Maam. Along this drive the road borders the shores of Lough Corrib, the silent glazed lake of Connemara, golden in the sunset.

CLONFERT

THE MEADOW OF THE GRAVE

St. Brendan founded this monastery in the 6th century, and of particular interest is the beautifully carved 12th-century Irish Romanesque door of the cathedral. The craftsmanship is regarded as the finest in the country. Located near Shannonbridge a few miles from the Shannon River.

CLONMACNOISE

This early Christian monastery was founded in 547 by St. Ciaran on the lands donated by Diarmaid MacCerbhaill. Legend is that Diarmaid himself built the first wooden church for the monastery and soon after became high king, due to the prayers of St. Ciaran.

Clonmacnoise is situated near a fiord of the Shannon at what is believed to be the center of Ireland, at the junction of three kingdoms: Connacht, Munster, and Meath. The monastery was one of the most important in Ireland, and the last high king, Ruaidhrai Ua Conchubhair, is buried there.

Many of the churches still stand. The smallest, St. Ciaran's, and the largest, the Cathedral, are both good examples of Irish Romanesque architecture. O'Rourke's Tower was erected in 1124 and stands 62 feet in height. There is also a vast collection of early grave slabs with Irish inscriptions. Two sandstone high crosses, dated about the early 19th century, remain intact. The Cross of the Scriptures is particularly interesting in its depiction of the Last Judgment and the Crucifixion. The lowest panel of the cross shows two figures believed to be Diarmaid and Ciaran clasping a post.

(Clonmacnoise is a few miles south of the main road, midway between Athlone and Ballinasloe.)

CONNEMARA COAST

Most travelers bypass the most beautiful haunting area of *Iar Chonnachta,* the rugged wild coast of Connemara. The road saddles the rocky edge of the Atlantic from Galway Bay to Spiddal and on to Costelloe and Carraroe. The area is the last pocket remnant of the ancient Gaelic nation. The Irish language is still the first language, and, for years, the Connemara Gaeltacht was the source of inspiration for Ireland's Celtic revival at the beginning of the century.

Bogs stretch along the countryside. The white thatched cottages are parceled by bracelets of gray granite. Possibly because it's so desolate, the sun gestures with extraordinary plays of light. Many of Ireland's artists have been drawn to the Connemara landscape, such as Seamus O'Sullivan, Norah Maguinness, and Charles Lamb. Lamb lived in Carraroe, and there is a permanent exhibit of his work in the village. Today one of Ireland's leading artists and sculptors, Edward Delaney, has a home there.

GALWAY

THE CITY OF THE TRIBES

Galway has for hundreds of years been the gateway to Iar Chonnachta, the last fragment of the Celtic nation. During the Norman and English invasions over the years the Irish were pushed to the banks of the city, the Claddagh, which was a tiny fishing village. "Neither O nor Mac shall swagger through the streets of Galway" was the 16th-century edict by the invaders. During the Troubles the thatched cottages scattered along the quay were burned and have been replaced with modern buildings. The Spanish Arch is the only remaining remnant of the wall that encircled the city with its 14 gates and towers.

In medieval days Galway thrived as a merchant port with Spanish trading in wine and other goods. The Lynch Stone commemorates this connection, and one of the most famous episodes of the city. In 1493 James Lynch Fitzstephen was Mayor of Galway. On one of his business trips to Spain, by way of returning the kindness of his Spanish host, he offered to bring the man's only son back with him for a visit to Ireland. In a rage concerning the affections of a local woman, Lynch's son stabbed the Spanish visitor. He confessed to his father. Against entreaties of the townspeople and his wife, Fitzstephen arrested, tried, and convicted his son. On the day of the execution, the hangman could not be found, so the father himself hanged his son from the window of his home for the townspeople to view. This act of justice is recalled in the word "lynching."

Eyre Square is the city's 18th-century town green. At the top of the square is the statue to Padric O'Conaire by Albert Power. Galway has been the center for the Irish language movement, and the statue commemorates this Gaelic poet, novelist, and short story writer. The Brown Doorway has been preserved as an example of 17th-century architecture.

The Church of St. Nicholas was founded by the Normans in 1320 and is the second largest ancient church in the country. Tradition is that Christopher Columbus prayed in the church with Rice de Culvey, a Galway sailor who accompanied him on his voyage to the New World. The church represents many periods of Irish architecture and is of interest because the aisles are wider than the nave.

GORT

THOOR BALLYLEE
(Peterswell 8)

> *I, the poet William Yeats,*
> *With old mill boards and sea-green slates,*
> *And smithy work from the Gort forge,*
> *Restored this tower for my wife George,*
> *And may these characters remain*
> *When all is ruin once again.*

William Butler Yeats bought this four-story 16th-century Norman keep in 1917 for £35, as a refuge for him and his young wife George. Thor Ballylee had many fascinations for Yeats. The local witch Biddy Early had said: "There is a cure for all evil between the two mills of Ballylee." Though Yeats never found the curing herbs.

The keep stands alongside the Cloone River and has been restored to much of its original design. Yeats, as ever, was clear in his specifications. In his "Prayer on Going into My House" he writes:

> *No table or chair or stool not simple enough*
> *For shepherd lads in Galilee, and grant*
> *That I myself for portions of the year*
> *May handle nothing and set eyes on nothing*
> *But what the great and passionate have used*
> *Throughout so many varying centuries.*

Frances McNally, a white-haired, extroverted woman, lovingly cares for Thor Ballylee. With every question you could ask about Yeats of his neighbors, Lady Gregory of

Coole Park or Edward Martyn of Tullira Castle, her eyes
sparkle as she answers. The bookshop is filled with works of
literary Ireland. There's a tearoom across the lane with delicious cakes, tea, and coffee. Be sure to rent a tourifon to
listen to Yeats describe his home.

> *I declare this tower is my symbol;*
>   *I declare*
> *This winding, gyring, spiring treadmill*
>   *of a stair is my ancestral stair.*
> *That Goldsmith and the Dean, Berkeley*
>   *and Burke have travelled there.*

Open: March — October
Daily 10 A.M. - 6 P.M. (9 P.M. July and August)

Only a few miles down the road is Coole Park, which was
once the home of Lady Augusta Gregory, and the haven for
so many Irish writers of the Literary Revival. As you approach Lady Gregory's demesne you pass through a twined
arboral tunnel. All that remains of those gatherings, where
Lady Gregory coached, calmed, and encouraged so many
talents, is the copper beech with a dozen carved initials: JMS,
S'OC, WBY, Æ, VM, and towering above them all, GBS.
Many of her friends described Coole Park over the years, but
it was Yeats who penned the final tribute, as she lay dying in
1931:

> *We were the last romantics – chose*
>   *for theme*
> *Traditional sanctity and loveliness,*
> *Whatever's written in what poet's name*
> *The book of the people; whatever most*
>   *can bless*
> *The mind of man or elevate a rhyme;*
> *But all is changed, that high horse*
>   *riderless,*
> *Though mounted in that saddle Homer*
>   *rode*
> *Where the swan drifts upon a darkening*
>   *flood.*

INISHBOFIN

This large granite island, off the fishing village of Cleggan, has been touched by every phase of Irish history. In the 7th century St. Cloman founded a monastery. Don Banco's fort is believed to have been built by the captain of the Spanish Armada. In later years the island was used as a concentration camp for priests and rebels. The island is a beautiful, peaceful patch for a day's picnic. There are only a few inhabitants now and a colony of seals. You can reach the island by mail boat. Inquire in the Pier Bar, the fisherman's local, which is filled with old navigational maps and nautical gear.

COUNTY SLIGO

DIVERSIONS

SLIGO

YEATS COUNTRY

Though he was born in Dublin, and soon afterward the family moved to London, William Butler Yeats spent his childhood summers with his grandfather, William Pollexfan, the local rector, in the dramatic Sligo countryside. In later years his returns to Sligo were infrequent, his time spent between Dublin, London, Thor Ballylee, and France. But in much of his poetry he often returned to those summers' innocence in the countryside, which held the roots of his imagination, ancient, magical, and romantic. Much like his brother, Jack B., his inspiration fed from the woodlands, lakes, and mountains, its people and it mythical legends.

Before Yeats died in the South of France in 1939, he left instructions for his burial in every detail:

Under bare Ben Bulben's head
In Drumcliffe churchyard Yeats is laid,
An ancestor was rector there
Long years ago, a church stands near,
By the road an ancient cross.
No marble, no convenient phrase;
On limestone quarried near the spot
By his command these words are cut:

Cast a cold eye
on Life, on Death.
Horseman, pass by!

Today it's exactly as Yeats described in Drumcliffe churchyard. In the distance great Ben Bulben's head sweeps toward the Donegal mountains. At the foot of the western base is the spraying mist of Glencar's waterfall.

There is a waterfall
Upon Ben Bulben side
That all my childhood counted dear;
Were I to travel far and wide
I could not find a thing so dear.

During the summers William B. and his brother Jack would ride the countryside, trying to find the places and sources of ancient legends. West of Sligo town is the Glen of Knocknarea. At the summit of the mountain is the grave of the legendary Queen Maeve, the romantic warrior Queen of Connacht. Her cairn (stone burial mound) is over 30 feet tall and 200 feet in diameter. She was also believed to be the Queen of the Immortal Faeries. In Yeats's play, *The Land of Heart's Desire,* a fairy takes a young bride to the land of Tir na nOg (Land of Eternal Youth) at the foot of Knocknarea.

...Away, come away:
Empty your heart of its mortal dream.
The winds awaken, the leaves whirl round,
Our cheeks are pale, our hair is unbound,
Our breasts are heaving, our eyes agleam...

The hill of the Glen of Knocknarea overlooks Lough Gill. This silver-splintered pool and its scattered islands was the source of Yeats's best-known poem, *The Lake of Inishfree.*

I will arise and go now, and go to
    Inishfree,
And a small cabin build there, of clay
    and wattles made;
Nine bean-rows will I have there, a hive
    for the honeybee,
And live alone in the bee-loud glade.

And I shall have some peace there, for
    peace comes dropping slow,
Dropping from the veils of the morning
    to where the cricket sings;

There midnight's all a glimmer, and noon
  a purple glow,
And evening full of the linnet's wings.

I will arise and go now, for always
  night and day
I hear lake water lapping with low
  sounds by the shore;
While I stand on the roadway, or on the
  pavements grey,
I hear it in the deep heart's core.

Yeats's burrowing the rich ground eclipsed a hundred centuries. He was the ancient poet, the wisp of the court, and left his legacy.

Swear by those horsemen, by those women
Complexion and form prove superhuman,
That pale, long visaged company
That air in immortality
Completeness of their passions won;
Now they ride the wintry dawn
Where Ben Bulben sets the scene.
That we in coming days may be
Still the indominitable Irishry.

LISSADEL
LISSADEL HOUSE

Near the Yeats relics is the ancestral home of the Gore-Booth family on the shores of Sligo Bay. After building three other homes in the area since the 16th century, the Gore-Booths chose Lissadell to build their Georgian mansion with its swirling views of Ben Bulben range, Sligo Bay, and Knocknarea. William B. Yeats often came to visit the famous sisters, Eva Gore-Booth, the poet, and Countess Markievicz. Yeats enjoyed the life of the Big House in Lissadell, but they were the declining generation. Eva left for London to help organize the women's labor movement, while Constance became a leader of the 1916 Rebellion. She was sentenced to death, but her execution was stayed because she was a woman.

Open: May 1 — September 30
Daily except Sunday 2:30 - 5:15 P.M.

COUNTY MAYO

HOTELS   COUNTRY HOUSES   FARMS

BALLINA

BELLEK CASTLE (C)
(Ballina 507)

After you pass through the turreted stone entrance, it's another mile, along the winding lane, before you reach the doors of Bellek Castle. The former baronial manor is surrounded by 3,000 acres of private woodlands and parks, extending to the marshy banks of the River Moy, famous for its trout and salmon catch.

Since Marshall and Joyce Doran acquired the castle, they have restored each room on the main floor to its original elegance, filling each with unusual period antiquities. In the entranceway are the original stone floors of the castle, and parts of the walls in the Great Hall are sections of the old castle built before the present structure in the 17th century. The Armada Bar was constructed from the timbers salvaged from a galleon along the Mayo coastline. Past the striking large 13th-century fireplace, imported from Jersey, is the Castle Armory, which is filled with interesting medieval weapons and a crossbow dating back to 1600.

Climbing the stairs to the second floor, you will find the atmosphere changes. Each door opens into a gay, brightly decorated room, some with four-poster beds, some with private sitting rooms and adjoining kitchenettes. All rooms are with private bath.

Back to the main floor for dining in the grill room, *Granuaille,* named after the 16th-century Mayo pirate queen. While you dine at hand-carved wooden refectory tables, you watch the chef cooking the steaks and grills over the medieval Celtic oven. Certain evenings during the summer there is medieval entertainment. Pleasantly, Bellek Castle is one of the least expensive castle visits.

Season: All year round
Luncheon: Residents preferred
Dinner: 7:00 - 9:00

CASTLEBAR
*BREAFFY HOUSE HOTEL (H)
(094-22033)

Breaffy House is one of the most pleasant blendings of the
old and new in the country. The modern additions easily
extend from the grand older stone mansion. Nearby is a
9-hole golf course, and many sporting amenities: fishing,
shooting, pony trekking, flying at the Castlebar airport.

The gentle hand of Una Lee, the director, touches every
area of the hotel with perfection. It's run as if it were her
home. The rooms are modern, and all have baths or showers. The dining room is an all-glass extension with sweeping
views of the hotel's sixty wooded acres. The chef's creations
range from superb Continental cuisine to the best of Irish
fare. Una Lee's staff is one of the best in the country.

Season: All year round   Closed Christmas Week
Luncheon: 1:00 - 2:30
Dinner: 7:00 - 9:30   AE

TURLOUGH PARK HOUSE (F)
(Castlebar 453)

Home of the famous "Fighting Fitzgeralds." Mrs. V. M.
Fitzgerald and her son, Patrick Butler, open their
19th-century country house from May to September. The
house is a mixture of Victorian-Gothic filled with antiques
and memorabilia of the eccentric Fitzgerald clan. Mrs. Fitzgerald oversees the cooking, and if she's not too tired at the
end of the day, she may join you in front of the roaring
oversized fire and tell some of the stories of her family. Eight
bedrooms. Good Irish cooking. Wine license.

CONG

*ASHFORD CASTLE (C)
(094-22644)

Ashford Castle is quite simply one of the most breathtaking places in all of Europe. Over the centuries it's been expanded from a medieval battlement to a magical Victorian fairy-tale castle. As you approach there's an unworldly stillness surrounding the castle, set on a few hundred acres of lusty Connemara countryside along the romantic silver shores of Lough Corrib.

As you pass through the massive oak entrance doors, Ashford these days is a pleasing mixture of awesome elegance and military memorabilia. The castle originally was a military stronghold of the Norman de Burgos, and suits of armor line the reception foyer recalling those medieval days in Mayo. More opulent years followed, and in the late 19th century Lord Ardilaun acquired Ashford. Over the next thirty years he lovingly transformed the military base to much of its present luxury, He filled the house with fine paintings and objets d'art. The Great Hall and reception rooms are walled with magnificent woodcarvings and stonework. He and his wife Olive planted over one million trees and created over twenty-five miles of walks through this magical forest. The demesne is seeped with folklore, and it is believed that it was here that the ancient invaders of Eire, the Fir Bolgs, battled and defeated the Tuatha de Danann.

Wings have been imperceptibly added for the guest rooms, decorated in contemporary manner and all overlooking either Lough Corrib or the River Cong. In the East wing suites are available with private sitting room and cocktail bar.

For the traveler Ashford has something for everyone. For over a century Ashford has been famed as a sporting paradise, especially for hunting, shooting, and fishing. One of the most popular shoots is run by Lord Oranmore and Browne, whose family owned Ashford Castle during the 18th century. Reservations for this shoot, which attracts the international set, can be made through the hotel. For the fisherman there is Lough Corrib, Ireland's second largest lake, filled with oversized Irish salmon and trout. On the grounds is a private 9-hole golf course and tennis courts. Even if you don't fish, the hotel will arrange boating trips and picnic visits to some of those mysterious islands scattered on the lough...over 365 of them.

Dining at Ashford is a few hours of splendor. The castle dining room is walled in mirrors, reflecting the glitter of the Waterford chandeliers and the silhouettes of carved Doric pillars. Each evening the chef prepares specialties from the days catch on Lough Corrib, and the smoked salmon and trout are cured in the castle's own smokehouse. Other choices include elaborate French cuisine and pastries. Since Ashford has long been a haven for sophisticated travelers, the wine list is one of the finest in the country.

Season: April — January   AE, DC, V
Luncheon: 1:00 - 2:30
Dinner: 7:00 - 9:00

MULRANY
GREAT WESTERN HOTEL (H)
(Mulrany 3)

In the old days the railroad system stretched as far as Achill Island, and the Great Southern Hotels chose one of the most beautiful lush spots in the West for its hotel at the entrance to Achill. The hotel is hidden in a forest of rhododendrons , plants, and trees, over one hundred acres, before the turn to the island. The hotel has been modernized and a swimming pool and tennis court added. The food is good Irish fare and a reasonable wine list. Often in the evenings the hotel offers traditional entertainment.

Season: April — January   AE, DC,
Luncheon: 12:30 - 2:30
Dinner: 7:00 - 9:00

NEWPORT

*NEWPORT HOUSE (CH)
(Newport 12 and 61)

Long ago the gourmand world decided that French honor was the highest you could achieve. Mr. Francis Mumford-Smith achieved an official honor, the Relais de Gourmand, one of France's most coveted recommendations. The food at Newport House is superb, the wine list unusual and carefully chosen. Upstairs the guest rooms throughout are fine elegant complements to the hotel's awarded standard. Mr. Mumford-Smith's white Georgian house set on the edge of Clew Bay is another era's elegance.

Season: April-September 30   AE, DC,
Luncheon: 12:45-2:15
Dinner: 7:00-9:00
Best to make reservations in advance.

ANTIQUES TRAIL

WESTPORT

CARRAIG DONN
Hughes Family
Bridge Street
(Westport 80)

BUYERS MARKET

WESTPORT

WESTPORT HOUSE

Over the past few years the Earl of Altamont has restored the mansion's dungeons below the main house and created a vast shopping arcade with over a dozen shops. An antique shop, pottery market, art gallery, gift and craft shop, heraldic shop, and Irish fashion shop. There are also tearooms to stop in during your tour of Westport House.

Hours: See below under Westport

DIVERSIONS

ACHILL ISLAND

Only a long thin bridge connects the mainland with this piece of Ireland oozing into the Atlantic. Achill is the largest of Irish islands, over 30,000 acres of crusty bog and purple heather, and its scenery one of the most spectacular in Ireland. Craggy cliffs rise 700 feet above the water, fencing the vast boglands and tiny villages of the island from the Atlantic. Along the edges are fans of crystal white beaches, and in the month of May these beaches are cluttered with fishermen gathering the basking sharks for the month season. If you are a climber, the views from Achill Head are breathtaking in the distance, Clare Island, the Mayo Mountains, and Croaghan Mountain rising from the sea 2,000 feet. There are a half dozen tiny villages on the island, and from the bridge the road fans in several directions. Take the Atlantic Drive for the most startling vistas. In the village of Dugort boats may be hired to visit the seal caves in the cliffs. The village of Doonagh was the home of Captain Boycott, and during the land wars the tenants refused to pay the taxes, hence the word "boycotting." At Keel village is Trawmore Strand stretching along two miles of coastline. There are a few restaurants and pubs on the island and a pottery industry at Keel, but the trip to Achill is a day for enjoying one of the most beautiful wildernesses of Ireland.

CLARE ISLAND
and
CLEW BAY

The ancient glacial drifts have left ragged drumlins surrounding and sinking into the windy inlet of Clew Bay along the Mayo Coast. Wedged in the valleys along the bay are the seaport towns of Westport and Newport. Guarding the entrance to Clew Bay is Clare Island, home of the legendary 16th-century Grace O'Malley, *Granuaille,* Warrior Queen of the West, whose adventures on land and sea have been handed down for centuries. From Clare Island Granuaille ruled the western coast, levying taxes on all boats entering Irish ports. She also led the rebellions against Elizabeth I. Elizabeth offered Grace a title, which she declined, pointing out that they were at least equal, she being the Queen of Connacht. In the ruined 15th-century Clare Abbey is a skull reputed to belong to Granuaille, and the inscription on the stone slab translates "O'Malley powerful on land and sea." Clare Island is five by three miles and accessible by mail boat from the tiny fishing village port of Roonagh Quay near Louisborough. The trip takes about 50 minutes. The population of Clare Island has dwindled to only a hundred islanders. Bring a picnic and climb to the summit of Slievemore with its sweeping views of Croagh Patrick and the Mayo coast and the Connemara mountains.

BALLINTUBBER ABBEY

Often referred to as "the abbey that refused to die," because it is the only church in the English-speaking world in which the Mass has been said continuously for almost 760 years. Though the present church was built in the 15th century, the Abbey was founded in 1224 by Cathal O'Conor, King of Connacht. It was here that Saint Patrick founded one of his churches in the 5th century, and nearby is the well in which he baptized his first converts. The name in Irish, *Baile Tobair Padraig*, means "homestead of the well of Patrick." During the persecutions of Henry VIII the Abbey was stripped of its lands and possessions, but the Mass continued. During these times the church was unroofed, but restoration was completed on its 750th anniversary in 1966. The Abbey is located one mile off the main Castlebar/Galway road, eight miles south of Castlebar.

BELMULLET

Almost every area of Ireland has a place that seems forgotten for hundreds of years. In this northern point in the West it's the Mullet Peninsula, with sixteen miles of untampered nature, clear bay beaches, sand dunes, and solitary cliffs. Off its coast are dozens of small beautiful islands for those who prefer a private, tranquil land. The area is cluttered with antiquities, stone forts, ancient crosses, beehive huts, and so on. Two miles off the coast is the island of Inishglora, with the monastic remains of Saint Brendan the Navigator, who died in A.D. 577. Saint Brendan is believed to have traveled to the New World before Columbus. Legend is that the Children of Lir regained their mortal bodies here after living as swans for 900 years, and are buried on the island.

CONG
CONG ABBEY

Only the remains of this "royal abbey" exist, so called because it was founded by Turlough Mor O'Conor, King of Connacht, at the beginning of the 12th century. Rory O'Conor, the last High King of Ireland, is buried in the church with his daughter and son. Restoration of the Abbey was begun by Benjamin Lee Guinness. The cross in the center of town is only part of the 14th-century original. It was destroyed by Cromwellians and later restored.

LOUISBOROUGH
CROAGH PATRICK

This is the holy mountain of Ireland, rising 2,500 feet above Clew Bay, and is the site of an annual pilgrimage up the conical-shaped mountain on the last Sunday in July. Saint Patrick is said to have fasted forty days of Lent on Croagh Patrick's sweeping summit to secure that the Irish would never lose their faith. The pilgrimage of tens of thousands begins at Murrisk Abbey, and the journey ends on the summit. Many make the climb in their bare feet on their knees in penance.

WESTPORT
WESTPORT HOUSE

This granite Georgian mansion is the ancestral home of the Marquess of Sligo, and was built on the site of the ancient castle of the O'Malleys. As was fitting for the local lords of Mayo, their home commands swirling views of Clew Bay emptying into the Atlantic, Clare Island, and the holy mountain of Croagh Patrick.

In the 15th century Colonel John Browne built the original house for his wife, the great-great-granddaughter of Grace O'Malley. In 1730 Robert Castels, a German architect, who also built Carton and Russburough and Leinster House, completed the East front of the mansion. By 1778 the house was completed by James Wyatt, who was one of the greatest of English architects. The house is a treasure of fine paintings, including one by Joshua Reynolds of the 1st Earl of Altamont, along with an impressive collection of English and Irish silver, Waterford glass, period clothing, and a library filled with Irish books and manuscripts.

The house has been beautifully restored in every detail by the present 10th Marquess of Sligo, who has also turned part of the demesnes into the Westport Zoo park. The birds and animals have been selected by the Fossetts, Ireland's famous circus family. The grounds are filled with baby elephants, lion cubs, monkeys, bears, raccoons, seals and more. The young, attractive Earl of Altamont is continuously expanding the activities at Westport House, which now includes cottages to rent, horse-drawn caravans, pony riding, and salmon and trout fishing. Additional information is available direct from Westport House.

Open: April 1 –– mid-October   Daily 2:00 - 6:00 P.M.
    May 10 –– Sept. 5   Daily 10:30 A.M. - 6:30 P.M.

COUNTY DONEGAL

HOTELS COUNTRY HOUSES FARMS

BARNESMORE
ARDNAMONA ESTATE (CH)
(Donegal 92)

This white stone and clapboard country house, only a few miles from Donegal Town, is ideal for the traveler who prefers peace and privacy. Ardnamona is hidden along the banks of Loch Eske in a valley of palm, fern, and rhododendron shrubs. The house was built by Sir Arthur Wallace in 1834 as his country estate and was only opened to the public a few years ago. The atmosphere is cozy, and the house is filled with overstuffed furniture, period antiques, and interesting French prints. Bedrooms are simple but tastefully done, and the menu is good fare if unimaginative. For travelers who prefer something remote.

Season: All year round
Dinner: 7:00-9:00

KILLYBEGS
KILLYBEGS HOTEL (H)
(Killybegs 120)

A perfect stop while touring the breathtaking Donegal coast. Set in the harbor town of Killybegs, one of the loveliest fishing villages in Ireland. The hotel is large and the décor modern.

During the summer months there's the Killybegs International Arts Festival with actors visiting from Dublin and London, art shows of local and international talent, and the air is filled with traditional music. The hotel has its own cabaret evenings, and the bar is usually filled with local and visiting fishermen who'll entertain you with fascinating, if hard-to-believe, lore. The chef's specialty is fish and the local catch is some of the finest in the country.

Season: June — September
Luncheon: 12:30-2:30
Dinner: 7:00-9:00

RATHMULLEN
*RATHMULLEN HOUSE (CH)
(Rathmullen 4)

One of the most gracious and elegant of country houses, another choice of France's *Relais de campagne,* located near the far tip of Donegal's lush, remote countryside. The main house sits high on a hill overlooking miles of the silent waters of Lough Swilly and surrounded by acres of award-winning gardens and plantings. The hill slopes toward a halfmile of sandy beach on the edge of the lake.

Bob and Robin Wheeler have restored all twenty-one bedrooms to a wonderful Old World atmosphere. Recently, they built twenty chalets around the grounds, which are perfect for families, each with its own living room, kitchenette, bath, and sleeping four to six persons per chalet.

Meals at Rathmullen House seem as if you're dining in the garden, but actually you're in a beautiful glass enclosed addition. This is Bob Wheeler's domain. A superb chef, he prepares courses and courses, changing the menu daily. It's imaginative, Continental, and Irish cuisine. All the vegetables and fruits are fresh from the garden. The wine list is extensive and impressive, but order your white wine before the meal, since the bottles are not chilled in advance. Both before and after the sumptuous meal be sure to join Francie, the barman, in the white stucco cellar bar around the blazing turf fire. He's an invaluable friend for getting to know the area and its history.

On the grounds are grass tennis courts, croquet, excellent

swimming in Lough Swilly, and nearby are 9- and 18-hole golf courses. The hotel will arrange for boating and deep-sea fishing.

Season: Mid-April — September 30   AE, DC,
Luncheon: 1:00-2:00
Dinner: 7:30-8:45

ROSSNOWLAGH
ROSSNOWLAGH MANOR ESTATE (CH)
(072-65477)

Pat and Nonie Reidy opened their "sporting lodge" only a few years ago, but have quickly gained an enviable sportsman trade. It's a modern house set between towering sand dunes. Overside the dunes is a three-mile private beach on the ocean. Across the road hundreds of swans drift on the pond, which is also stocked with duck and geese. There's something for almost every interest, swimming, surfing, deep-sea fishing, shooting, and horse-drawn caravans. Golf, hunting, and pony trekking can be arranged nearby.

Mrs. Reidy is a Cordon Bleu cook and serves some of the finest food in the area. There are only seven rooms, and the stay is a visit with the Reidy family, since you are never sure just how many of the children, nine in all, will also be on hand. Since this is a sporting lodge, the theme is carried through to the décor of the rooms. One in African design, another in a fishing scheme. Definitely for those who prefer the "sporting life."

Season: All year round
Dinner: 7:00-9:00

THE SAND HOTEL (H)
(072-65343)

Rossnowlagh is the jewel of Donegal resorts, with its miles of sun-bleached sand bordering Donegal Bay. At the Sand Hotel the ocean rolls beneath your window. The hotel is modern, and all rooms are available with private bath. You can ride horseback along the beach, golf nearby, or arrange for deep-sea fishing or water skiing. In the evenings during the season there's entertainment, or table tennis or billiards. The menu is standard Irish fare, and the wine list adequate.

Season: Easter — September 30   AE
Luncheon: 1:00-2:30
Dinner: 7:00-9:00

RESTAURANTS AND PUBS

ARDARA
NANCY'S

Nancy's great-grandmother started the pub, and it's been in the same family for over 200 years. A great place to hear traditional Irish music, especially fiddle playing.

BARNESMORE GAP
BIDDY O'BARNES

Along the main road of the Barnesmore Gap, between Donegal town and Ballyboofey, is this famous old pub, and it's just as it's been for over a hundred years, complete with oversized hearth fire, chickens strolling in and out, and local shanachies on the odd day. No food served here, just good drink and good crack.

ANTIQUES TRAIL

DONEGAL
THOMAS ANTIQUES
Sean Thomas
Market Square
(Donegal 144)

BUYERS MARKET

ARDARA

This is the best town for purchasing Donegal tweeds. There's a cluster of over a half dozen stores that specialize in this knobby, durable fabric. You can buy by the bolt or already made up in suits, skirts, jackets, table mats or almost anything else you can imagine.

BUNDORAN

THE GALLERY ART CENTER

Just before you enter the town of Bundoran heading north on the left is this unique gallery in an old castle keep. It's filled with unusual metal etchings reproducing 19th-century drawings of Irish scenery and landscapes and works of Irish artists. Worth a visit.

Open: Daily 10:00 A.M.-5:00 P.M.

DUNFANAHY

THE GALLERY

Plan to spend a few hours sifting through Alan and Moira Harley's Gallery. There are some fine handcrafts and antiques to be found, though the prices are relatively high.

Open: Weekdays 10:00 A.M.-10:00 P.M.

DIVERSIONS

BARNESMORE GAP

This road winds a scenic trail through Croaghaum, or the Blue Stack Mountains, rising from the solitary, lonely Donegal landscape. For hundreds of years this was one of the most dangerous and feared of Irish passes, with its woods harboring bandits and robbers in the narrow gorge.

CREESLOUGH

DOE CASTLE

This small town on the inlet at Sheep Haven was the ancestral home of the MacSweeny tribe. The family was invited by the O'Donnell clan to settle here from Scotland. It was at Doe Castle that Red Hugh O'Donnell was fostered, and later attacks were mounted from Doe against the Plantations of Ulster. A good example of an ancient fortified castle surrounded on three sides by the sea and a moat on land. Still standing are a 55-foot keep, a bawn, and round towers. Nearby is the graveyard of the MacSweeny family.

DONEGAL

The town was given its name *Dun na aGall* (Fort of the Foreigners) during the Viking occupation, but became important in Irish history as the seat of the O'Donnells, the kings of Ireland, and remained so until the "Flight of the Earls" in 1607. Soon afterward the town was planted by Sir Basil Brooke, and its layout altered along English lines, including the Diamond, or market place.

DONEGAL CASTLE

The castle was originally built by Red Hugh O'Donnell in 1505, and ruins of the original tower still stand. Later, in 1610, Sir Basil incorporated the original castle within his new Jacobean structure. Of special interest is the finely carved Jacobean fireplace.

THE ABBEY

Near Lough Eske the remains of the Franciscan Abbey of Donegal. It was founded by Red Hugh O'Donnell and his wife in 1474, and the founders are buried at the Abbey. Over the centuries its possession shifted between the Planters and the Irish, and was finally blown up in 1601. At the temporary home of the Friary at Bundrowes, between 1623 and 1626, four Franciscans compiled the *Annals of the Four Masters* (mentioned earlier in this book). A 25-foot-high obelisk stands in the Diamond in their honor.

DOOCHARNEY

For those who want a scenic drive in the fabulous untouched countryside of Donegal, approach this tiny village by the moor from Dungloe. Wind down the road, the "Doocharney Corkscrew," into the lush Glen of Gweebarra along the Gweebarra River. The river eventually pours into the Atlantic. Take this tour through the heather and gorse-filled hillsides; you won't be disappointed.

GLENCOLUMCILLE

Not so many years ago this seaside village was one of the most desolate outposts in Ireland, remote from the rest of the world, bordered by the raging Atlantic and threatened by complete desertion. Then, almost a decade ago, Father James McDyer, a parish priest, decided to organize a few lingering families of Glencolumcille to form what would eventually become one of the most productive county cooperatives in Ireland. He began with a vegetable co-op, and then expanded to include a processing co-op, a hand-knitting co-op, and a metal craft co-op. Today the seaside town is booming with activity.

Of special interest to the traveler is Holiday Village, a cluster of twenty cottages designed and thatched in traditional style, complete with turf fires, but modernized with central heating, refrigerators, and cookers. Write: Glencolumcille Holiday Village (or ring Glencolumcille 3 for reserving a cottage.) Cottages are available all year round. There's no better way to get close to the heart of Ireland.

If you can come for only a day's stay, be sure to visit the Folk Village, with its period cottages filled with traditional household items, fixtures, farm tools and more. During the season teas are served during the daytime, and in the evenings there are ceilis. The craft shop is filled with local handcrafts.

INISHOWEN PENINSULA

This peninsula is a bird's-eye view of Ireland untouched, bordered by Lough Swilly, Lough Foyle, and the Atlantic. An entire circle of the peninsula is over a hundred miles of bays and inlets. Plan to spend at least a day to tour the scenic drive, and don't miss the views from the heights of Mamore Gap, which fan the heather-covered hills and burnt bogs of Donegal. In the distance rises majestic Malin Head, the solitary tip of Ireland's most northerly point.

SLIEVELEAGUE

Another day's journey for some of the most breathtaking scenery. Begin with the ascent of Slieveleague in the town of Carrick. Slieveleague is a most awesome, majestic sight, with its ancient cliffs rising almost 2,000 feet from the sea. It is believed to be the highest marine cliff in Europe. Beware of the drive up the mountain from Teelin. It's only for the experienced driver, but it is one of the most exciting drives. Atop the cliffs, surrounded by fields of heather, is an ancient oratory. An appropriate place for a holy site.

DUBLIN CIRCLE

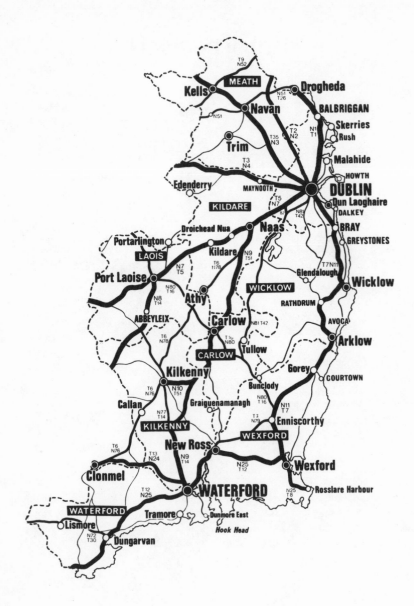

Courtesy of Irish Tourist Board

COUNTY DUBLIN

HOTELS   COUNTRY HOUSES   FARMS

DUBLIN

*SHELBOURNE HOTEL (H)
St. Stephen's Green
(766471)

This red-and-white Victorian hotel stands at the edge of St. Stephen's Green. A stay in the Shelbourne is a touch of Dublin's 18th-century elegance. Many of the bedrooms have been renovated over the years, and just recently six suites were completely redone. The Horseshoe Bar is the most gracious of Dublin drinking spots, walled in mirrors, with red leather banquettes lining the walls. It's been the favorite gathering place for decades of Dublin's finest, especially the horsey set. Jimmy, the head bartender, and his assistants, John and Sean, offer the quickest, most convivial service in Dublin.

The Shelbourne has three restaurants: the Main Dining Room, the Saddle Room, and the Grill. Chef Maurice O'Looney oversees all three, but his superb culinary creations appear in the Main Dining Room. He's a genius with French sauces and puffy French desserts. Be sure not to leave Dublin without tasting his Veal Ludovic or his Crème Brulée. Next door is the Saddle Room, which specializes in excellent grills, roasts, and seafood. It's preferred by those who want a more relaxed atmosphere. Both present excellent wine lists. By the Kildare Street entrance is the Grill Room if you want a quick, inexpensive meal.

Season: All year round   AE, CB
Main Dining Room: 12:30-2:30; 6:30-10:30
Closed Sunday

Saddle Room: 12:30-2:45; 6:00-11:15

Sunday 12:30-2:00; 6:00-9:00

Grill: 10:30-11:00 (Closed Sunday)

A special note on the Shelbourne: The entire staff is one of
the finest, most efficient in the country, or in Europe for that
matter.

*ROYAL HIBERNIAN (H)
Dawson Street
(772991)

This elegant jewel of a hotel caters to the elite international
travelers to Dublin, and has maintained the highest hotelier
standards since its first days as a coaching inn. The graceful
interior of the main floor is Georgian, with large, high-
ceilinged reception rooms. The bedrooms are decorated in
soft colors and floral prints with sheer voile curtains and
satin puffs on the beds.

Chef Roger Noblet has been with the hotel for over sixteen
years and prepares exquisite French cuisine in the Lafayette
Room. A few of his specialties are: Brochette de Fruits de Mer
and Rognons au Vieil Armagnac. During the year Chef Noblet features special international evenings with Italian,
Swiss, German, and other Continental food. The décor of
the Layfayette Room has been styled after Maxim's in Paris
and its service is faultless. The wine list is impressive.

On the floor below are two other popular restaurants, the
Buttery and the Bianconi Grill. The Buttery is a favorite for an
elegant intimate luncheon, but be sure to ring Jack ahead of
time, since it's very difficult to secure a table some days. If
you just want cocktails George always stocks the bar with
all sorts of obscure liqueurs, etc.—the best bartenders in
Dublin for accommodating the "exotic requests of Americans." (The Irish consider anything exotic that isn't straight
whiskey with a splash of water.)

Next door is the Bianconi Grill, which serves the tastiest
food of grill rooms in the city at the least expensive prices.
Especially recommended is the poached or grilled salmon.

Lafayette Room: 12:30-3:00; 6:30-10:30   AE, CB, DC
   Sunday 1:00-2:30; 6:30-9:30
Buttery: 12:30-2:30 (Closed Sunday)
Bianconi Grill: 11:00 A.M.-11:00 P.M. (Closed Sunday)
La Rotisserie: 12:00-10:45 (Closed Sunday)

*SACHS (H)
Morehampton Road
(680995)

Though a relatively new hotel in Dublin, Sachs is a jewel of period elegance, whose clever renovator amalgamated a terrace of Regency houses along the lush tree-lined Morehampton Road. The bedrooms and suites carry through the period atmosphere and are filled with antiques and rich lush décor. The key to Sachs, however, is Jack Donnelly, the ebullient handsome manager and one of Ireland's leading hoteliers. Jack's keen perception as host to his guests cause international visitors and Dubliners alike to flock to the hotel. Guests usually gather in the Liberties Bar and then later ajoin upstairs for a superb supper of Continental cuisine. During the day a marvelous luncheon is served in the Bar with such specialties as: Smoked Salmon Paté, Dublin Bay Prawn Salad, Cheese Pancakes, Cider Baked Limerick Ham and Sherry Trifle. Sachs is not to be missed.

Season: All year round   AE, CB
Luncheon: 12:30-2:30
Dinner: 7:00-10:00

GRESHAM HOTEL (H)
Upper O'Connell Street
(746881)

As you pull up to the blue canopied entrance, you're reminded of the opulence of the finest European hotels. Past the front doors of the lobby the famous Waterford chandeliers still hang, and there is still some Regency furniture scattered around. But the Gresham has changed management so often in the past few years it is hard to say what it is these days. What it is not is the grande dame of past years run by Timothy "Toddy" O'Sullivan, Ireland's legendary hotelier. For decades it was *the* hotel in Dublin, set on the broad historic boulevard of O'Connell Street. Today the area is cluttered with fast food shops and junk boutiques. The rooms are still well kept and tastefully decorated. The main restaurant is now called the Savarin, and the food is good, but certainly not memorable. The new management has a long way to go to retreive the Gresham's past reputation for elegance and excellence.

Open: All year round   AE, CB, DC
Luncheon: 12:30-2:30
Dinner: 6:30-11:15

*THE BERKELEY COURT HOTEL (H)
Lansdowne Road, Ballsbridge
(601711)

When P.V. Doyle, one of Ireland's most successful hoteliers, decided to create this new hotel obviously, nothing was to be spared. The hotel opened in the summer of 1978 and was built on three acres of land in the former Botanic Gardens of Trinity College. The lobby is filled with antiques (almost too many), and on the far wall is an enormous tapestry designed by Patrick Scott, one of Ireland's leading artists. The hotel has over two hundred rooms, and they are decorated in modern hotel fashion, not too imaginative. Amenities not found in other Dublin hotels: an indoor heated swimming pool, sauna and hairdressing salons. Michael Governey is the hotel manager, and this personable professional is one of the most highly regarded managers in the country, and he has acquired a very good staff.

Eugene McSweeney is the chef de cuisine and his creations in the Berkeley Room are ambitious and skilled. Some exceptional specialities are: Potiquet de Beurre de Saumon

Fumé (smoked salmon paté), Le Casserolette de Filet de Sole (fillets of sole poached with white wine, served in a pastry case served on a bed of saffron mushrooms with tomatoes).

Season: All year round   AE, CB, DC
Berkeley Room: Luncheon: 12:30-2:30
Dinner: 7:00-11:00
Coffee Shop: 7:30-Midnight

(It would be unfair not to warn: The Berkeley Court is very expensive by Dublin standards.)

BUSWELL'S (H)
Molesworth Street
(764013)

When people travel, they tend to want to find that small intimate hotel no one knows about. Well, unfortunately, people *know* about Buswell's, and adore it. Located on a small street, not far from St. Stephen's Green and Dawson Street. The rooms tend to be small and simply decorated. The staff is warm and accommodating. A wonderful "find." The restaurant offers good solid Irish fare, but nothing too exciting.

Season: All year round

KILLINEY

*FITZPATRICK CASTLE (C)
Killiney Hill
(851533)

One of the most popular castle hotels, located nine miles from Dublin, high on a hill overlooking Dublin Bay and the city lights. Paddy Fitzpatrick is a top host-patron, and with his wife Eithne he opened the castle to guests after completely renovating it in 1972. It's hard to imagine a castle on a

300-acre estate so near the heart of the city. The castle dates back to 1741, but was in crumbling condition when Paddy took it over. Now there are fifty modern, beautifully decorated rooms, some with four-poster beds, all with bath and shower; a large indoor swimming pool; squash courts; saunas; tennis courts; and a mini golf course. There are three suites complete with sitting room, kitchenette, and one with a romantic four-poster.

Dine in the candlelit Victorian Room. The menu varies from unusual Continental choices to excellent Irish fare. Good wine selection. Have a drink before or after dinner in the Dungeon Bar by the open turf fire. Paddy is inventive in finding good entertainment for his guests. On Sunday mornings there's a lively jazz session.

Season: All year round   AE, DC,
Luncheon: 12:30-2:00
Dinner: 6:30-11:00

RESTAURANTS AND PUBS

DUBLIN

SNAFFLES
47 Lower Lesson Street
(760790)

Unless you keep a keen eye out, you'll miss the entrance to one of Dublin's finest restaurants, a small intimate room in the basement of a Georgian house along Lesson Street. Soon after the Tinnes opened their restaurant it became regarded as a gastronomic haven. The menu is limited, but usually faultless. Some of Snaffles specialties are unusual and not to be missed: a rich, tart Snaffles mousse, smoked mackerel paté, kidneys sautéed in brandy, and excellent game in season. Afterward, try a fluffy grape pud covered with caramel glaze, or a grapefruit sorbet. If you have any trouble deciding what to order, Hugh or Jimmy, excellent waiters from the now closed Russell, will help you along. Fine impressive wine list. The restaurant is tiny, so always book in advance.

Luncheon: 12:30-2:30   AE, DC,
Dinner: 7:00-11:00
Closed Sunday, dinner Monday, lunch Saturday.

LE COQ HARDI
29 Pembroke Road
(689070)

Don't be misled by the unassuming entrance to this basement restaurant under the Landsdowne Hotel. Chef/Patron John Howard has devised one of Dublin's most sophisticated restaurants. Mr. Howard blends Ireland's bountiful resources with the best French preparations. To start try his Plateau de Fruits de mer (a cold selection of fresh Irish seafood) or the unusual Coq Hardi Smokies (smoked haddock, tomato, cheese and cream cooked "en cocotte"). The soups are homemade and very rich. In fact, most of the dishes here are rich: Vol au Vent Vendredi is Mr. Howard's own creation in a pastry case filled with seafood in a light cream sauce. The beef selections include Entrecote au Poivre et Cognac (sirloin steak sauteed in crushed peppercorns with mushrooms and brandy). The cheese tray has a good variety. The desserts are not quite as imaginative as the rest of the menu.

Luncheon: 12:30-2:30   (Closed Saturday)   AE
Dinner: 7:30-11:00
Closed Sunday

THE GREY DOOR
22 Upper Pembroke Road
(763286)

Barry Wyse and P.J. Daly have opened probably the most innovative restaurant in Dublin in sometime. The fare here is

Russian — and not just borscht soup and blinis, but genuine robust country-style Russian. Their chef is thirty-one-year-old Eammon Walsh, who has trained in Helsinki and Finland. Some of its delicious specialties are: Pelmans á la Sibrienne (minced beef encased in pastry and coated with a mustard sauce), Filet Novgorod (filet steak on a bed of thinly sliced sauerkraut, fried barley mushrooms, caviar, and sour cream), Sole Kirgis (sole flavored with tarragon, horseradish, capers, and dill). To finish off this dizzyingly exotic meal order an Armenian Kiss (coffee laced with Russian brandy-based liqueur).

Luncheon: 12:15-2:30   (Monday-Friday)   AE
Dinner: 6:30-12:30   (Monday-Saturday)

TANDOORI ROOMS
27 Lower Lesson Street
(762286)

What else could a terribly elegant, refined man like Mike Butt create but a terribly elegant restaurant? Tandoori Rooms is one of two restaurants in an old Georgian house (the other is also Mike's, the Golden Orient). Mike specializes in Tandoori food, a kind of Indian cuisine, which derives its name from *tandoor* (a mud oven). The food is marinated for hours in spices and herbs. Some of his fascinating specialities are: Teetar Bhoona Angoori (pot roast pheasant Tandoore), Saffron marinated chicken, King scallops and Dublin jumbo prawns Falfaraizi, Aubergine frite or Provencal. He serves such exotic sweets as Mango sorbet and Jelebi Kulfi. Also included on the menu are simple grills for those who can't enjoy the spicy food. Mike goes to the market every day to choose his ingredients for that evening and insists on everything being fresh. The cellar dining room is candlelit with tasteful Islamic touches. A man of incredible range, he commissioned Edward Delaney to design fascinating Celtic centerpieces for his tables. A restaurant not to be missed. Upstairs, in the Golden Orient, the atmosphere is informal, and Mike serves very good curries. A good late night spot.

Dinner: 7:00 P.M.-1:00 A.M.   AE, DC,
Closed Sunday

THE BAILEY
2 Duke Street
(773055)

For years the Bailey was one of the favorite pubs of Dublin literati, and just beyond the entranceway is the door to No. 7 Eccles Street, where Molly and Leopold Bloom lived in *Ulysses*. A few years ago the old pub was renovated and upstairs is the grand restaurant. You dine along leather banquettes, and there are lots of ferns hanging round the windows. The specialties are elaborate and rich. Especially good is the Beef Stroganoff in a very spicy sauce or creamy moules marinière. Be sure to have the house salad, prepared at your table. A rather good wine list.

Luncheon: 12:30-3:00   AE, CB, DC
Dinner: 6:30-11:15
Closed Sunday

SHRIMPS WINE BAR
1 Anne's Lane
(713143)

If you are disappointed by finding Grafton Street laced with McDonalds, Baskin-Robbins, and other American-style restaurants, then turn from Grafton towards Dawson and again at Anne's Lane. There is Sheila Tynan's lively bistro. Only eight tables bank the emerald green and mirrored walls. There's an adequate bar and a glowing fire, when the weather cools. Sheila oversees the menu, which changes daily. Some of her specialties are unusual: fresh crab claw salad, rabbit and prune terraine, and a hot curried tarte. Wine license only.

Open: 12:00-11:00 P.M.
Closed Sunday

THE LORD EDWARD
23 Christchurch Place
(752557)

A treasure for those who love fresh seafood. The only thing on the menu that's not from the sea is the dessert. Fish of a dozen varieties, broiled, boiled, grilled, sautéed, or in a rich creamy sauce, whichever way you prefer. Unfortunately, the vegetables are not quite up to standard and neither are the sweets, but you're going for the fish anyway. The restaurant is located in the Liberties, the old section of Dublin, and is named after Lord Edward Fitzgerald, a beloved Irish patriot, who led the United Irishmen in the '98 Rising. The restaurant's atmosphere is Edwardian (what else?). The dining room seats only 50-odd, so book in advance.

Luncheon: 12:30-2:30   AE, DC,
Dinner: 6:00-10:45
Closed for luncheon on Saturday and all day Sunday

UNICORN
11 Merrion Row
(762182)

Renato Sidoli's Unicorn is one of the most popular restaurants with Dubliners, especially members of the Dail (the Irish Parliament). Located just one block away from St. Stephen's Green, this small restaurant serves the finest Italian cuisine. Mr. Sidoli is a host-patron in the Old World style, and every once in a while during your meal he checks at your table to see that all is going well. Around the corner down a narrow lane is the Unicorn Minor, an excellent place for lunching. Delicious creamy fettucine, lasagna, and tiny pizzas. During the day Domenica Fulgona, a warm personable Italian woman, looks after you at the Minor. Fine selection of Italian wines.

Unicorn Minor: 10:30-7:30
Unicorn: 6:00-10:30
Closed Sunday

LUNCHEON SUGGESTIONS

There are four very good places for luncheon if you don't want anything elaborate at reasonable prices.

NATIONAL GALLERY
Merrion Street West
Monday-Saturday:
  10:00-5:30
Thursday: 10:00-9:00
Sunday: 2:30-5:00

Restaurant in lovely gallery setting with a menu offering typical Irish fare: smoked salmon, Dublin prawns, baby spring lamb, and so on.

MURPHS
21 Batchelors Walk
(along the Quay)
Monday-Saturday:
  10:00-11:00
Closed Sunday

If you are yearning for American-style food: plump juicy hamburgers, varied omelettes, club sandwiches, salads, and pizzas . . . this is the best there is in Dublin.

MITCHELL'S WINE BAR
Kildare Street
(Hours unknown at
  press time)

The famous purveyors of wines and spirits Mitchell & Sons, have turned their basement into a delightful place serving very good soups, sandwiches, and cold platters.

BEWLEYS CAFES LTD.
79 Grafton Street
Monday-Friday: 9:00-5:00
Saturday: 9:00-1:00
Closed Sunday

Established in 1840. Old tradition of period tearooms. Tasty sandwiches, rich pastries, and the best tea and coffee in Dublin.

DUBLIN PUB CRAWL

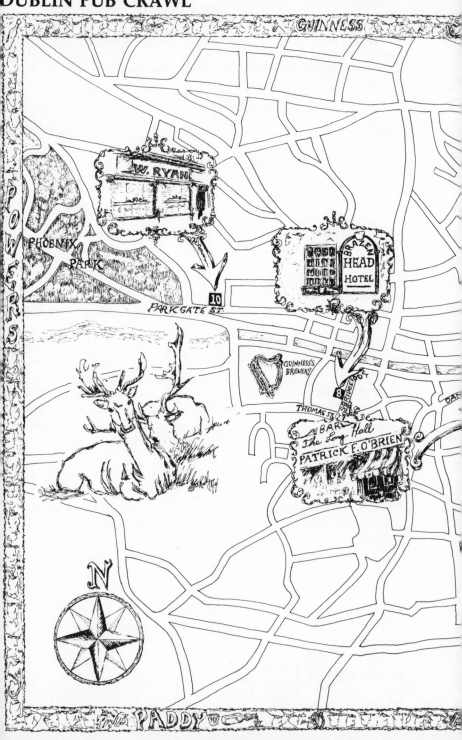

DUN LAOGHAIRE

TRUDI'S
107 Lower Georges Street
(805318)

The Kiernan's have created a lively, informal restaurant in this harbor town, which is a pleasant distraction from Dublin's center city. The menu offers tempting, varied specialties: potted crab, smoked salmon paté, lamb kidneys in brandy cream and mustard sauce, roast breast of pigeon in black cherry sauce, along with dishes for the less adventurous. The wine list offers French, Italian, and Austrian wines at reasonable prices. In fact, all prices at Trudi's are reasonable.

Dinner: 7:30-11:00   AE
Closed Sunday

HOWTH

KING SITRIC
East Pier
(325235)

After a half dozen visits, I would have to say that the King Sitric is the finest restaurant in the Dublin area. A meal at Aidan McManus's restaurant is close to faultless. This tiny white Georgian house sits on the edge of the secluded harbor at Howth. Aidan was trained as a chef in Switzerland, and his specialty is seafood. Begin with the unusual Thyme and Stilton mousse or moules marinière in a light airy sauce, or a thick rich soupe de poisson. The next suggestion gets a little more difficult — everything is so tempting . . . grilled turbot steak, prawns frits, black sole meunier, scallops in vermouth, and huge, luscious, oversized lobsters. During the shooting season there's wild duck, teal, roast woodcock, widgeon, and roast pheasant. Each day bushels of fresh vegetables arrive for the evening's meal. At the end of the feast Aidan prepares an indecent creation of airy meringues covered with vanilla ice cream and a rich chocolate sauce. Excellent wine list.

Dinner: 6:30-11:30   AE, DC,
Luncheon: 1:00-2:00 (Monday-Friday, May-October)
Closed Sunday

RATHFARNUM
KILLAKEE HOUSE
Killakee Road
(906-645)

Chef/Patron Josef Frei created this deliciously continental restaurant in the renovated art center alongside the road winding up through the Dublin Mountains below the Hell Fire Club (see page 317). Mr. Frei is Swiss-born and his specialties tend to be very generous, rich, and full-flavored, so be sure to be near ravenous when you arrive. Particularly recommended: Hors d'oeuvre Variés, Beignets de Fromage (deep-fried pastry filled with cheese, ham, and spinach), Sole Farcie du Maison (filet of sole poached in white wine and filled with scallops, prawns and mushrooms in a light cream sauce). For those who prefer something simpler but memorable: Carré d'Agneau Roti (a spicy rack of lamb). Be sure to sample the fresh vegetable platter. If there is any strength left for dessert, both Crepe Suzettes and Bananes Flambés are prepared at the table.

Luncheon: 12:30-3:00   AE
Afternoon Tea: 3:00-6:00
Dinner: 7:30-11:30
Closed Monday
(The Art Gallery and Craft Shop are open 8:00-11:00 P.M.)

SANDYCOVE
MIRABEAU
Marine Parade
(809873)

Sean Kinsella took over Mirabeau a few years ago and has created a very good restaurant along the seashore in this old Victorian house. The bar overlooks the sea, and you sip your drinks by the open turf fire. Sean has an international flair, and his menu is varied and wide-ranging. Best choice would be seafood. Rich French desserts. *However*, be forewarned. His prices are staggering and pretentious. He has had enough complaints to have adjusted them, but it's doubtful.

Dinner: 7:30-11:00   AE, DC,
Closed Sunday

BUYERS MARKET

Like all cities, Dublin has thousands of shops to browse through, but here are a few suggestions that offer the finest in their special-ties and will serve as a good beginning. Grafton Street, off St. Stephen's Green, is a good place to start. Ireland's two finest department stores, Switzer's and Brown Thomas, are the Harrod's of Dublin and are across the street from one another. They're the best places to purchase Waterford crystal. They also carry fine Irish pottery and linen. Head over toward Dawson Street via Duke Street, and on the right is Duke Lane. Tucked away there in a small shop at No. 9 is the Weaver's Shed. This tiny shop is filled with unusual imaginative goods, tweeds, scarves, tablemats, bags, blankets. A half block over is Dawson Street and Cleo's, *the* place for the finest quality Aranwear, tweed jackets, coats and cloaks, hand-crocheted shawls and skirts, and many other finds. At the bottom of Dawson Street is Nassau Street. At No. 39 is Kevin & Howlan for men's clothing. Hun-dreds of kinds of the finest of Donegal tweed jackets, slacks, suits, hats and caps, scarves and ties. They may be taken right from the rack, or, if you prefer, you may choose your fabric and order what you want to be made up.

Walk down along the quays to Ha'penny Bridge gracefully arching across the Liffey. The Bridge was built in 1816 to replace the ferry taking people over to the south side of Dublin. It was so called because there was a half-penny toll. Today there's no toll, and directly across the bridge is the Dublin Woolen Company

Ltd. You could almost do all your shopping here. Rooms are filled with bolts of tweed fabric and linen, Aran handknit wear, pottery, and fine handcrafts.

Dublin has never been known as a couturier center, but two of Ireland's leading designers have an international reputation for custom made clothing: Sybil Connolly, Seven Merrion Square, and Ib Jorgenson, 24 Fitzwilliam Square. Plan to spend money when you pass through their elegant portals. Slightly less expensive but of very good quality is Ib Jorgenson's Boutique on Molesworth Street.

The making of Irish lace flourished as a craft for over a hundred years in 18th century Ireland and then died out. For the past ten years a very talented, attractive woman, Deirdre Ryan, has been collecting this delicate workmanship from attics and homes around the country, then redesigning and refurbishing it. Her shop "Design On You" is in Monkstown (Tel: 801549) and is a must for anyone who treasures the unusual. Don't miss it.

If you have little time to browse through tiny shops and ferret out special finds, head for the Kilkenny Shop on Nassau Street, the Bloomingdale's of Dublin. It has something for everyone. All of the design done in the workshops in Kilkenny is available there along with the best of design around the country. The prices tend to be higher, but shopping there is a time-saver. If you are getting hungry or want a tea break during your shopping spree, the Kilkenny Kitchen on the second floor is open from 9:30 A.M. to 5:30 P.M.

For the bibliophile I have three suggestions: For the antiquarian and rare books, Fred Hanna, 29 Nassau Steet; for Irish contemporary and classic, Hodges & Riggis, 20 St. Stephen's Green. If you're looking for a special remembrance or present from Ireland I have a few selections: *Irish Houses and Castles*, by Desmond Guinness and William Ryan; *Dublin, A Portrait,* by V.S. Pritchett. Or a subscription to *Ireland of the Welcomes.* Betty Healey edits this superb quarterly magazine in cooperation with the Irish Tourist Board, and it's filled with fascinating articles each month. It's available at almost every newsstand. Be sure to pick up a copy, and if you'd like to have it sent when you return home, write to: Ireland of the Welcomes, Baggot Street Bridge, Dublin.

ANTIQUES TRAIL

One of the most pleasant pastimes in Dublin is antique hunting, and these shops are open from 10:00 A.M. to 6:00 P.M. weekdays and until 1:00 P.M. Saturdays. For those who prefer browsing the flea markets there's the Dandelion Market on St. Stephen's Green near the top of Grafton Street, which has over thirty antique stalls open on Saturdays. During the first of August is the Antique Dealers Fair, which is held in the Mansion House on Dawson Street. Over fifty dealers from all over the country arrive for a fortnight fair. Below are a few of Dublin's dozens of antique shops and stalls. The finest auctions are held in the Adams Rooms next door to the Shelbourne Hotel. You'll have to check for details to see if there's an auction going on while you're in Dublin.

EDWARD BUTLER
ANTIQUES
14 Batchelors Walk
(743485)

Fine old established shop. 18th-century furniture and pictures. Quality items.

H.E. DANKER
10 South Anne Street
(777009)

Fine jewelry, silver, and paintings.

THE GEORGIAN SHOP
54 South William Street
(774437)

A fine shop with many pieces of Georgian furniture, clocks and mantlepieces.

HIBERNIAN ANTIQUES
1 Molesworth Place
(763824)

Small but very fine shop. Irish Bellek china, furniture, pictures and glass.

GERALD KENYON
26 South William Street
(773945)

One of the best sources for Irish 18th- and 19th-century furniture.

R. McDONNELL LTD.
16 Kildare Street
8/9 Molesworth Street
(762614)

Mr. McDonnell is chairman of the Irish Antique Dealers Association. Specializes in 18th- and 19th-century furniture.

MISSION ANTIQUES
45/46 Clarendon Street

Run by the Carmelites. Proceeds go to the missions. Priests are notorious for acquiring a wide range of antiques in Ireland.

MITCHELL ANTIQUES
40 Clarendon Street
(773922)

Very small shop. Mainly mantlepieces and brass.

JOHN O'REILLY
Fine Art Showrooms
27 South Anne Street
(772142)

Regarded as one of the best in Dublin. Antique jewelry, silver, objets d'art, 18th- and 19th-century furniture, paintings, porcelain, bronzes, and old Waterford glass.

REMBRANDT ANTIQUES
24 South Anne Street
(779374)

Nice small shop. General range.

J.W. WELDON
55 Clarendon Street
(771638)
18 South Anne Street
(772742)

Both are small shops and cater to those interested in high quality silver.

JANE WILLIAMS
23 Molesworth Street
(767857)

Small prints, small silver objects, and 18th-century and early 19th-century furniture.

LOUIS WINE LTD.
31/32 Grafton Street
(773865)

The finest in Ireland. The shop has one of the largest antique silver collection in Europe. Also deals in jewelry and early pictures.

ENTERTAINMENT

Much of Dublin's evening entertainment has been covered in the Theatre and Music chapters in Part One. Check listings there for information. Here are a few other suggestions for Dublin during the tourist season.

DUBLIN

JURY'S IRISH CABARET
(767511)

Deciding to spend an evening at Jury's Irish Cabaret depends on whether you enjoy an evening put on for tourists. If you do, Jury's is the best and most professional in the country. You have a choice of going along for dinner or just seeing the show. The meal is good and exactly what you can expect considering the number of people served and the time in which it has to be served. The program includes storytelling, step-dancing, and harpers. Since it was first put on over fifteen years ago, over one million people have seen the show.

Dinner: 7:30   AE, CB, DC
Cabaret: 8:15

HOWTH

ABBEY TAVERN
(322006)

In the quiet seaside village of Howth, on the north of Dublin Bay, is the Abbey Tavern, one of the most popular spots for visitors who want a rollicking evening of ballad singing and Irish entertainment. You can either plan to dine at the Abbey in the candlelit restaurant, with open turf fires, on the seafood menu, or join in later next door in the barn as the Abbey singers roar a medley of ballads, patriots' songs, and haunting airs. An evening at the Abbey can be a spontaneous free-for-all, and you're never sure what the program will include. During the season the Tavern is packed, so be sure to ring ahead for reservations.

Entertainment usually begins around 8:30 P.M.
Dinner: 7:00-11:30   AE, DC,
Closed Sunday

DIVERSIONS
DUBLIN
TOURIST TRAIL

One of the most useful booklets put out by a tourist board is the *Dublin Tourist Trail*. It's a sign-posted trail of Dublin City available at the Dublin Tourist Office at 51 Dawson Street or 14 Upper O'Connell Street. Keep a sharp eye out for the signs along the way indicating the path for this three-hour tour. The booklet is witty and filled with fascinating information as you pass along Dublin's streets. Be sure to get a copy before setting out for full details of your tour of Dublin's monuments. Following is a general itinerary of the principal spots.

Begin at O'Connell Street and the General Post Office. This was the site of the Easter Rebellion in 1916. As you cross the Liffey you're passing into Georgian Dublin. Visit College Green and the granite halls of Trinity College, then amble around Merrion Square and on to Fitzwilliam Square. The rows of stately Georgian houses have all been refurbished to their old charm.

The Tourist Trail continues north of the city to Dublin Castle, housing the state apartments with their exquisite Georgian décor, which are open to the public. Turn back down toward the city center to St. Stephen's Green. The Green is in the heart of Georgian Dublin and is one of the most beautiful city parks in Europe. Dublin for centuries was shredded by political upheavals and rebellions, and this placid patch of green is filled with political memorabilia. As you enter the Green you will see the memorial to those who died in the Boer War, and just past the gate is a memorial to O'Donovan Rossa, a Fenian leader. The park was a gift to Dublin by Sir Arthur Guinness in 1880. At the entrance of the Green in front of the Shelbourne Hotel is a strikingly power-ful statue of another Irish hero, Wolfe Tone, who founded the Society for United Irishmen in 1791. The statue is the work of Edward Delaney. Just inside the gates is a haunting cluster of bronzes called "The Famine," a reminder of Ireland's tragic blight, also done by Delaney.

Pass by and visit Leinster House, one of the stateliest of Georgian mansions, which now serves as the house for the Irish Parliament. Another fine building is Mansion House on Dawson Street, the official seat of the Lord Mayor of Dublin since 1715.

Back over O'Connell Bridge, following the Liffey as it empties into the sea, is the Four Courts, built between 1786 and 1802 by one of the finest of Irish architects, James Gandon. During its heyday it housed the courts of the King's Bench, Chancery, Exchequer, and Common Pleas.

Should you prefer to take a tour of Dublin or the surrounding countryside by bus for the day C.I.E. (the Irish Transport Company) has over thirty tours during the high season. For information and bookings inquire at the: Passenger Sales Office, 59 Upper O'Connell Street (Tel: 746301). For over-night and extended tours: Passenger Information, 35 Lower Abbey Street (Tel: 330777).

PHOENIX PARK and ZOO

One of the largest and most beautiful parks in Europe, with over 2,000 acres of grass, gardens, and trees. Herds of deer roam the park. The grounds are filled with horseback riders, Gaelic footballers, and polo players. Located in Phoenix Park is Aras an Uachtarain, the residence of the President of Ireland, which was formerly the Viceregal's lodge. Nearby is the residence of the American ambassador. Phoenix Park is a lovely spot to view the silhouette of Dublin, called a city, but more of a bulging parish!

GUINNESS BREWERY

This stop is for those who are fascinated by the making of Ireland's creamy, frothy national drink. This brewery is the largest in Europe, occupying 60 acres in the city center, and produces 3½ million glasses of stout a day. Enter on James Street and join the tours, which are conducted continuously from 10:00 A.M. to 3:00 P.M. You'll learn all about the processes, and finish up in the Tasting Room. Here you can decide for yourself about this unusual "wine of Ireland."

(Special Note: Last season these tours were discontinued because of extensive renovation work. Check with the Brewery to see if the tours have been resumed.)

DUBLIN MOUNTAINS and
THE HELL FIRE CLUB

If you have a Sunday afternoon to spare and want to do a little touring but stay near Dublin, rent a car and wind around the outskirts of the city to the Dublin mountains and the Hell Fire Club. Take the road to Rathfarnum, and when you've passed through the town, turn right at the Yellow House pub. Follow signs to the Killakee Arts Center (about two miles). About a quarter of a mile past the art center you'll have to park your car and climb the rest of the way up the hill to the 16th-century club, which was a popular meeting place for the rakes of Dublin. The views of Dublin City, the Bay, and the Wicklow Hills are breathtaking on a clear day. A Judge Walsh once wrote this description of the antics at the Hell Fire Club:

> Some of the bucks associated together under the name of the "Hell Fire Club," and among other infernal proceedings, it is reported that they set fire to the apartment in which they met, and endured the flames with incredible obstinacy, till they were forced out of the house in derision, as they asserted, of the torments of a future state. On other occasions, in mockery of religion, they administered to one another the sacred rites of the Church in a manner too indecent for description.

HOWTH
HOWTH CASTLE GARDENS

This overwhelming castle on the north side of Dublin Bay has been the ancestral home of the St. Lawrence family for thirty-four generations. There's a fascinating legend attached to the castle:

"Grace O'Malley, the Warrior Queen of Connacht, was returning from England, when weather forced her to put in at Howth. She proceeded to the castle at Howth, then, as now, held by a Norman family of St. Lawrence. She found the gate shut and was refused admittance on the plea that the family were at dinner. Incensed at such a breach of Irish hospitality, she returned to her ship and found, playing on the shore, a young boy, heir to the Howth titles, whom she carried off with her to County Mayo. She released him only when a solemn pledge was given her that never again would the gates be shut during dinner nor hospitality refused to a traveler in need of refreshment. This pledge was faithfully carried out at Howth Castle up to recent years. An extra place was always laid for dinner and the gate remained open while the meal was in progress."

The exquisite gardens are open to the public, and tea and refreshments are served at the Deer Park Hotel.

Open: 8:00 A.M.-sunset

MALAHIDE
MALAHIDE CASTLE
(450263)

Much of Dublin is being destroyed by property speculators so the saving of Malahide Castle in 1976 by a determined group of tourism organizations was awesome. In 1973 the unmarried, heirless Lord Talbot de Malahide died, ending his ancestral line, which reached back 800 years. In the 12th century Henry II gave the title of Lords of Malahide to the Talbot family. Except for a dozen years' absence forced by Cromwell, the same family lived on until 1973.

In 1976 many of the paintings and furnishings were sold by Christie's, but before the auction the National Gallery purchased the collection of family portraits. By purchase and donation many of the original hangings and carpets have been restored. Malahide Castle has one of the most extensive collections of Irish furniture in the country. The Great Hall is filled with portraits of people connected to this Anglo-Norman-Irish family — Carolan, the harper; Jonathan Swift, Grattan, and Daniel O'Connor.

The late Lord Talbot was an impressive horticulturalist, and his gardens have been preserved. Malahide Castle and its 200-acre demesne should not be missed.

Open: Monday-Saturday 10:00 A.M.-5:00 P.M.
        Sunday 2:00 P.M.-5:00 P.M.
Closed January

SANDYCOVE

JAMES JOYCE TOWER

This Martello tower was one of seventy-four erected along the Irish coast. James Joyce immortalized the tower by using it in the opening scene for his masterpiece, *Ulysses*. In 1904 he lived in the tower with Oliver St. John Gogarty. The tower fell into disrepair, but a few years ago a generous Dublin businessman, Thomas Keating, refurbished it and gave it over to the Tourist Board as a Joyce museum. It is filled with Joycean memorabilia. The tower is located nine miles from Dublin near Dun Laoghaire.

Open: May-September
Monday-Saturday: 10 A.M.-1:00 P.M.; 2:00-5:15 P.M.
Sunday: 2:30-6:00 P.M.

COUNTY WICKLOW

HOTELS   COUNTRY HOUSES   FARMS

AVOCA

*VALE VIEW HOTEL (H)
(042-5236)

Mr. and Mrs. Mahon O'Brien run a wonderfully cozy country inn on a hill above the "Meeting of the Waters." Staying at Vale View is a few days in a home rather than a hotel. Only ten bedrooms, and Mr. O'Brien doesn't intend to expand, nor does he print a brochure. He likes the numbers and guests as they are. The walls of the paneled bar are filled with dozens of prints — Mrs. O'Brien refers to her husband as a "print maniac." You'll soon realize Mr. O'Brien has a deep sense of history and art. Mrs. O'Brien oversees the intimate candlelit dining room, and she's a superb Cordon Bleu cook, ranging from Paella to Steak Diane. Fine selection of ninety-five wines. There are great stables, a syndicate for pheasant shoots, and golf courses at Woodenbridge.

Season: All year round
Luncheon: 12:30-2:30
Dinner: 7:00-10:00

WICKLOW

KNOCKROBIN HOUSE (F)
(040-2344)

At times referred to as a "little spot of Bavaria" in the Irish countryside. Mrs. Bittel is a warm, ebullient lady, who vacationed in Ireland for years and finally bought Knockrobin to settle in. The house is an elegant farmhouse on its own park land along the Murrough River, a mile from Wicklow town. The house is filled with fascinating *bavarois,* mahogany and oak furniture and Biedermeier antiques. The large-size bedrooms upstairs have German beds with puffy down quilts.

Mrs. Bittel is a clever cook, and her menus combine Bavarian and Irish specialties.

Season: All year round   AE
Luncheon: (Sunday only) 1:00-3:00 ·
Dinner: 7:00-9:00
(Dining room closed Sunday and Monday evenings)

RESTAURANTS AND PUBS
ANNAMOE
ARMSTRONG'S BARN
(0404-5194)

A little over a year ago Paul Tullio and his wife took over this renovated bar/restaruant from the Peter Robinsons. Unfortunately, at first reports the food is way below the high standards maintained by the previous owners. This could be understood as first-year "growing pains." What is impossible to understand is the very high prices of the new management. Do not misunderstand. The food is good and the menu varied, with such offerings as: Beetroot Soup, Sweetbreads in Black Butter, Chinese Beef, and Swedish Pork Casserole, but the quality in no way equals the prices. There's a good wine list with expensive price tags.

Dinner: 7:30-10:00   AE
Closed Sunday and Monday

LARAGH
LARAGH INN
(0404-5141)

Down the road from Annamoe to Glendolough is the village of Laragh and the Laragh Inn. This lovely white inn along the banks of a rippling stream is simply excellent. William and Moira Lloyd have spent the last few years redoing the old pub, restoring the wood-beamed ceiling and grand stone fireplace.

During the summer season Moira returns to the kitchen,

and she's a fabulous cook. For luncheon she presents a cold buffet — platters filled with smoked trout, homemade paté, Limerick ham and roast chicken, dozens of cheeses and *the* most delicious pecan pie. In the evening the dining room is cozy and warm and filled with candlelight. Red-and-white checkered cloths cover the tables. The menu depends on what Bill can find fresh at the markets and the choice changes each evening.

Season: All year round
Luncheon: 12:30-2:30
Sandwiches and snacks all day long
Dinner: 7:30-10:00
Closed for dinner Sunday and Monday

(Meals served only from mid-April to end of October)
Book ahead for reservations

ROUNDWOOD
ROUNDWOOD INN
(818107)

While you are touring the Wicklow countryside, be sure to visit this attractive inn. It was built over 300 years ago as a coaching stop and ever since has been a haven for travelers. It's a maze of rooms with open hearth fires, oak-beamed ceilings, and shelves filled with copper and pewter ware. The inn is owned by Florian Binsack, who presents a menu specializing in Austrian and Swiss dishes, all well prepared, even if the vegetables are canned from time to time. All during pub hours marvelous snacks are served in the lounge of baskets filled with smoked salmon, roast chicken, and ham.

Season: All year round
Luncheon: 12:45-2:30
Dinner: 7:00-10:00
Call ahead for reservations

DIVERSIONS

If I were asked where I would first return, I would have to say to the glens and hills of Wicklow. Ancient acres created from the palette of winsome gods. After days in Wicklow you never seem to remember seeing any people, just endless countryside. On misty days there's a melancholy bluish haze over the land, but on a good day lavish brush strokes of color sweep the landscape, as romantic as a Monet painting, yet more vivid. Grassy hills gold with gorse rest against the sky under blankets of purple heather. Villages, glens, and lakes have magical whimsical names like Glenmacnass (Glen of the Hollow of the Waterfall), Poulaphoca (Puck's Hole), Glenmalure (Glen of the Lover of Skirmishes), and the towering mountain Mallaghcleevaun (Featherbed).

There's a wise old Irish expression, "Better the half-said thing." And a tour of Wicklow needs no wordy embellishment. So in this "Diversion" I'll give you only markers, and let you make your own discoveries. The best way to see Wicklow would be by bicycle, as the young kids from Dublin do, but for the sake of time a car will do. Take the road out of Dublin along the Bay to Bray. Bray was an old Victorian resort, which over the years has lost much of its charm. If you have the time, stop along the coast at Bray Head and then cut over the hills to the village of Enniskerry. You've already entered into one of the hundreds of Wicklow's lush glens. Follow the signs to Powerscourt Demesne. Sadly, Powerscourt, one of the most breathtaking of Irish estates, burned because of a faulty chimney, but the grounds are still intact, and the gardens and views are fabulous. Also be sure to visit the Powerscourt waterfall. As you leave, take the road to Glencree, which links to the Military Road. This narrow winding road was built by the English during the '98 Rising to capture rebels hidden in the wild Wicklow Hills. Not far from where the roads meet is a sign saying "Private No Admittance." Park your car and climb the nearest hill for a view of Lough Bray, one of a half dozen "black lakes" of Wicklow. Off on the left is Sugarloaf, a golden mound rising hundreds of feet, teasing you to climb it.

For the next eight miles you wind over the crusty bogs till you reach a crossroads at Sally Gap. Here there's a decision, to turn or not. If you go straight on, the winding Military Road curves around the hills and lonely glens, and leaves you in Laragh. If you turn to the left, you pass by the haunting black lakes of Lough Dan and Lough Tay and Luggula. On Sundays Luggula's generous owner welcomes travelers to park their cars and walk the grounds to the banks of the lakes.

Either way the roads meet at Laragh, and there you can begin your tour of Glendolough, the brilliant glen between two lakes, where St. Kevin founded his monastery in the 6th century. So much has been written about St. Kevin. He must have been a man of instinctive brilliance to have chosen such a breathtaking site, since he could not have seen the sweeping vistas in those days, when Wicklow was a dense primeval forest. As the legend goes, it seems St. Kevin could have been a bit more tolerant toward the poor girl who pursued him to his cell trying to seduce him, whom he finally either throttled or killed. Glendolough is one of the most romantic spots in the world. Poor dear girl. The place has some fine remnants of early Christian Ireland, including St. Kevin's Kitchen and beehive.

After Glendolough turn back toward Laragh. Turn right toward Rathdrum and weave your way down this wonderful road alongside the Avonmore River. The first time I traveled the road I was with a friend from Dublin. About a mile down the road he stopped the car and, turning to me with a strange glow, sighed, "I've been looking for this road for ten years." He had come to work in Dublin from Limerick, and one of his first weekends some friends had taken him for a tour of Wicklow. This tiny narrow road had made a profound impression on him, but its exact location had been lost in the haze of a reeling tour. As he started the car up again he said, "You see, it's one of the most beautiful roads in Ireland."

At Rathdrum is Avondale House, which was the residence of Charles Stewart Parnell, one of Ireland's famed patriots. Three of the rooms are open to the public. Travel then to Ashford to visit Robert Walpole's Mount Usher Gardens. Over twenty acres of flowers and trees from all over the world.

Russborough House in Blessington, the home of Sir Alfred and Lady Beit, was recently opened to the public. This 100-room Palladian style house was designed in the mid 18th century by the German architect Richard Cassells for Joseph Lesson, a Dublin brewer. Russborough houses an art collection that is regarded as one of the great private collections in the world. Included in its collection, valued at over thirty million pounds, is Vermeer's "The Letter," and Velazquez's "The Moorish Kitchenmaid," along with works by Goya, Rubens, Gainsborough, and others. In the summer of 1974 armed robbers stole nineteen pictures from Russborough, but all were recovered undamaged.

Open: Easter-October
      Wednesday, Saturday, Sunday and Bank holidays
      2:30-6:30

For years John Millington Synge lived in the Wicklow Hills. It was here he gathered his material for one of his most acclaimed plays, *In The Shadow of the Glen,* and many other loving limns of Wicklow. For some these lines from his "Prelude" are familiar, but I wouldn't want to leave them out as you drive over the Wicklow hills:

Still south I went and west and south again,
Through Wicklow from the morning till the night,
And far from cities, and the sights of men,
Lived with the sunshine, and the moon's delight.

I knew the stars, the flowers, and the birds,
The gray and wintry sides of many glens,
And did but half remember human words,
In converse with the mountains, moors, and fens.

COUNTY WEXFORD

HOTELS　COUNTRY HOUSES　FARMS

FOULKSMILL

MILL HOUSE (F)
(051-63685)

Mrs. Redmond's house is a lovely vine-covered Georgian farmhouse overlooking the River Cormac. Just below the farmhouse is an old water-powered corn mill built in 1851. It is one of the few remaining in Ireland. You're more than welcome any time to watch the workings of the mill. Count on homemade Irish bread and fresh farm produce.

Season: May — September

HORETOWN HOUSE (F)
(051-63633)

Horetown House is an 18th-century Georgian manor house whose original structure was built in 1692 by a Puritan family of twenty-two. It is a perfect spot for those who love the outdoors, especially riding. There are twenty fine riding horses, over 200 acres of ground for your rides, and an all-Ireland cross-country course. During the winter there are the fox hunts with the Wexford Hounds Club. Mrs. Young, who owns Horetown, is a great source of information and history of the area. If you request, Mrs. Young may arrange for the "Mummers" to come and perform at Horetown.

Season: All year round

RATHASPECK

RATHASPECK MANOR (F)
(053-22661)

Out the road from Wexford, a few miles toward Johnstown Castle, is Mrs. Cuddihy's 300-year-old Georgian manor. You'll know you've arrived at Rathaspeck when you pass by the "Alice in Wonderland" gatehouse. There are seven huge bedrooms, and a putting green on the grounds.

Season: May — September

TOMHAGGARD
*BARGY CASTLE (C)
(Tomhaggard 3)

Bargy Castle has been in Maeve Davidson's (née de Burgh) family for over 800 years, and for the past fifteen years she and her husband, Colonel Charles Davidson, have opened their elegant castle to visitors. The rooms are filled with memorabilia of this great Norman family, which descended from Charlemagne. There are eighteen bedrooms exquisitely decorated. Some with four-poster beds and one with wood paneling dating back to the 16th century. Over 200 acres of grounds, which include tennis courts, pony traps, boats on the lake, private salmon and trout fishing, and a horse-drawn coach.

Meals at Bargy are a few glorious hours. The tables adorned with Waterford and 18th-century Irish silver. Along the wall in the dining room is a 17th-century sideboard that belonged to Jonathan Swift. Course after course is a gourmet treat. If you're in the south, be sure to visit Colonel Davidson and his wife.

Season: mid-May — mid-September
Dinner: 7:00-9:00

RESTAURANTS AND PUBS
NEW ROSS
THE GALLEY
(051-21723)

For a few hours each day Dick Fletcher hosts a gourmet

cruise up the Barrow and Nore rivers on his *New Ross Galley*. The nice part about this boat is that if you happen not to know a thing about boats, you don't have to do a thing, just sit back and enjoy the courses and courses of Mr. Fletcher's gourmet food and watch the passing countryside. There's a souvenir menu, which also provides a map of the area and all sorts of other information, historical, botanical, and folkloric.

The *New Ross* departs three times a day: at 12:30 for luncheon; 3:00 for tea, and 7:00 for dinner. Luncheon is a cold buffet, which may include trout, salmon, quiche, and salad. Dinner becomes elaborate, for Mr. Fletcher insists on using only fresh local produce. Tea includes dozens of homemade breads, scones, and cakes. During the cruises there's a fully licensed bar.

Be sure to reserve ahead — the boat seats only forty or so passengers. It's a lovely, lazy way to see the Nore and Barrow Valleys. The schedule is a little complicated.

Sailings: March 30-October 30
Daily: June—August
Docked: Monday, Tuesday, Sunday dinner during April—May, September—October; after September 15 docked for dinner daily

WEXFORD
THE CROWN BAR
Monck Street

Tucked away in one of the narrow lanes in Wexford is the Crown Bar, but it is no ordinary pub. The Crown has been in the Kelly family for over a hundred years, the longest ownership of any pub in the country. But the pub itself is not that unusual. What is unusual is Mr. Kelly and his "mini museum" in the back room. Plan to spend a few hours with this gentle, intriguing man, who over the years has accumulated a trove of military memorabilia to make any museum envious. There's a 12th-century suit of chain mail, sabers, powder horns, brass muzzled guns, and military hats of many nations. Before John Kennedy's death, Mr. Kelly sent the President one of the famous pikes the Irish had used during the Wexford Rising in 1798, in which the President's great-grandfather took part.

ENTERTAINMENT

GOREY

FUNGE ART CENTRE
Rafter Street
(055-21470)

Five years ago a young, dynamic artist named Paul Funge began an arts center in this southern town. Its success is phenomenal for such a short time. The purpose of the center is geared toward involvement of the locals in the arts, but it's an alive center of entertainment for travelers as well. During the year there are dozens of programs and activities, including exhibitions, publications, workshops, and performing arts. It seems as though all of Ireland's leading artists and performers have stopped by at Gorey to lend a hand to Paul Funge's exciting project. Ring ahead to find out the evening's program or just drop by.

Open: All year round

WEXFORD

OPERA FESTIVAL

(See end of section in Part One on Rural Theatre and check with Local Tourist Board for specific program information.)

"MUMMERING"

This is a traditional entertainment you'll find only in County Wexford, whose origins have become obscured. Some believe it was brought here by shipwrecked Cornish sailors, but there is still no proof. We do know it's a form of English folk dance set to Irish music. The performance is done by a dozen men, each representing a character in Irish history, wearing white shirts and dark pants with yellow and green sashes. Each holds a wooden "sword." There's a lengthy monologue in which all are introduced, and then they begin their fascinating, ritualistic mime. Most mummers are very old today. The art has been passed down through generations. You'll have to check with the local tourist office to see where the mummers may be. They perform free of charge.

DIVERSIONS

BARGY and FORTH
These south Wexford baronies of Bargy and Forth are not so much a plate to visit as something curious to know about. For over 500 years, as late as the end of the last century, a curious civilization lingered in this area. The people spoke a dialect of Chaucerian English and kept their medieval customs and folklore. They were descendants of the Anglo-Norman invasion, with Welsh-Flemish origins, who remained isolated from the surrounding Irish in speech and custom.

COURTOWN
If you have a desire to find miles of beaches, six in all, Courtown is one of the best seaside visits. During the season there are a great many tourists, but you can still find some solitary dunes and stretches for walks and sunning.

ENNISCORTHY
This small village overlooking the banks of the River Slaney was the site for the first attack of the 1798 Rebellion, one of the bloodiest in Ireland's history. In the town square is a statue of Father John Murphy, pike in hand, who headed the insurrection. Nearby, above the town, is Vinegar Hill, where the insurgents were finally defeated. Enniscorthy Castle is one of the few castles remaining in Ireland not in ruins. It was an ancient Norman keep believed to have been built by Raymond the Great. In the 16th century it was the home of the poet Edmund Spenser.

HOOK PENINSULA

In this narrow, rocky peninsula in the south of County Wexford stands one of the four oldest lighthouses in the world. The building itself is over 700 years old, but a light has been burning for navigators at Hook for over 1500 years. Directly opposite the inlet is Crook Castle in County Waterford. In 1650 Cromwell said he would take Waterford "by Hook or by Crook." Nearby at Tacumshane is a thatched working windmill, the only one in Ireland.

KILMORE QUAY

Around the country there are a few traditional villages, which have all been refurbished by the Tourist Board or an interested party, but Kilmore Quay is an authentic Irish village. Narrow streets wind around the harbor lined with traditional thatched white cottages. From the harbor at Kilmore Quay you may hire a boat to go to the Saltee Islands.

JOHN F. KENNEDY NATIONAL PARK

By the slopes of Sliabh Coilthe, and near the Kennedy family homestead at Dunganstown, is this parkland dedicated to the memory of the late President, which was opened in 1968. Included on the 400-acre park is an arboretum and a horticultural college.

SALTEE ISLANDS

Great Saltee Island is located five miles off the Wexford Coast and has been called the "most beautiful resort for birds in Great Britain and Ireland." In his sensitive, fascinating account of his travels in Ireland, *The Way That I Went,* Robert Lloyd Praeger wrote of the Great Saltee: "Their colonies form a wonderful sight in June. On a recent visit a careful observer estimated the number of birds in the water on the lee side of the Great Saltee as over two million." Swallows, wrens, larks, gannets, oyster catchers, magpies, jackdaws, puffins, and more nest on the islands. The island is only a mile and a half long and a quarter mile wide, and at times there is a "housing shortage"! As you approach, strange cries awaken the island, warning of your arrival. Launches may be hired at Kilmore Quay, but they tend to be expensive.

WEXFORD

This southern harbor town was the port for invaders for over 600 years. First came the Norsemen, then the Normans filling the countryside with such names as Sinnott, Roche, Staffords, Fitzhenry, and de Burghs. Each invader fortified the city, and the Westgate Tower is the only remaining one of five towers that once flanked the city walls. These ancient walls are belicved to have been built around 1200. The Bull Ring within the city walls is a remnant of the Normans, whose favorite pastime was baiting the bulls. Also, within the old city walls are the ruins of Selskar Abbey, where in 1172 King Henry came for Lent to atone for his murdering Thomas à Beckett, Archbishop of Canterbury and the Prelate of England.

Wexford was the birthplace of Admiral James Barry," the Father of the American Navy," and a statue in his honor stands at the harbor on Crescent Quay. Farther down the street, on the site of White's Hotel, was the birthplace of the Alaskan explorer, Sir Robert McClure, who discovered the Northwest Passage. Since Wexford was the stronghold of intruders' oppression, it was the inevitable place for one of Ireland's bloodiest insurrections, the Rebellion of 1798. Leaving Wexford town, it's a sad memory, looking at Wexford Bridge, to recall the days of its use as an Irish scaffold.

COUNTY WATERFORD

HOTELS   COUNTRY HOUSES   FARMS

DUNMORE EAST

Just a few miles south of Waterford town is the charming fishing village of Dunmore East. Tiers of brightly colored houses climb the hills overlooking the Atlantic. The village is off the usual tourist trail and has managed to retain its sleepy, Old World charm. During the summer season the harbor is filled with sailboats and fishing trawlers, and there's a sandy beach in the harbor cove. In Dunmore East there are three fine hotels, all of good quality. High on a hill overlooking the harbor is John Kelly's Haven Hotel, an old Victorian mansion, which serves excellent roasts and grills. During the season in the evening there's entertainment and a discotheque. Slightly smaller in size are the Ocean Hotel and the Candlelight Inn. They're situated a few hundred yards up from the ocean. The rooms are small and simply decorated. The atmosphere is warm, and you are immediately greeted as an old friend. The treat at both is the menu of dozens of choices of local fish caught daily from the neighboring Atlantic. At the Candlelight is your own private swimming pool. Dunmore East is off the beaten track and perfect for those who prefer being by the sea.

HAVEN HOTEL (H)
(051-83150)

Season: May-September 30

Luncheon: 1:00-2:30

Dinner: 7:00-10:00

AE, DC,

OCEAN HOTEL (H)
(051-83136)

Season: All year round
Luncheon: 12:30-2:30
Dinner: 7:00-10:00

CANDLELIGHT INN (H)
(051-83125)

Season: All year round
Dinner: 7:00-9:30

WATERFORD

FOXMOUNT FARM (F)
(051-74308)

The Kent's Foxmount Farm is one of the best guesthouse farms in the country. Spend the days watching the workings of a real dairy farm, and in the evenings enjoy a meal of the fresh farm produce and homemade breads and cakes. The farm was built in 1700, and there's over 200 acres of land, farmed by Mr. Kent. There are only six bedrooms, so be sure to book ahead.

Season: May — September

RESTAURANTS AND PUBS

DUNMORE EAST
DOWNS BAR

These days it is awfully difficult to find an authentic country pub, but not far from Dunmore is this genuine thatched cottage pub cum grocery store. In the evenings the locals gather in around the open turf fire for stories, news, and, some evenings, traditional music. At first the locals may be reserved, but eventually they'll warm up, just give them time. Down the road a little is Eileen White's pub, which is billed as a real country pub but has been modernized in the last few years and is just another bar and not particularly frequented by the locals.

ANTIQUES TRAIL

WATERFORD
THOMAS O'NEIL
O'Connell Street

CONRAD NICHOLLS
Mall House
33 The Mall
(051-32749)

BALLYDUFF
CARRAGINE ANTIQUES
Carragine Lodge
(Ballyduff 6)
Mrs. J. Benson

ENTERTAINMENT

WATERFORD
INTERNATIONAL FESTIVAL OF LIGHT OPERA

During the month of September opera buffs arrive from Britain, the Continent, and the United States for a fortnight of opera performances. It's the only festival in the world where amateur opera companies can compete, and the response has been overwhelming. Even those sophisticated urban critics arrive by the carload, so be sure to book well in advance. The program has ranged to include the *Desert Song*, *The Mikado*, and *No, No, Nanette*. C.I.E. runs special trains between Dublin and Waterford during the festival. Reservations for all fourteen performances can be made with the festival booking office in Waterford or any Tourist Board office.

THEATRE CLUB
10 Henrietta

During the season this tiny 45-seat theatre presents a medley of Irish plays from the best of Irish writers. Current information and reservations can be obtained from the Tourist Board.

DIVERSIONS

KNOCKEEN
A few miles south of Waterford town, on the way to Annestown, is the village of Knockeen. Near the town is a well-preserved ancient portal dolmen with a 13-foot overslab supported by upright granite slabs. (For the history of dolmens, see below under Carlow, Browne's Hill Dolmen.)

LISMORE CASTLE
Driving through the sylvan Waterford countryside, along the edges of the Blackwater River, you arrive at Lismore,

with its dramatic medieval castle. It was originally the residence of the Bishop of Lismore, and in the 18th century became the property of the Devonshire family. During the summer months it's the holiday residence of the Devonshire family, one being Adele Kingman-Douglas, Fred Astaire's sister! The gardens are open to the public.

Open: mid-May — September
Tuesday to Friday 2:00-5:00 P.M.

WATERFORD

The thing you have to remember about visiting Irish cities is that they were foreign inventions and the Irish have never felt compelled to improve their looks. Waterford is no exception. Just plan on a short visit, since there are a few interesting spots, such as Reginald's Tower. It's steeped in fascinating history. It was built in 1003 as a part of the city's walled fortification. Almost seventy years later, in the top-floor Banquet Hall, King Dermot MacMurrough's daughter, Eav, was married to Strongbow, the Norman conqueror. The marriage sealed Ireland's fate as a Norman conquered land. Enormous restoration has been done in the tower. On the second floor is a museum collection, which includes King John's 11th-century sword and mace and the original charters granted to the city.

Alongside the tower is the "stronghold," which unfortunately has been modernized, but has kept the original city retaining wall dating around 1100 with its "sally ports." These are the small apertures through which sailors would board their ships to raid and plunder ships on the Waterford seas.

Open: Monday through Friday 9:30 A.M. - 6:00 P.M.
Saturday 9:30 A.M. - 12:30 P.M.

WATERFORD GLASS FACTORY
(Waterford 3311)

It's not too chancy to assume that if you've heard of Ireland, you've heard of Waterford Crystal. If you've come this far you must visit their new factory and see the workings of this fascinating craft. The original factory was opened in 1729 with foreign artisans brought to Ireland to teach the locals the delicate craft. Waterford closed its doors in the mid-19th century and did not reopen to its original capacity until 1952.

The tour at Waterford takes you through every process, from glass blowing, before 1500° ovens, through the fine chiseling of their trademark patterns, to the elaborate show-rooms in the main room displaying the finished Waterford. Be sure to book reservations for tours in advance during the busy summer high season. Check with Waterford or the Tourist Board for the hours, since they may be extended.

Tours: Every half hour 10:30 A.M.-3:30 P.M.
Monday through Friday

COUNTY CARLOW

HOTELS   COUNTRY HOUSES   FARMS

BAGENALSTOWN
OLD RECTORY (F)
(0503-25283)

Mrs. Young's Old Rectory is a charming 100-year old cut-stone farmhouse. It is situated midway between Carlow and Kilkeeny. Only five bedrooms, each tastefully done. Fishing nearby in the river Barrow.

Open: All year round

DIVERSIONS

CARLOW
BROWNE'S HILL DOLMEN

Dolmens were megalithic tombs consisting of three or more standing stones roofed over with a single vast boulder. Browne's Dolmen is a particularly fine example, whose capstone weighs over 100 tons, with four upright granite slabs.

Legend is that these dolmens were built by two young lovers, Diarmuid and Grainne, to sleep under at night while fleeing from the wrath of the aging king, who wanted Grainne for himself. There are over 300 "Diarmuid and Grainne beds" over the country.

COUNTY MEATH

RESTAURANTS AND PUBS

SLANE

SLANE CASTLE RESTAURANT
(041-24207)

When the young Earl and Countess of Mount Charles came back from England to live at Slane Castle three years ago, they decided to open a restaurant. They converted the servants' hall in this Gothic-style castle designed by James Wyatt, and guests now dine by romantic candlelight by a roaring fire. Tommy FitzHerbert, a well-known restaurateur around Dublin, is chef. A particularly good specialty of the house is game (in season), which is shot on the estate and all the vegetables are grown in the castle garden. Another specialty is fresh salmon caught in the nearby Boyne River. The castle's setting in the rolling Meath countryside is breathtaking, so plan to drive up before sunset.

Open: All year round   AE
Dinner 7:00-11:00
Closed Monday and Tuesday

DIVERSIONS

BOYNE VALLEY

A circle of the Boyne Valley hedges forty centuries of Ireland with it's rich vernal land, covered with relics of the collisions of centuries. Only perhaps in Rome could you find such a rare trove of the pagan and Christian worlds. Sculpted high crosses are scattered nearby moss-covered fairy grounds and megalithic tombs. Battle-worn castles linger beside the crumbled abbeys. You can walk the center of the valley along the banks of the River Boyne. Watching the rippling water, those ripples, like tiny furled chapters of its past unfolding, flowing along, endlessly along.

Almost everyone has heard of Tara, the ancient seat of the High Kings of Ireland. Some, when they visit the hill rising only 500 feet from the surrounding Meath countryside, have been disappointed with their visit. But Tara is the place for the imagination. Nothing remains today, no ruins, except a few markers left by archaeologists to designate the ancient court. If you visit Tara, imagine the royal court in the days of Ireland's High Kings. One hundred and forty-two kings ruled in all, long before records of Greece and Rome. Still standing at Tara is the *Lia Fail* (Stone of Destiny), an oblong stone, which it was believed would roar three times when a true High King sat upon it at his inauguration. There were five chariot roads leading away from Tara crossing all of Ireland. During the Great Harvest Feast in August these roads would be filled with princes, peasants, druids, and musicians, all traveling to Tara. Twelve portal doors were opened, and all would be welcomed for the feast. The banquet hall alone would hold up to 1,200 people. Cormac MacArt in the 3rd century established an enviable cluster of learning centers at Tara for literature, metal work, and military training. Unfortunately, his reign ended when he received facial wounds during a battle. Brehon Law forbade anyone with physical blemish to rule. Tara for centuries was the source of Irish resurgence against the invaders of Eire. Even as late as 1843, centuries after the ancient order and buildings had crumbled, Daniel O'Connell, the Great Liberator, held a mass meeting at Tara demanding the dissolution of the Union. The protest was attended by over a million Irishmen. Unfortunately, most of the archaeological traces of Tara were literally torn apart by a delegation from a group calling itself British Israel after World War One. They were obsessed with the idea that the Arc of the Covenant was buried at Tara, and proceeded to tear apart every blade and mound.

If your imagination is tiring and you'd now like more concrete relics of the life of the ancients, turn toward Newgrange, Dowth, and Knowth. Within a few miles radius of each other these ancient burial mounds, rising over 40 feet from the ground are some of the finest examples of neolithic passage graves in Europe. Very little is known about the graves, other than they were built almost 4,500 years ago. Who were these navigators up the Boyne? Why they chose these locations for the burial of their royalty is unknown. Newgrange is by far the most impressive. Larger than the others, but subtler than those of Stonehenge in England, Newgrange rises 45 feet and has a 100-yard diameter. The exterior is covered in white quartz pebbles. Circling the mound are 12-foot-high stone slabs, and excavation has shown there originally were 36 stones forming a complete ring. Over 180,000 tons of stone in all were used at Newgrange. But it is the mysterious hieroglyphics chiseled in the curbstone, mystical spirals, and lozenges whose meaning other than decorative is still unknown. Pass through the entrance to the 62-foot passage grave, kept dry all these centuries by its corbelled roof. It is also unknown whether cremation or burial took place within the tomb. The ancient pagans were sun worshipers, and in recent years it was learned that only once a year, on December 21, the sun pierces the entrance through to the center of the grave. Newgrange was accidentally discovered in 1700 by a group of road diggers, and has been preserved as an archaeological site. A few miles down the road is Dowth, another of these neolithic burial mounds, which is believed also to have been used for festive occasions. At Dowth there are beehives believed to have been added during Christian times. The final grave is Knowth, the most expansive of the three, including eleven satellite tombs on over a half dozen acres. The designs of this mound include serpents, spirals, and broken circles.

Another ancient site is the town of Teltown (or *Tailte*) near Kells. In the town have been found the remains of ancient ports and dried-up lakes. It was at Teltown the ancient Irish held the Celtic Olympic Games. The games were begun in 370 during the reign of Lugh Lamhfhada in commemoration of his foster mother "Tailte." The fields were filled with chariot racing, wrestling, running. It's believed that the lakes were filled and used for fake naval battles. The fair continued to be held every August until the reign of Roderick O'Connor, the last King of Ireland.

In A.D. 433, during the reign of King Laoghaire, change began in the Irish order. King Laoghaire was at Tara preparing for the Great Harvest Festival. In the distance, on the hill in Slane, he saw a fire and was enraged, since no fires were to be lit before the inaugural bonfire at Tara. He traveled to Slane himself and found it was St. Patrick lighting his Pascal fire to celebrate Easter. It was at this meeting that St. Patrick is said to have explained the mystery of the Trinity to the pagan king by using the shamrock, and converted his first believers. From that time on Ireland would never again be completely pagan.

During the following centuries the seed of the new Christian order flourished with the establishment of three Cistercian monasteries in the Boyne Valley. The first was at the Old Mellifont (meaning Honey Fountain) on the banks of the River Mattock. Many of the ruins of the 13th-century structures still stand, giving an easy view of the design of these monasteries. The most interesting structure remaining is the baptistry, Lavabo. The monastery was surrounded by rich farmland, which the monks worked, and there is a mill nearby. At Bective, near the somnolent village of Kilmessan, another abbey was founded and planned along the lines of other Cistercian monasteries. It stands on a private demesne of over 200 acres alongside the Boyne. These monasteries grew to hold great power, and at one time the Abbott of Bective held a peer's seat in Parliament, one of the fifteen within the Pale. The abbey at Monasterboice is probably the best known. Its sculpted high crosses are the finest in Ireland, particularly Muirdeach's Cross. The cross is over 14 feet high, and the shaft is made of one stone. There have been many arguments over the years concerning the meanings of the panels. Some say they are depictions of the Danes and the Irish, the pagans and the Christians, and others insist they are scenes from the Old and New Testament. You can decide for yourself. The round towers guarding the abbey remind us of the hazardous life the monks led. They were constantly assaulted, and retreated to these towers, some as tall as five stories, for protection.

In July, 1690, the lazy River Boyne was the barrier between the armies of William of Orange and James the Second. The defeat of

James at the Battle of the Boyne signaled the downfall of the Stuarts and the beginnings of Catholic and Irish persecution, which would continue another 200 years. During the battle over a thousand untrained Irish soldiers died trying to restore James the Second to power. At nearby Athumney Castle, a few miles from Navan, Sir Lancelot Dowdall heard the news of King William's victory and "swore that the Prince of Orange would never get the opportunity to rest under his roof." He set fire to his castle, and from a hill across the river he watched it burn to the ground. The next day he left to live on the Continent.

Trim is the last stop along the Boyne Valley. A tiny peaceful town, which recently won a "tidy town" award from the Government. Attractive kudos have not always been forthcoming. In his book about the Boyne Sir William Wilde, the father of Oscar, wrote that the town had sunk "in dirt, laziness and apathy." The result of centuries of invaders plundering, building, and trampling its peaceful land. Many of the remnants and ruins of its turbulent history still stand. King John's Castle was owned by the Dunsany family and the keep dates back to 1200. Later it became a stronghold of the de Lacys, Norman settlers. The lands in Trim were given to Hugh de Lacy by Henry the Second, but he didn't live very long to enjoy it. His particular interest was the destruction of abbeys, and he was soon murdered by a local farmer. The Yellow Tower across the river has been described as the most lofty remnant of Anglo-Norman architecture in the country. Its Gothic steeple once stood 125 feet high. In the center of the town is an enormous column in honor of the Duke of Wellington. The Duke preferred to think of himself as an Englishman. The story told is that someone accused him of being an Irishman and reminded him he was born in Ireland. To which he replied: "If you are born in a stable, that doesn't make you a horse." (This same remark has been attributed to at least three other Anglophiles.)

(If you want more information about the Boyne Valley before your tour, there have been dozens of books written that can easily be found in Dublin. Plan to spend the day and bring along a picnic. A perfect ending would be a dinner at Mullaghfin House.)

COUNTY KILKENNY

RESTAURANTS AND PUBS

KILKENNY

KYTELER'S INN
Kiernan Street
(056-21888)

This may be your first and only time to dine in the homestead
of a bona fide witch, Dame Alyce Kyteler. She lived in
Kilkenny in the beginning of the 14th century, and outlived
four husbands. Well, outlived is *one* way of putting it. She's
said to have murdered all four in the stone dungeons below,
where you dine. Around the time the fifth husband disappeared, she was charged with heresy and witchcraft, and
sentenced to be burned at the stake, but she managed to
escape to England. One of her followers, Petronilla of Meath,
was burned in her place.

Some evenings at the inn are Medieval Witchcraft Banquets, and during the tourist season there's *Seisun*, an evening of folk ballads, music, and dancing. Even if you visit
Kyteler's on an off night and there's no entertainment, the
menu has a variety of grills and fish and a good wine list.
Luncheon usually offers a choice of two or three specialties.

Open: All year round
Luncheon: 12:30-2:30
Dinner: 7:00-10:00

BRIDGE HOUSE BAR (TYNAN'S)

When you're visiting Kilkenny be sure to stop in for a few
"jars" at Tynan's. Everyone's imagined what they think an
Irish pub looks like, and Tynan's is one of the half dozen or
so in the country that don't disappoint. On the right as you
enter is a wall of antique apothecary drawers left from the
days when Tynan's was not only a pub, but a grocery and

drug store. Soft leather banquettes line the mirrored walls. The bar is solid mahogany with the original brass gas lamps (which still work!). Along the other side of the bar are the oversized wooden kegs they used to store the whiskey in. As I said before, Tynan's is one of the few pubs that look like what you've always imagined a pub would.

BUYERS MARKET

KILKENNY
KILKENNY DESIGN WORKSHOPS

The design workshops are located in the renovated 18th-century stables of Kilkenny Castle. Visit the center and watch a weaver, a potter, a silversmith, or a woodturner demonstrate their crafts. The Irish have been famous over centuries for their handcraft, but at Kilkenny the methods and designs of centuries have been modernized. Much of the work at the design center is done by commission, but many kinds of goods, including jewelry, textiles, furniture, glassware, and ceramics, are available at the Design Center Shops. The prices are relatively high, but you are paying for the best in design and craftsmanship.

Shop Hours: Monday-Friday 9:00 A.M.-5:45 P.M.
   Saturday 10:00 A.M.-5:45 P.M.
   Sunday 11:00 A.M.-5:45 P.M.

Workshops: Monday-Friday 9:00 A.M.-6:00 P.M.

RUDOLF HELTZEL
Rothe House
(056-21497)

Rudolf Heltzel carries the finest glass and pottery in the country, but his specialty is jewelry. Intricate, unusual settings in silver and gold, diamonds, emeralds, moonstones, garnets, sapphires. He also does exquisite bracelets and necklaces. A true craftsman.

ENTERTAINMENT

KILKENNY
KILKENNY ARTS WEEK

This is a week-long celebration of the arts in Ireland. Historic Kilkenny is the perfect background for its guests and performers. Every night there are poetry readings, and in its first few years the finest of Irish poets have appeared: Seamus Heany, John Montague, Thomas Kinsella, Ted Hughes. In the evenings, in the 13th-century St. Canice's Cathederal, are concerts of musical works ranging from medieval to Bach to Aaron Copeland. At Rothe House and Kilkenny College are exhibitions of works by Irish artists, too numerous to mention. It's the finest of festivals in Ireland and not to be missed if you are in the country the last week in August. (Check with the Tourist Board for the program and dates, since they vary each year.)

DIVERSIONS

KILKENNY

The town of Kilkenny is the most perfect example of a medieval town in the country. Its importance during the Anglo-Norman occupation was second only to Dublin within the Pale. After the Anglo-Norman invasion, King Edward the Third granted three earldoms in Ireland: Desmond, Kildare, and Ormonde. The Norman Butler family settled and fortified the town of Kilkenny. James Butler purchased Kilkenny Castle from William Marshall, the Earl of Pembroke, in the 14th century. The next four centuries the Butlers ruled this Anglo-Gaelic settlement. Many Parliaments were held at Kilkenny Castle in the 14th, 15th, and 16th centuries, the most famous of which produced the Statutes of Kilkenny. This effort to prevent the assimilation of the Normans into the Irish culture eventually failed, but the Irish were driven to the north of the city, to Irishtown, on the adjoining slope overlooking the Nore. This is the site of St. Canice's Cathedral. The origins of the town of Kilkenny date back to the 6th century when St. Kieran   and St. Canice founded a monastery there. The Cathedral is 13th-century Gothic and was restored to its present condition in the mid-19th century.

Rothe House is of particular interest, since it is one of the only remaining Tudor-style buildings in the country. Rothe House was a merchant's house in medieval days and was believed to have been built between 1594 and 1610. There were, originally, three houses surrounded by cobblestone courtyards. Merchandise was displayed in the arched store front. The coat-of-arms of the original owner, John Rothe Fitzpiers, and his wife, Rose Archer, are carved on the front facade of the building. The interior has been restored by the Kilkenny archaelogical society, which includes the family's living quarters and banquet hall. The Rothe family deserted the house for the Continent during the Flight of the Wild Geese in 1609.

Open: June 1—October 1
Daily 10:30 A.M.-12:30 P.M.
    3:00 P.M. - 5:00 P.M.
All year round
Sunday 3:00 P.M.-5:00 P.M.

DUNMORE CAVES

These caves have been described as the "darkest places in Ireland." The natural caverns were formed by the action of water with limestone. There are four passages leading to a central chamber. In the chamber stands a giant stalactite called the "Market Cross." Entrance is in the face of a cliff 60 feet high.

JERPOINT ABBEY

This beautiful Cistercian monastery once owned 6,500 of the surrounding acres near Kilkenny town. Today the monastery stands in quiet ruin. Enough remains to give the visitor a limn of its former grandeur. The abbey was founded in the

12th century, planned on the model of European monasteries. Fine examples of Hiberno-Romanesque architecture. Especially interesting are the fine, delicate stone carvings, which include one of St. Christopher, a Butler Knight and his lady, a friar and his rosary, cats, dragons, and squirrels and fascinating abstracts. Be sure to climb to the top of the abbey for the ranging views of Kilkenny in the distance and the local countryside.

COUNTY KILDARE

HOTELS   COUNTRY HOUSES   FARMS

CASTLEDERMOT
KILKEA CASTLE (C)
(053-45156)

This storybook castle, with its turreted battlements, sits on 110 acres of rolling Kildare plains. It was built in this romantic setting as a fortress for the Earls of Kildare in the 12th century. It is believed to be the oldest inhabited castle in Ireland. The interior of the castle has been modernized, but has retained its baronial heritage. All fifty-five rooms have been tastefully decorated, and each commands sweeping views of the countryside. When Kilkea was renovated, the owner built one of the only "health spas" in the country, which includes sauna cabinets, ultraviolet and infrared treatments, gymnasium, massages, and a health restaurant. On the grounds are a private stable and fishing rights in a private estuary for the use of the guests.

Season: All year round   AE
Dinner: 7:45—9:45

STRAFFAN
BARBERSTOWN CASTLE (C)
(01-288206)

Two wonderfully eccentric ladies run Barberstown Castle only ten miles from the city of Dublin. It would be impossible to describe the architecture of Barberstown other than as a medley of Victorian, Norman, and Georgian. The interior is a maze of rooms filled with cozy "kitch," and all the lampshades and pictures are just a *little* tilted. Up the main staircase to the second floor is a row of romantic bedrooms done in soft colors and delicate floral fabrics with fabulous oversized bathrooms. Up a few more steps is the stone-walled Tower Room with its brass beds and shelves filled with pewter. A door on its right wall leads to a secret passage to one of the towers. Back on the main floor is the bar cluttered with love seats and overstuffed chairs. On weekends Ignatius plays the piano, and the singing and music can go on until dawn. If you are near Dublin, be sure to stay in this wonderful hotel.

Season: All year round   AE, DC,
Dinner: 7:30-9:00

RESTAURANTS AND PUBS

THE CURRAGH
JOCKEY HALL
(045-41416)

Near the famous Curragh race track is a small, low white 19th-century house, Jockey Hall, where Monica and Paul McCloskey prepare some of the finest meals in the country. Paul is a graduate of Lausanne and favors a Continental menu using the finest of Irish fare. The atmosphere is usually jubilant as owners and jockeys arrive for the winner's celebration. The dining room, which seats thirty-five, has been decorated with Monica's impressive porcelain collection. Be sure to call ahead and book, since it's one of the most popular places in Ireland. Even if you don't particularly like the races, plan to make a trip through the lush Kildare countryside for an evening at Jockey Hall.

Dinner: 6:00-12:00   AE
Closed Sunday

BUYERS MARKET

TIMOLIN MOONE

THE PEWTER MILL

The medieval craft of pewterware all but died out during the 17th and 18th centuries. During the past few years the Pewter Mill, located in old oak-beamed workshops, has been reviving the art. This tiny little shop is becoming *the* place to find the finest in Irish pewter. The shop is tiny, in one of the tiniest villages (only four or five buildings), so be sure not to pass by this little store.

Open: Monday — Saturday 10:00 A.M.-5:00 P.M.

ENTERTAINMENT

CELBRIDGE
FESTIVAL IN GREAT IRISH HOUSES

For the past decade the Irish Georgian Society has presented concerts in the great 18th-century mansions around the Dublin area such as Castletown House, Russborough, Clonalis, and Slane Castle. Major international celebrities perform, and the evenings have had enormous critical acclaim. This year the Festival will begin June 3rd and continue for two weeks. Unfortunately, as we went to press specific details on performances were not available. For details contact the:

> Festival Secretary
> Irish Georgian Society
> Castletown House
> Celbridge
> (Tel: 288252)

ROBERTSTOWN
ROBERTSTOWN CANDLELIGHT BANQUET
(045-60204)

Robertstown is not your usual tourist banquet evening. In this tiny rural village on the banks of the Grand Canal you will spend a few hours as close as you will ever come to relaxed 18th-century living. Arrive around 7:30 P.M. for a visit to the Falconry of Ireland. It's one of the finest houses of this bird of prey in the world. At about 8:00 cross over the canal and board a horse-drawn barge, which has been renovated to model the old fly boats used between Dublin and Shannon hundreds of years ago. (The fare in those days was a mere six shillings for first-class passage.) A mug of whiskey punch is served as you laze down the canal. Within the hour you're back at the Grand Canal Hotel for the Candlelight Banquet. The menu is, well, overwhelming: Mulligatawny Soup, Broiled Salmon, Roast Turkey, Beef and Saddle of Mutton (you don't have to choose, you can have them all!!), Hill of Allen potatoes, fruit bowls, and cheeses. Through it all Spanish wine pours and pours. During the banquet there's traditional entertainment.

(You can arranged to travel to Robertstown by charter bus. Contact C.I.E.: Dublin 746301, and they will make reservations for the evening for you.)

DIVERSIONS

CELBRIDGE
CASTLETOWN HOUSE

Through the indomitable efforts of   the Honorable Desmond Guinness and his Irish Georgian Society, the finest of Palladian houses, Castletown, was salvaged from total ruin. Though when Mr. Guinness took over Castletown, it had all but crumbled. Over the past few years he and volunteers have restored the graceful house to its past elegance.

Castletown was built in 1722 by William Connolly, Speaker of the House of Irish Commons. The architect, an Italian, Allessandro Galilei, used the finest in Irish building material, oak, marble, and even recommended using Irish silver for the locks and gates. The interior rooms are filled with period portraits, paintings, and antiques. Especially interesting is the Print Room, which Lady Louisa Connolly did herself, and which is the only one remaining in Ireland. If for no other reason you should visit Castletown to see the delicately carved plasterwork throughout the house, done by two Italian brothers, the Francinis, whose work will fascinate. On the grounds is a whimsical 140-foot obelisk known as "Connolly's Folly." Follies were popular during the 18th century. Landlords had them built to give locals work during the famines. The Irish Georgian Society is headquartered at Castletown and would appreciate any donations for the continuing preservation of Georgian buildings in Ireland.

Open: April 1 — September 30 11:00 A.M.-6:00 P.M.
  Closed Tuesdays
  October — March Sunday only 2:00-5:00 P.M.

Dinner is served each evening by candlelight and often there is entertainment. The country-style food is quite good and combined with the romantic 18th-century setting of Castletown, it provides a perfect ending for a day of touring.

Open: All year round
Dinner: 7:00-11:00
Must book reservations (Tel: 288502)

EPILOGUE

Reading over these pages I see that some things have been left unsaid. When you come to Ireland you'll have your own maze of experiences, travel your own ground. You'll leave guilty at the amount of indiscriminate pleasure, and later you may feel a longing.

I think of something an Irishman said to me who was concerned that I was writing a book: "Don't write too much, explain too much. Leave a little mystery."

Woodtown Manor
Rathfarnham
1976

GLOSSARY

An lar (on lar)	City center
An Taoiseach (on Tee-shack)	Prime Minister
An t-Uachtarán (on Ook-taran)	President
Baile Atha Cliath (Bawlya Awaha Klee)	Dublin
Banba (Bawn-ba)	Ireland
Béaltaine (Beeowlthin)	pagan feast of summer
Bord Failte (Board Fawltah)	Irish Tourist Board
brehons (bray-hons)	keepers of the law
ceardaighe (care-dee)	class of tradesman
ceili (kay-lee)	dance
Ceoltóirí Chualann (Keyol-tori Koolun)	a musical group
coarb (korb)	successor
Coras Iompair (Koras Oompar Eireann Airun)	Irish Transport Company
cruit (krit)	harp
clairseach (klauirshak)	harp
Daer Fuidirs (Dare Foodears)	slaves from a conquered land
derbfine (daireb-feen)	four generations of landowners
Dinnshenchas (Din-shen-a-hus)	lore of high places
Druids (Drew-ids)	keepers of the supernatural
Eire (Airah)	Ireland
filid (fee-lee)	poets of ancient Ireland
Fir (fear)	men
Fir Bolg (Fear-Bolg)	mythical inhabitants of ancient Ireland

Fohlar (Fawler)	Ireland
fleadh cheoil (flah-key-ol)	music festival
geantraighe (gan-tree)	pleasant music
goltraighe (gol-tree)	sad music
lein (lean)	gold
Lugnasad (loonasa)	pagan feast of autumn
Mna (men-aw)	lady
Oifig an Phoist (Offig un Phuist)	Post Office
Oilmeac (e-milk)	pagan feast of spring
oireachtas (ore-ee-aktas)	gathering
Samain (sau-in)	pagan feast of winter
Seanchas Mor (Shankus mor)	book of Irish lore
shanachies (shan-a-keys)	storytellers
sidh (shee)	fairy mound
suantraighe (soon-tree)	lullaby
Táin (Tah-in)	ancient saga of a cattle raid
Tuatha de Danann (Tooa de Dann)	tribe of the goddess Danu
tuatha (too-a)	tribe

SELECTED BIBLIOGRAPHY

BARRINGTON, Jonah, *Personal Sketches*

BEHAN, Brendan, *Brendan Behan's Island - An Irish Sketchbook*. Great Britain: Hutchinson, 1962

BOWEN, Elizabeth, *Bowen's Court*. New York: Knopf, 1942

CORKERY, Daniel, *The Fortunes of the Irish Language*. Cork: Mercier Press, 1956

DARLINGTON, C.D., *The Evolution of Man and Society*. London: Allen & Unwin, 1968

DAVIES, John, *Discoveries of the True Causes Why Ireland Was Never Entirely Subdued*. London: 1610

EDGEWORTH, Maria, *Tales of Fashionable Life: Ennui*, London: J. Johnson, 1812-13

EVANS, Estyn, *Prehistoric and Christian Ireland*, 8 v. London: Batsford, 1966

FLOOD, J.M., *The Life of Chevalier Charles Wogan*. Dublin: Talbot Press, 1922.

GWYNN, Aubrey, S.J., ed., *Irish in the West Indies*. *Analectia Hibernica*, No. 4, Oct., 1932, Irish Manuscripts Commission

GWYNNE, Stephen, *Experiences of a Literary Man*. London: Butterworth, 1926

HEANEY, Seamus, *North*. London: Faber & Faber, 1975; New York, Oxford University Press, 1976

HOGAN, James, "The Irish Law of Kingship with Special Reference to Ailech & Cenel Eoghaim." Proceedings of the Royal Irish Academy. Vol. XL, Sect. 3, No. 3, 1932

HOAGLAND, Kathleen, ed., *Thousand Years of Irish Poetry*. Greenwich: Devin-Adair, 1947

HYDE, Douglas, *Legends of Saints & Sinners*. Dublin: Talbot Press

INGLIS, Brian, *West Briton*. London: Faber & Faber, 1962

IRISHMAN, An, *My Country*. Edinburgh & London: William Blackwood & Son, 1929

JOYCE, P.W., *A Smaller History of Ancient Ireland.* Dublin: Gill, 1906

KANE, Sir Robert, *Industrial Resources of Ireland.* Dublin: Hodges & Smith, 1845

KEANE, John B., *Self Portrait.* Cork: Mercier Press, 1964

KINAHAN, George Henry, *Manual of the Geology of Ireland,* 8 v. London: 1878

MacERLEAN, John C., S.J., *The Poems of David O'Brudair.* London: Irish Texts Society, 1910

MacFIRBIS, Dualtagh, *Genealogical Tracts I,* edited by Toirdhealbhach O Raithbheartaigh. Dublin: Irish Manuscripts Commission, The Royal Irish Academy, 1932

MacLIAMMOIR, Michael, *Theatre in Ireland.* Dublin: Cultural Relations Committee of Ireland, 1950

McMANUS, M.J., *Irish Cavalcade, 1550-1850.* London: Macmillan; Dublin: Browne & Nolan, 1939

MEYER, Kuno, *Selections of Ancient Irish Poetry.* London: Constable, 1959

MONTAGUE, John, *The Rough Field.* Dublin: Dolmen Press, 1972

MOORE, George, *Hail and Farewell,* 3 v. New York:Appleton, 1911-14; London: Heinemann, 1933

MURPHY, Denis, S.J., *Cromwell In Ireland: A History of Cromwell's Irish Campaign.* Dublin: M.H. Gill & Sons, 1883

O'CALLAGHAN, J.C., *Irish Brigades in the Service of France.* Glasgow: R.T.Washburne, 1869

O'CURRY, Eugene, *On the Manners and Customs of the Ancient Irish.* Williams, 1873

O'SULLIVAN, Donal, ed. *"The Memoirs of Arthur O'Neil,"* from *Carolan.* London: Routledge & Kegan Paul, 1958

PLUMMER, Charles, *Lives of the Irish Saints.* Oxford: Clandon Press, 1922

PRAEGER, Robert Lloyd, *The Way That I Went.* Dublin: Allen Figgis, Riverrun series, 1969

SOMERVILLE, Edith, *Irish Memories*. New York: Longmans, 1918

THACKERAY, William Makepeace, *Irish Sketchbook*. Chapman & Hall, 1842

WELLS, Warre, *An Irish Apologia*. Dublin & London: Mansuel, 1917

YEATS, William Butler, *Collected Works*. New York: Macmillan, 1951

YOUNG, Arthur, *Tour in Ireland* (1776-1779). London: 1780

INDEX